ADVANCED C

Second Edition

Herbert Schildt

Osborne **McGraw-Hill**
Berkeley, California

Osborne **McGraw-Hill**
2600 Tenth Street
Berkeley, California 94710
U.S.A.

For information on translations and book distributors outside of the U.S.A., write to Osborne **McGraw-Hill** at the above address.

A complete list of trademarks appears on page 395.

1234567890 DODO 898

ISBN 0-07-881348-4

CONTENTS

INTRODUCTION

I have been fortunate to be able to write the kind of programming book that I have always wanted. Years ago, when I started to program, I tried to find a book that had algorithms for such tasks as sorts, linked lists, simulations, and expression parsers in a straightforward presentation. I wanted a book that would give me insight into programming, but I also wanted a book that I could take off the shelf to find what I needed when I needed it. Unfortunately, I never found the exact book I was looking for — so I decided to write it.

This book explores a wide range of subjects and contains many useful algorithms, functions, and approaches written in the C language. C is the de facto systems programming language, as well as one of the most popular general-purpose professional programming languages available. A wide variety of C compilers is available for virtually all computers, and many are quite inexpensive. I used both Microsoft C and Turbo C; however, with only a few exceptions, any ANSI Standard compiler will compile and run all code in this book. (Users with nonstandard C compilers will need to make only slight, if any, changes.)

Chapter 1 covers sorting and searching. Chapter 2 deals with stacks, queues, linked lists, and binary trees. (You may think that's a lot to cover in one chapter; however, the subjects go together nicely and form a solid unit.) Chapter 3 discusses dynamic allocation. Chapter 4 explains the various C memory models. Chapter 5 presents an overview of operating-system interfacing and assembly language linkage. Chapter 6 covers statistics and includes a complete statistics program. Codes, ciphers, and data compression are the topics of Chapter 7, which also includes a short history of cryptography. Chapter 8 details several random number generators and then discusses how to use them in two simulations. The first simulation is a check-out line in a store; the second is a random-walk portfolio management program.

Chapter 9 is my personal favorite because it contains the complete code for a recursive descent parser. Years ago, I would have given just about anything to have had that code! If you need to evaluate expressions, Chapter 9 is for you. Chapters 10 and 11 discuss conversions from other languages, efficiency, porting, and debugging.

H.S.

If you would like to obtain an IBM PC-compatible diskette that contains all of the programs and algorithms in this book, please complete the order form and mail it with payment enclosed. If you are in a hurry, you can call (217) 586-4021 (the number of my consulting company) and place your order by telephone.

Please send me _____ copies, at $24.95 each, of the programs in this book. Foreign orders: Please add $5.00 for shipping and handling.

Name: _____

Address: _____

City: _____ State: _____ ZIP: _____

Telephone: _____

diskette size: 5 1/4" _____ 3 1/2" _____

Method of payment: check _____ Visa _____ MC _____

Credit card number: _____

Expiration date: _____

Signature: _____

Send to:
    Herbert Schildt
    RR 1, Box 130
    Mahomet, IL 61853

This is solely the offering of the author. Osborne-McGraw/Hill takes no responsibility for the fulfillment of this offer.

1

SORTING AND SEARCHING

In the world of computer science, perhaps no other tasks are more fundamental or as extensively analyzed as those of sorting and searching. These routines are used in virtually all database programs, as well as in compilers, interpreters, and operating systems. This chapter introduces you to the basics of sorting and searching. Since sorting data generally makes searching the data easier and faster, sorting is discussed first.

SORTING

Sorting is the process of arranging a set of similar pieces of information into an increasing or decreasing order; specifically, given a sorted list **i** of **n** elements,

$$i_1 <= i_2 <= \ldots <= i_n$$

Even though many C compilers supply the standard **qsort( )** function as part of the standard library, the study and understanding of sorting is important for three main reasons. First, a generalized function like **qsort( )** cannot be applied to all situations. Second, because **qsort( )** uses parameters in order to operate on a wide variety of data, it runs more slowly than does a similar sort operating on only one type of data. Run time increases because of the extra processing time needed to handle various data types. Finally, as you will see, the Quicksort algorithm that is used by **qsort( )** may not be the best sort for specialized situations, although it is very good for general cases.

There are two categories of sorting algorithms: the sorting of arrays, both in memory and in random-access disk files; and the sorting of sequential disk or tape files. This chapter will focus on the first category because it is of most interest to the microcomputer user. However, the general method of sorting sequential files will also be introduced.

The main difference between sorting arrays and sorting sequential files is that each element of the array is always available. This means that any element may be compared or exchanged with any other element at any time. In a sequential file, however, only one element is available at any one time. Because of this difference, sorting techniques differ greatly between the two.

Generally, when information is sorted, a small portion of that information is used as the *sort key* on which comparisons are based. When an exchange must be made, the entire data structure is transferred. In a mailing list, for example, the ZIP code field might be used as the key, but the entire name and address accompanies the ZIP code when the exchange is made. For the sake of simplicity examples of the various sorting methods presented here will focus on sorting character arrays. Later, you will learn how to adapt any of these methods to any type of data structure.

Classes of Sorting Algorithms

There are three general methods that can be used to sort arrays:

- By exchange
- By selection
- By insertion

Imagine a deck of cards. To sort the cards by *exchange*, you would spread the cards, face up, on a table and then proceed to exchange out-of-order cards until the deck is ordered.

To sort by *selection*, you would spread the cards on the table, select the lowest-value card, and take it out of the deck. Then, from the remaining cards on the table, you would select the lowest card and place it behind the one already in your hand. This process would continue until all of the cards were in your hand. Because you always selected the lowest card from those remaining on the table, when the process was complete the cards in your hand would be sorted.

To sort by *insertion*, you would hold the cards in your hand, taking one at a time. As you took cards from the deck, you would place them into a new deck on the table, always inserting them in the correct position. The deck would be sorted when you had no cards in your hand.

Judging Sorting Algorithms

There are many different algorithms for each of the three sorting methods. Each algorithm has its merits, but the general criteria for judging a sorting algorithm are based on the answers to the following questions:

- How fast can the algorithm sort information in an average case?
- How fast are its best and worst case?
- Does the algorithm exhibit *natural* or *unnatural* behavior?
- Does it rearrange elements with equal keys?

How fast a particular algorithm sorts is of great concern. The speed with which an array can be sorted is directly related to the number of comparisons and the number of exchanges required, with exchanges taking more time. A *comparison* occurs when one array element is compared to another; an *exchange* happens when two elements are swapped in the array. Later in this chapter you will see that some sorts require an exponential amount of time per element to sort, and some require logarithmic time.

The best- and worst-case run times are important if you expect to encounter best- and worse-case situations frequently. Often a sort will have a good average case but a terrible worst case, or vice versa.

A sort is said to exhibit *natural* behavior if it works least when the list is already in order, harder as the list becomes less ordered, and hardest when a list is in inverse order. How hard a sort works is based on the number of comparisons and moves that must be executed.

To understand the importance of rearranging elements with equal keys, imagine a database that is sorted on a main key and a subkey—for example, a mailing list with the ZIP code as the main key and the last name within the same ZIP code as the subkey. When a new address is added to the list and the list is sorted again, you do not want the subkeys to be rearranged. To guarantee this, a sort must not exchange main keys of equal value.

In the following sections, representative sorts from each class of sorting algorithms are analyzed to judge their efficiency.

The Bubble Sort

The best-known (and most infamous) sort is the *Bubble sort*. Its popularity is derived from its catchy name and its simplicity. However, it is one of the worst sorts ever conceived.

The Bubble sort uses the exchange method of sorting. It makes repeated comparisons and, if necessary, exchanges of adjacent elements. Its name comes from the method's similarity to bubbles in a tank of water, where each bubble seeks its own level. In this simplest form of the Bubble sort

```
/*The Bubble sort. */
void bubble(item, count)
char *item;
int count;
{
  register int a,b;
  register char t;

  for(a=1; a<count; ++a)
    for(b=count-1; b>=a; --b) {
      if(item[b-1] > item[b]) {
        /* exchange elements */
        t = item[b-1];
        item[b-1] = item[b];
        item[b] = t;
      }
    }
}
```

item is a pointer to the character array to be sorted and **count** is the number of elements in the array.

The Bubble sort is driven by two loops. Since there are **count** elements in the array, the outer loop causes the array to be scanned **count−1** times. This ensures that, in the worst case, every element is in its proper position when the function terminates. The inner loop performs the actual comparisons and exchanges. (A slightly optimized version of the Bubble sort will terminate if no exchanges occur, but this also adds another comparison to each pass through the inner loop.)

This version of the Bubble sort can be used to sort a character array into ascending order. For example, this program sorts a string typed in from the keyboard:

```
void bubble();

/* sort driver */
main()  /* sort a string from the keyboard */
{
  char s[80];

  printf("enter a string:");
  gets(s);
  bubble(s,strlen(s));
  printf("the sorted string is: %s\n", s);
}
```

To illustrate the way that the Bubble sort works, here are the passes used to sort the array **dcab**:

initial d c a b
pass 1   a d c b
pass 2   a b d c
pass 3   a b c d

When analyzing any sort, you must determine how many comparisons and exchanges will be performed for the best, average, and worst cases. With the Bubble sort, the number of comparisons is always the same because the two **for** loops will still repeat the specified number of times, whether the list is initially ordered or not. This means that the Bubble sort will always perform $1/2(n^2-n)$ comparisons, where n is the number of elements to be sorted. This formula is derived from the fact that the outer loop of the Bubble sort executes $n-1$ times and the inner loop $n/2$ times. Multiplying these together gives the formula.

The number of exchanges is 0 for the best case—an already sorted list. The numbers are $3/4(n^2-n)$ for the average case and $3/2(n^2-n)$ for the worst case. It is beyond the scope of this book to explain the derivation of these cases, but you can see that as the list becomes less ordered, the number of elements that are out of order approaches the number of comparisons. (There are three exchanges in a Bubble sort for every element out of order.) The Bubble sort is called an *n-squared algorithm* because its execution time is a multiple of the square of the number of elements. A Bubble sort is very bad for a large number of elements because execution time is directly related to the number of comparisons and exchanges.

For example, if you ignore the time it takes to exchange any out-of-position element, you can see that if each comparison takes 0.001 seconds, then sorting 10 elements will take about 0.05 seconds, sorting 100 elements will take about 5 seconds, and sorting 1000 elements will take about 500 seconds. A 100,000-element sort, the size of a small phone book, would take about 5,000,000 seconds, or about 1400 hours—about two months of continuous sorting! Figure 1-1 shows how execution time increases in relation to the size of the array.

You can make some improvements to the Bubble sort to speed it up—and help its image a bit. For example, the Bubble sort has one peculiarity: an out-of-order element at the large end, such as the **a** in the **decab** array example, will go to its proper position in one pass, but a misplaced element in the small end, such as the **d**, will rise very slowly to its proper place. Instead of always reading the array in the same direction, subsequent passes could reverse direction. Greatly out-of-place elements will travel more quickly to their correct position. Shown here, this version of the Bubble sort is called the *Shaker sort* because of its shaking motion over the array:

```
/* The Shaker sort - an improved bubble sort. */
void shaker(item, count)
char *item;
int count;
{
  register int a, b, c, d;
  char t;

  c = 1;
  b = count-1; d = count-1;

  do {
    for(a=d; a>=c; --a) {
      if(item[a-1] > item[a]) {
        t = item[a-1];
        item[a-1] = item[a];
        item[a] = t;
        b = a;
      }
    }
    c = b+1;
    for(a=c; a<d+1; ++a) {
```

```
    if(item[a-1] > item[a]) {
       t = item[a-1];
       item[a-1] = item[a];
       item[a] = t;
       b = a;
     }
  }
  d = b-1;
} while (c <= d);
}
```

Although the Shaker sort does improve the Bubble sort, it still executes on the order of n^2 because the number of comparisons is unchanged and because the number of exchanges has only been reduced by a relatively small constant.

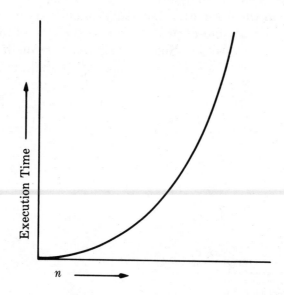

Figure 1-1.   The execution time of an n^2 sort in relation to array size

Sorting by Selection

A *Selection sort* selects the element with the lowest value and exchanges that with the first element. Then from the remaining $n-1$ elements, the element with the next-lowest value is found and exchanged with the second element, and so forth, up to the last two elements. For example, if the selection method were used on the array **bdac**, each pass would look like this:

    initial   b d a c
    pass 1   a d b c
    pass 2   a b d c
    pass 3   a b c d

A simple form of the Selection sort is shown here:

```
/* The Selection sort. */
void select(item, count)
char *item;
int count;
{
  register int a, b, c;
  char t;

  for(a=0; a<count-1; ++a) {
    c = a;
    t = item[a];
    for(b=a+1; b<count; ++b) {
      if(item[b] < t) {
        c = b;
        t = item[b];
      }
    }
    item[c] = item[a];
    item[a] = t;
  }
}
```

Unfortunately, like the Bubble sort, the outer loop executes $n-1$ times and the inner loop $1/2(n)$ times. This means that the Selection sort requires $1/2(n^2-n)$ comparisons, which makes it too slow for a large number of items. The number of exchanges for the best case is $3(n-1)$ and for the worst case is $n^2/4+3(n-1)$.

For the best case (the list is ordered) only $n-1$ elements need to be moved, and each move requires three exchanges. The worst case approximates the number of comparisons. Although the average case is beyond the scope of this book to develop, it is $n(\ln n+y)$ where y is Euler's constant (about 0.577216). This means that although the number of comparisons for the Bubble sort and the Selection sort is the same, the number of exchanges in the average case is far less for the Selection sort.

Sorting by Insertion

The *Insertion sort* is the last of the simple sorting algorithms. The Insertion sort initially sorts the first two members on the array. Next, the algorithm inserts the third member into its sorted position in relation to the first two members. Then the fourth element is inserted into the list of three elements. The process continues until all elements have been sorted. For example, in the array **dcab**, each pass of the Insertion sort would look like this:

```
initial   d c a b
pass 1    c d a b
pass 3    a c d b
pass 4    a b c d
```

A version of the Insertion sort is shown here:

```
/* Sorting by straight insertion. */
void insert(item, count)
char *item;
int count;
{
    register int a, b;
    char t;

    for(a=1; a<count; ++a) {
        t = item[a];
        b = a-1;
        while(b>=0 && t<item[b] ) {
            item[b+1] = item[b];
            b--;
        }
        item[b+1] = t;
    }
}
```

Unlike the Bubble sort and the Selection sort, the number of comparisons that occur while the Insertion sort is used will depend on how the list is initially ordered. If the list is in order, then the number of comparisons is $n-1$. If the list is in inverse order, then the number of comparisons is $1/2(n^2+n)-1$, while its average is $1/4(n^2+n-2)$.

The number of exchanges for each case is as follows:

best	$2(n-1)$
average	$1/4(n^2+9n-10)$
worst	$1/2(n^2+3n-4)$

Therefore, the number for the worst case is as bad as those for the Bubble and Selection sorts, and the number for the average case is only slightly better.

The Insertion sort does have two advantages, however. First, it behaves *naturally:* it works the least when the array is already sorted and the hardest when the array is sorted in inverse order. This makes the Insertion sort useful for lists that are almost in order. Second, it leaves the order of equal keys unchanged: if a list is sorted using two keys, then it remains sorted for both keys after an Insertion sort.

Even though the number of comparisons may be fairly good for certain sets of data, the fact that the array must constantly be shifted means that the number of moves can be significant. However, the Insertion sort still behaves naturally, with the least exchanges occurring for an almost sorted list and the most exchanges for an inversely ordered array.

Improved Sorts

Each algorithm shown so far had the fatal flaw of executing in n^2 time. For large amounts of data, the sorts would be slow — in fact, at some point, too slow to use. Every computer programmer has heard, or told, the horror story of the "sort that took three days." Unfortunately, these stories are often true.

When a sort takes too long, it may be the fault of the underlying algorithm. However, a sad commentary is that the first response is often "let's write it in assembly code." Although assembler code will almost always speed up a routine by a constant factor, if the underlying algorithm is bad, the sort will be slow no matter how optimal the coding. Remember, when the run time of a routine is relative to n^2, increasing the speed of either the coding or the computer will only cause a marginal improvement because the rate at which the run time increases changes exponentially. (The graph in Figure 1-1 is shifted to the right slightly, but the curve is unchanged.) Keep in mind that if something is not fast enough in C, it won't be fast enough in assembler. The solution is to use a better sorting algorithm.

In this section, two excellent sorts will be developed. The first is the Shell sort, and the second is the Quicksort, which is generally considered the best sorting routine. These sorts run so fast that if you blink, you will miss them.

The Shell Sort

The *Shell sort* is named after its inventor, D.L. Shell. However, the name seems to have stuck because its method of operation resembles sea shells piled upon one another.

The general method, derived from the Insertion sort, is based on diminishing increments. Figure 1-2 gives a diagram of a Shell sort on the array **fdacbe**. First, all elements that are three positions apart are sorted. Then all elements that are two positions apart are sorted. Finally, all those adjacent to each other are sorted.

It may not be obvious that this method yields good results, or even that it will sort the array, but it does both. This algorithm is efficient because each sorting pass involves either relatively few elements, or elements that are already in reasonable order; therefore each pass increases the order of the data.

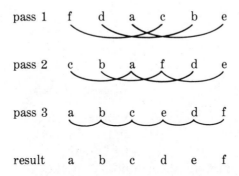

Figure 1-2.   The Shell sort

The exact sequence for the increments can be changed. The only rule is that the last increment must be 1. For example, the sequence 9, 5, 3, 1 works well and is used in the Shell sort shown here. Avoid sequences that are powers of 2 because, for mathematically complex reasons, they reduce the efficiency of the sorting algorithm. (However, even if you used them, the sort would still work.)

```
/* The Shell sort. */
void shell(item, count)
char *item;
int count;
{

  register int i, j, k, s, w;
  char x, a[5];

  a[0]=9; a[1]=5; a[2]=3; a[3]=2; a[4]=1;

  for(w=0; w<5; w++) {
    k = a[w]; s = -k;
    for(i=k; i<count; ++i) {
      x = item[i];
      j = i-k;
      if(s==0){ s = -k;
```

```
    s++;
    item[s] = x;
  }
  while(x<item[j] && j>=0 && j<=count) {
    item[j+k] = item[j];
    j = j-k;
  }
  item[j+k] = x;
 }
}
}
```

You may have noticed that the inner **while** loop has three test conditions. The **x<item[j]** is a comparison necessary for the sorting process. The tests **j>=0** and **j<=count** are used to keep the sort from overrunning the boundary of the array **item**. These extra checks will degrade the performance of the Shell sort to some extent. Slightly different versions of the Shell sort employ special array elements, called *sentinels*, which are not actually part of the array to be sorted. Sentinels hold special termination values that indicate the least and greatest possible elements. In this way, the boundary checks are unnecessary. However, using sentinels requires a specific knowledge of the data, which limits the generality of the sort function.

The analysis of the Shell sort presents some very difficult mathematical problems that are beyond the scope of this book. However, execution time is proportional to $n^{1.2}$ for sorting n elements. This is a significant improvement over the n^2 sorts of the previous section; see Figure 1-3, which graphs an n^2 curve and an $n^{1.2}$ curve together. However, before you decide to use the Shell sort, you should know that the Quicksort is even better.

The Quicksort

The *Quicksort*, invented and named by C.A.R. Hoare, is generally considered the best sorting algorithm currently available. It is based on the exchange method of sorting. This is surprising if you consider the terrible performance of the Bubble sort, which is also based on the exchange method.

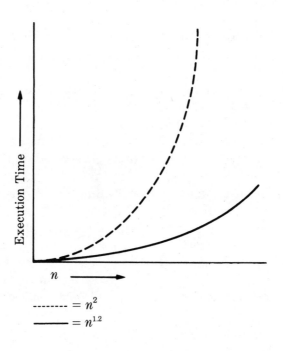

Figure 1-3. n^2 and $n^{1.2}$ curves

The Quicksort is built on the idea of partitions. The general procedure selects a value called the *comparand* and then partitions the array into two parts, with all elements greater than or equal to the partition value on one side and those less than the partition value on the other. This process is repeated for each remaining part until the array is sorted. For example, given the

array **fedacb** and the value **d** for the partition, the first pass of
the Quicksort would rearrange the array like this:

```
initial      f e d a c b
pass 1       b c a d e f
```

This process is repeated for each part (**bca** and **def**). The process
is essentially recursive; indeed, the cleanest implementations of
Quicksort are recursive algorithms.

The selection of the middle comparand value can be accomplished in two ways. The value can be chosen either at random or
by averaging a small set of values taken from the array. For
optimal sorting it is best to select a value that is precisely in the
middle of the range of values. However, this is not easy to do for
most sets of data. Even in the worst case—the value chosen is at
one extremity—Quicksort will still perform reasonably well.

The following version of Quicksort selects the middle element
of the array. Although this may not always result in a good choice,
it is a simple, quick technique, and still performs correctly.

```
/* The Quicksort entry function. */
void quick(item, count)
char *item;
int count;
{

   qs(item, 0, count-1);

}

/* The Quicksort function. */
void qs(item, left, right)
char *item;
int left, right;
{

   register int i, j;
   char x, y;

   i = left; j = right;
   x = item[(left+right)/2];

   do {
     while(item[i]<x && i<right) i++;
     while(x<item[j] && j>left) j--;
```

```
    if(i<=j) {
      y = item[i];
      item[i] = item[j];
      item[j] = y;
      i++; j--;
    }
  } while(i<=j);

  if(left<j)   qs(item, left, j);
  if(i<right)  qs(item, i, right);
}
```

Here, **quick( )** sets up a call to the main sorting function, called **qs( )**. While this maintains the same common interface for **item** and **count**, it is not essential, because **qs( )** could have been called directly using three arguments.

The derivation of the number of comparisons and the number of exchanges that Quicksort performs requires mathematics beyond the scope of this book. However, you can assume that the number of comparisons is n log n, and that the number of exchanges is approximately $n/6$ log n. These are significantly better than any of the sorts discussed so far.

The equation

$$N = a^x$$

can be rewritten as

$$x = \log_a N$$

This means, for example, that if 100 elements were to be sorted, Quicksort would require 100 * 2, or 200, comparisons because log 100 is 2. Compared with the Bubble sort's average of 990 comparisons, this number is quite good.

However, there is one nasty aspect of Quicksort that you should be aware of. If the comparand value for each partition happens to be the largest value, then Quicksort degenerates into "slowsort" with an n^2 run time. Generally, though, this does not happen.

You must take care though in choosing a method to determine the value of the comparand. Often the value is determined by the actual data that you are sorting. In large mailing lists where the sorting is often done by ZIP code, the selection is simple, because the ZIP codes are fairly evenly distributed and a simple algebraic function can determine a suitable comparand. However, in certain databases, the sort keys may be so close in value, with many having the same value, that a random selection is often the best method available. A common and fairly effective method is to sample three elements from a partition and take the middle value.

Choosing a Sort

Generally, the Quicksort is the preferred sort because it is so fast. However, when only very small lists of data are to be sorted (less than 100, for example), the overhead created by Quicksort's recursive calls may offset the benefits of a superior algorithm. In rare cases like this, one of the simpler sorts, perhaps even the Bubble sort, will be quicker.

Sorting Other Data Structures

Until now, the sorts have only been applied to arrays of characters. This has made it easy to present each sorting routine. Obviously, arrays of any of the built-in data types can be sorted simply by changing the data types of the parameters and variables to the sort function. However, it is generally complex data types like strings or structures that need to be sorted. (Remember, most sorting involves a key and information linked to that key.) To adapt the algorithms to sort other data structures, you need to change either the comparison section or the exchange section, or both. The basic algorithm itself will remain unchanged.

Because Quicksort is one of the best general-purpose routines available at this time, it will be used in our examples. The same techniques, however, will apply to any of the sorts described earlier.

Sorting Strings

The easiest way to sort strings is to create an array of character pointers to those strings. This allows you to maintain easy indexing, and it keeps the basic Quicksort algorithm unchanged. The string version of Quicksort shown here accepts an array of **char** pointers that point to the strings to be sorted. The sort rearranges the pointers to the strings, not the actual strings in memory. This version sorts the strings in alphabetical order.

```
void quick_string(item, count)
char *item[];
int count;
{
  qs_string(item, 0, count-1);
}

/* A Quicksort for strings */
void qs_string(item, left, right)
char *item[];
int left, right;
{
  register int i, j;
  char *x, *y;

  i = left; j = right;
  x = item[(left+right)/2];

  do {
    while(strcmp(item[i],x)<0 && i<right) i++;
    while(strcmp(item[j],x)>0 && j>left) j--;
    if(i<=j) {
      y = item[i];
      item[i] = item[j];
      item[j] = y;
      i++; j--;
    }
  } while(i<=j);

  if(left<j)  qs_string(item, left, j);
  if(i<right) qs_string(item, i, right);
}
```

The comparison step has been changed to use the function **strcmp()**, which returns a negative number if the first string is lexicographically less than the second, 0 if the strings are equal, or a positive number if the first string is lexicographically greater than the second. The exchange part of the routine has been left unchanged because only the pointers are being exchanged — not the actual strings. To exchange the actual strings, you would have to use the function **strcpy( )**.

The use of **strcmp( )** slows down the sort for two reasons. First, it involves a function call, which always takes time; second, the **strcmp( )** function itself performs several (and sometimes many) comparisons to determine the relationship of the two strings. If speed is absolutely critical, the code for **strcmp( )** can be duplicated in line within the **quick_string** routine. However, there is no way to avoid comparing the strings, since this is by definition what the task involves.

Sorting Structures

Most application programs that require a sort will need to have a group of data sorted. A mailing list is an excellent example because a name, street, city, state, and ZIP code are all linked. When this conglomerate unit of data is sorted, a sort key is used, but the entire structure is also exchanged. To understand this process, you first need to create a structure. For a mailing-list example, a convenient structure is

```
struct address {
  char name[40];
  char street[40];
  char city[20];
  char state[3];
  char zip[10];
};
```

The **state** is three characters long and **zip** is ten characters long because a string array always needs to be one character longer than the maximum length of any string in order to store the null terminator.

Since it is reasonable to arrange a mailing list as an array of structures, assume for this example that the sort routine sorts an array of structures of type **address** by the ZIP code field as shown here:

```
void quick_struct(item, count)
           /* setup */
struct address item[];
int count;
{
  qs_struct(item, 0, count-1);
}

/* A Quicksort for structures. */
void qs_struct(item, left, right)
struct address item[];
int left, right;
{

  register int i,j;
  char *x, *y;

  i = left; j = right;
  x = item[(left+right)/2].zip;

  do {
    while(strcmp(item[i].zip,x)<0 && i<right) i++;
    while(strcmp(item[j].zip,x)>0 && j>left) j--;
    if(i<=j) {
      swap_all_fields(item,i,j);
      i++; j--;
    }
  } while(i<=j);

  if(left<j)  qs_struct(item, left, j);
  if(i<right) qs_struct(item, i, right);
}
```

Notice that both the comparison code and the exchange code needed to be altered. Because so many fields needed to be exchanged, a separate function called **swap_all_fields( )** was created. You will need to create **swap_all_fields( )** in accordance with the nature of the structure being sorted.

Sorting Disk Files

There are two types of disk files: *sequential* and *random-access*. If
a disk file is small enough, it may be read into memory so that the
array-sorting routines presented earlier can sort it most efficiently. However, many disk files are too large to be sorted easily
in memory and require special techniques.

Sorting Random-Access Disk Files

Used by most microcomputer database applications, random-
access disk files have two major advantages over sequential disk
files. First, they are easy to maintain: you can update information
without having to copy the entire list over. Second, random-access
disk files can be treated as a large array on disk, which greatly
simplifies sorting. Applying this method means that you can use
the basic Quicksort with modifications to seek different records
on the disk, instead of having to index an array. Unlike sorting a
sequential disk file, sorting a random file in place means that a
full disk does not need to have room for both the sorted and
unsorted files.

Each sorting situation differs with the exact data structure
that is sorted and the key that is used. However, the general idea
of sorting random-access disk files can be understood by developing a sort program that sorts the mailing-list structure called
address that was defined earlier. This sample program assumes
that the number of elements is fixed at 100, but in a real application, a record count would have to be maintained dynamically.
The Mailing-List Sorting program is shown here:

```
/* Disk sort for structures of type address.
   This program sorts a random access disk file as if it
   were an array on disk.
*/

#include "stdio.h"
#define NUM_ELEMENTS 100   /* this is an arbitrary number
                              that should be determined
                              dynamically for each list */
```

```
struct address {
  char name[30];
  char street[40];
  char city[20];
  char state[3];
  char zip[10];
}ainfo;

void quick_disk(), qs_disk(), swap_all_fields();
char *get_zip();

main()
{
  FILE *fp;
  int t;

  if((fp=fopen("mlist","rb+"))==0) {
    printf("cannot open file for read/write\n");
    exit (0);
  }

  quick_disk(fp, NUM_ELEMENTS);
  fclose(fp);
  printf("List sorted.\n");

}

/* Quicksort for disk files entry function. */
void quick_disk(fp, count)
FILE *fp;
long int count;
{
  qs_disk(fp, 0L, count-1);
}

/* Quicksort for disk files. */
void qs_disk(fp, left, right)
FILE *fp;
long int left, right;
{

  long int i, j;
  char x[100], *y;

  i = left; j = right;

  strcpy(x, get_zip(fp, (long)(i+j)/2)); /* get the middle zip */

  do {
    while(strcmp(get_zip(fp,i),x)<0 && i<right) i++;
    while(strcmp(get_zip(fp,j),x)>0 && j>left) j--;

    if(i<=j) {
      swap_all_fields(fp, i, j);
      i++; j--;
    }
  } while(i<=j);

  if(left<j)  qs_disk(fp, left, j);
  if(i<right) qs_disk(fp, i, right);
}
```

```
/* Exchange two disk records. */
void swap_all_fields(fp, i, j)
FILE *fp;
long int i, j;
{

    char a[sizeof(ainfo)], b[sizeof(ainfo)];
    register int t;

    /* first read in record i and j */
    fseek(fp, sizeof(ainfo)*i, 0);
    fread(a, sizeof(ainfo), 1, fp);

    fseek(fp, sizeof(ainfo)*j, 0);
    fread(b, sizeof(ainfo), 1, fp);

    /* then write them back in opposite slots */
    fseek(fp, sizeof(ainfo)*j, 0);
    fwrite(a, sizeof(ainfo), 1, fp);

    fseek(fp, sizeof(ainfo)*i, 0);
    fwrite(b, sizeof(ainfo), 1, fp);
}

/* Return the zip code. */
char *get_zip(fp, rec)
FILE *fp;
long int rec;
{
    struct address *p;
    register int t;

    p = &ainfo;

    fseek(fp, rec*sizeof(ainfo), 0);
    fread(p, sizeof(ainfo), 1, fp);

    return ainfo.zip;
}
```

Several support functions had to be written to sort the address records. In the comparison section of the sort, **get_zip()** returns a pointer to the ZIP code of the comparand and the record being checked. The **swap_all_fields()** function performs the actual exchange of the data. Under most operating systems, the order of reads and writes has a great impact on the speed of this sort. The code, as it is written, forces a **seek** to record **i** and then a seek to **j**. While the head of the disk drive is still positioned at **j**, the data of **i** is written. This means that it is not necessary for the head to move a great distance. Had the code been written with the data of **i** to be written first, then an extra **seek** would have been necessary.

Sorting Random Access Files by Using Index Files

With some applications, it is not always necessary to physically sort the information contained in a disk data file. In these situations, another file, called the *index file*, is sorted in memory. It contains the sort keys and the data-file record numbers associated with each key. As you might expect, this approach greatly reduces the time it takes to sort the data.

To access a specific record in the data file, you first read the index file to find the location of the desired record in the data file. The example shown in Figure 1-4 helps make this process clear. Although the use of index files is quite simple, no example of this method is shown here because the length of the code prohibits its inclusion.

Sorting Sequential Files

Unlike random-access files, sequential files generally do not have fixed record lengths, and they may be organized on storage devices that do not allow easy random access. Therefore, sequential disk files are common because a specific application is best suited to variable record lengths or because the storage device is sequential in nature. For example, most text files are sequential.

Although sorting a disk file as if it were an array has several advantages, this method cannot be used with sequential files — there is no way to achieve quick access to any arbitrary element. For example, no quick way exists to reach arbitrary records of a sequential file that is located on tape. For this reason, it would be difficult to apply any of the previously presented array-sorting algorithms to sequential files.

There are two main approaches to sorting sequential files. The first approach reads the information into memory and sorts with one of the standard array-sorting algorithms. Although this approach is fast, memory constraints limit the size of the file that can be sorted.

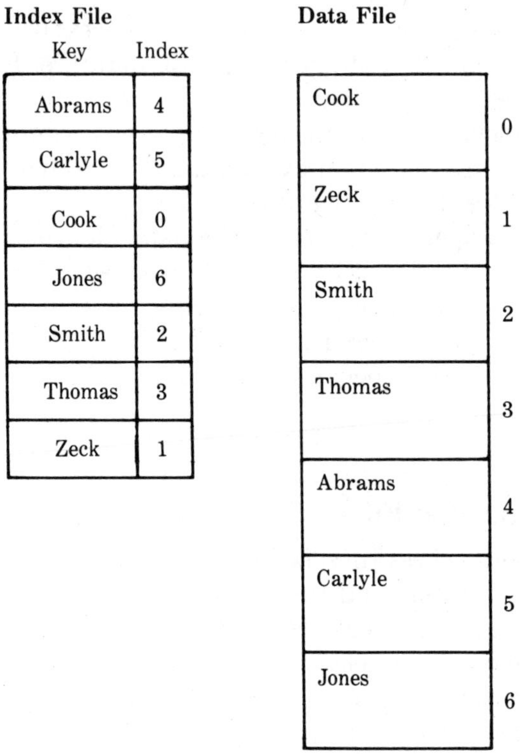

Figure 1-4.   Using an index file with a data file

The second approach, called a *Merge sort*, divides the file to be sorted into two files of equal length. Using these files, the sort reads an element from each file, orders that pair, and writes elements to a third disk file. This new file is then divided and the ordered doubles are merged into ordered quadruples. The new file is split again, and the same procedure is followed until the list is sorted. For historical reasons, this Merge sort is called a *three-tape merge* because it requires three files (tape drives) to be active at one time.

To understand how the Merge sort works, consider the following sequence:

    1 4 3 8 6 7 2 5

The first split produces

    1 4 3 8
    6 7 2 5

The first merge yields

    1 6 - 4 7 - 2 3 - 5 8

This is split again and becomes

    1 6 - 4 7
    2 3 - 5 8

The next merge yields

    1 2 3 6 - 4 5 7 8

The final split is

    1 2 3 6
    4 5 7 8

with the outcome

    1 2 3 4 5 6 7 8

As you may have guessed, the three-tape merge requires passes equal to $\log_2 n$ where n is the number of total elements to sort.

Here is a simple version of the Merge sort. It assumes that the input file is a character stream, such as a text file, and that the file is an even power of two in length. You can easily alter this version to sort any type of data file.

```
#include "stdio.h"

#define LENGTH 16   /* arbitrary */
void merge();

main(argc, argv)    /* merge sort for disk files */
int argc;
char *argv[];
{
  FILE *fp1, *fp2, *fp3;

  if((fp1=fopen(argv[1],"rw"))==0) {
    printf("cannot open file 1%s\n", argv[1]);
    exit(0);
  }

  if((fp2=fopen("sort1","rw"))==0) {
    printf("cannot open file 2\n");
    exit(0);
  }

  if((fp3=fopen("sort2","rw"))==0) {
    printf("cannot open file 3\n");
    exit(0);
  }

  merge(fp1, fp2, fp3, LENGTH);

  fclose(fp1); fclose(fp2); fclose(fp3);

}

/* A merge sort for even length files. */
void merge(fp1, fp2, fp3, count)
FILE *fp1, *fp2, *fp3;
int count;
{
  register int t, n, j, k, q;
  char x, y;

  for(n=1; n<count; n=n*2) {

    /* split file */
    for(t=0; t<count/2; ++t) putc(getc(fp1), fp2);
    for(; t<count; ++t) putc(getc(fp1), fp3);

    reset(fp1, fp2, fp3);

    for(q=0; q<count/2; q+=n) {
        x = getc(fp2);
```

```
      y = getc(fp3);
      for(j=k=0; ; ) {
   if(x<y) {
     putc(x, fp1);
     j++;
     if(j<n) x = getc(fp2);
     else break;
   }
   else {
     putc(y, fp1);
     k++;
     if(k<n) y = getc(fp3);
     else break;
   }
      }
      if(j<n)  {
        putc(x, fp1);
        j++;
      }
      if(k<n)  {
        putc(y, fp1);
        k++;
      }
      for(; j<n; ++j) putc(getc(fp2), fp1);
      for(; k<n; ++k) putc(getc(fp3), fp1);
   }
   reset(fp1,fp2,fp3);
   }
}

/* Rewind the files. */
reset(fp1, fp2, fp3)
FILE *fp1, *fp2, *fp3;
{
  rewind(fp1);
  rewind(fp2);
  rewind(fp3);
}
```

SEARCHING

Databases of information exist so that, from time to time, a user can locate and use the data in a given record as long as that record's key is known. There is only one method of finding information in an unsorted file or array, and another for a sorted file or array. Many compilers supply search functions as part of the standard library. However, as with sorting, general-purpose routines are sometimes too inefficient to use in demanding situations because of the extra overhead created by their generalization.

Searching Methods

Finding information in an unsorted array requires a sequential search, starting at the first element and stopping either when a match is found or when the end of the array is reached. This method must be used on unsorted data but can also be applied to sorted data. If the data has been sorted, then a *binary search* can be used, which will increase the speed of any search.

The Sequential Search

The sequential search is easy to code. The following function searches a character array of known length until a match is found with the specified key:

```
/* A sequential search function. */
sequential_search(item, count, key)
char *item;
int count;
char key;
{
   register int t;
   for(t=0; t<count; ++t)
     if(key==item[t]) return t;
   return -1;  /* no match */
}
```

This function returns either the index number of the matching entry if there is one, or −1 if there is not.

A straight sequential search will, on the average, test $1/2n$ elements. In the best case, it will test only one element and, in the worst case, n elements. If the information is stored on disk, the search time can be very long. But if the data is unsorted, this is the only method available.

The Binary Search

If the data to be searched is in sorted order, then a superior method, called the *binary search*, can be used to find a match. The method uses the "divide-and-conquer" approach. It first tests the middle element; if the element is larger than the key, it then tests the middle element of the first half; otherwise, it tests the middle element of the second half. This process is repeated until either a match is found or there are no more elements to test.

For example, to find the number 4 in the array **1 2 3 4 5 6 7 8 9**, the binary search would first test the middle element, which is **5**. Since this element is greater than 4, the search would continue with the first half, or

1 2 3 4 5

In this example, the middle element is **3**. This is less than 4, so the first half is discarded and the search continues with

4 5

This time the match is found.

In the binary search, the number of comparisons in the worst case is $\log_2 n$. With average cases, the number is somewhat better; in the best case, the number is 1.

You can use the following binary search function for character arrays to search any arbitrary data structure by changing the comparison portion of the routine.

```
/* A binary search function. */
binary(item, count, key)
char *item;
int count;
char key;
{
  int low, high, mid;

  low = 0; high = count-1;
  while(low<=high) {
    mid = (low+high)/2;
    if(key<item[mid]) high = mid-1;
    else if(key>item[mid]) low = mid+1;
    else return mid;  /* found */
  }
  return -1;
}
```

The next chapter explores different approaches to data storage and retrieval, which, in some cases, can make sorting and searching much easier tasks.

2

QUEUES, STACKS, LINKED LISTS, AND TREES

Programs consist of algorithms and data structures, and a good program is a blend of both. Choosing and implementing a data structure is as important as the routines that manipulate the data. The way information is organized and accessed usually is determined by the nature of the programming problem. Therefore, as a programmer, your "bag of tricks" must contain the right storage and retrieval method for any situation.

As data types become more complex, the way a programmer thinks of them bears less and less resemblance to the way they are actually represented in memory. For example, simple data types like **char** and **int** are bound tightly to their machine representations. In such a case, the value that an integer has in its machine representation closely approximates that which the programmer expects. Simple arrays, which are organized collections of the simple data types, are not quite as tightly bound as the simple types themselves, because an array may not appear in memory the way the programmer thinks it does. Even less tightly bound are **floats**, because the actual representation inside the machine does not match the average programmer's concept of a floating-point number. A structure, which is a conglomerate data type accessed under one name, is even more abstracted from the machine representation. Transcending the physical aspects of the data, the final level of abstraction concentrates on the sequence in which the data will be accessed (that is, stored and retrieved).

In essence, the physical data is linked to a "data engine" that controls the way information can be accessed by your program. There are four of these engines. They are

- A queue
- A stack
- A linked list
- A binary tree

Each method provides a solution to a class of problems, and each is essentially a "device" that performs a specific storage and retrieval operation on the information that it is given and the requests that it receives. The methods have two operations in common: they *store an item* and *retrieve an item*, where an item is one informational unit. This chapter shows you how to develop these mehthods for use in your own programs.

QUEUES

A *queue* is a linear list of information that is accessed in *first in, first out* order (sometimes called FIFO). The first item placed on the queue is the first item retrieved, the second item placed on the queue is the second item retrieved, and so on. This is the only means of storage and retrieval; random access of any specific item is not allowed.

Queues are very common in everyday life. For example, a line at a bank or a fast-food restaurant is a queue (except when rude patrons push their way to the front). To visualize how a queue works, consider two functions: **qstore( )** and **qretrieve( )**. The **qstore( )** function places an item onto the end of the queue, and **qretrieve( )** removes the first item from the queue and returns its value. Figure 2-1 shows the effect of a series of these operations.

Keep in mind that a retrieval operation removes an item from the queue, and if it is not stored elsewhere, destroys it. Therefore, even though the program is still active, a queue may be empty at any particular time, because all of its items have been removed.

Action	Contents of Queue
qstore(A)	A
qstore(B)	A B
qstore(C)	A B C
qretrieve( ) returns A	B C
qstore(D)	B C D
qretrieve( ) returns B	C D
qretrieve( ) returns C	D

Figure 2-1.   A queue in action

Queues are used in many types of programming situations. One of the most common is simulations (discussed in Chapter 8). They are also used for event scheduling (as in a PERT or Gantt chart) and for I/O buffering.

As an example of using queues, consider a simple event-scheduler program that allows you to enter a number of appointments. As each appointment is kept, it is taken off the list, and the next one is displayed.

The queue consists of an array of character pointers that point to a description of each appointment. The size of the queue is determined by the definition of the macro **MAX—EVENT**, which is set arbitrarily to 100 in this program, so the number of appointments is limited to 100. The maximum length of the description string is limited to 256 characters, including the **NULL** terminator.

The functions **qstore( )** and **qretrieve( )** are needed first for this simple appointment-scheduling program. They are shown here:

```
#define MAX_EVENT 100

char *p[MAX_EVENT], *qretrieve();
int spos;
int rpos;

/* Store an appointment. */
void qstore(q)
char *q;
{
  if(spos==MAX_EVENT) {
    printf("list full\n");
    return;
  }
  p[spos] = q;
  spos++;
}

/* Retrieve an appointment. */
char *qretrieve()
{
  if(rpos==spos) {
    printf("No appointments to perform.\n");
    return NULL;
  }
  rpos++;
  return p[rpos-1];
}
```

These functions require two global variables: **spos**, which holds the index of the next free storage location, and **rpos**, which holds the index of the next item to retrieve. (You can use these functions to maintain a queue of other data types simply by changing the base type of the array they operate on.) The macro **NULL** in **qretrieve( )** is defined in **stdio.h**, which must be included in the file that contains these functions.

The **qstore( )** function places pointers to new events (appointments) on the end of the list and checks to see if the list is full. The **qretrieve( )** function takes events off the queue while there are events to perform. With each new event scheduled, **spos** is incremented, and with each event completed, **rpos** is incremented. In essence, **rpos** "chases" **spos** through the queue. Figure 2-2 shows how this appears in memory as the program executes. If **rpos** and **spos** are equal, there are no events left in the schedule. Keep in mind that even though the information stored in the queue is not actually destroyed by the **qretrieve( )** function, it can never be accessed again and is in effect destroyed.

The entire program for this simple appointment scheduler is listed here. You may want to enhance it for your own use. Notice that the file **stdlib.h** is included in the program to ensure that the declarations necessary to C's dynamic allocation routines are included. If your compiler is not in agreement with the ANSI standard, then this file will probably be called **malloc.h** instead.

```
/* A simple appointment scheduler that demonstrates the
   use of a queue.
*/
#include "stdlib.h"      /* "malloc.h" on some systems */
#include "stdio.h"

#define MAX_EVENT 100

char *p[MAX_EVENT], *qretrieve();
int spos;
int rpos;
void enter(), qstore(), review(), perform();

main()
```

```
{
  char s[80];
  register int t;

  for(t=0; t<MAX_EVENT; ++t)
    p[t] = NULL; /* init array to nulls */

  spos = 0; rpos = 0;

  for(;;) {
    printf("Enter, List, Remove, Quit: ");
    gets(s);
    *s = toupper(*s);

    switch(*s) {
      case 'E':
        enter();
        break;
      case 'L':
        review();
        break;
      case 'R':
        perform();
        break;
      case 'Q':
        exit(0);
    }
  }
}

/* Enter the appointments. */
void enter()
{
  char s[256], *p;

  do {
    printf("enter appointment %d:", spos+1);
    gets(s);
    if(*s==0) break;  /* no entry */

    /* get memory to hold the appointment description */
    p = (char *) malloc(strlen(s));
    if(!p) {
      printf("out of memory.\n");
      return;
    }
    strcpy(p, s);  /* copy description */
    if(*s) qstore(p);
  }while(*s); /* stop entry on blank line */
}

/* See what's in the queue. */
void review()
{
  register int t;

  for(t=rpos; t<spos; ++t)
    printf("%d. %s\n", t+1, p[t]);
}

/* Remove an appointment from the queue. */
void perform()
{
  char *p;
```

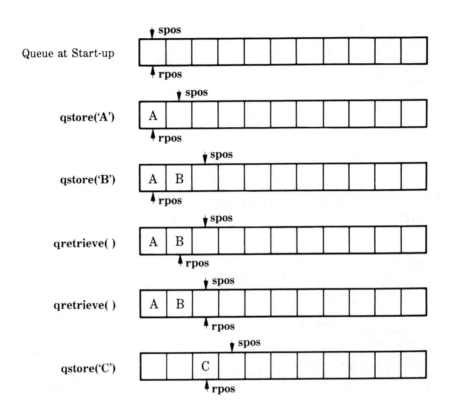

Figure 2-2. The retrieval index chasing the storage index

```
  if(!(p=qretrieve())) return;
  printf("%s\n", p);
}

/* Store an appointment. */
void qstore(q)
char *q;
{
```

```
  if(spos==MAX_EVENT) {
    printf("list full\n");
    return;
  }
  p[spos] = q;
  spos++;
}

/* Retrieve an appointment */
char *qretrieve()
{
  if(rpos==spos) {
    printf("No appointments pending.\n");
    return NULL;
  }
  rpos++;
  return p[rpos-1];
}
```

A short sample run of the appointment scheduler is shown here:

```
Enter, List, Remove, Quit: E
enter appointment 1: Jon at 9 about the phone system
enter appointment 2: Ted at 10:30 - wants that raise...humm.
enter appointment 3: lunch with Mary and Tom at Harry's
enter appointment 4: <cr>
Enter, List, Remove, Quit: L
1. Jon at 9 about the phone system
2. Ted at 10:30 - wants that raise...humm.
3. lunch with Mary and Tom at Harry's
Enter, List, Remove, Quit: R
Jon at 9 about the phone system
Enter, List, Remove, Quit: L
2. Ted at 10:30 - wants that raise...humm.
3. lunch with Mary and Tom at Harry's
Enter, List, Remove, Quit:
```

The Circular Queue

While studying the appointment-scheduler program, you may have thought of an improvement. Instead of having the program stop when the limit of the array used to store the queue was reached, you could have both the store index **spos** and the retrieve index **rpos** loop back to the beginning of the array. This would allow any number of items to be placed on the queue, as long as items were also being taken off. This implementation method, called a *circular queue*, uses the storage array as if it were a circle instead of a linear list.

To create a circular queue for the appointment-scheduler program, the functions **qstore( )** and **qretrieve( )** need to be changed as shown here:

```
/* Circular Queue store function. */
void qstore(q)
char *q;
{
  if(spos+1==rpos || (spos+1==MAX_EVENT && !rpos) {
    printf("List full\n");
    return;
  }
  p[spos] = q;
  spos++;
  if(spos==MAX_EVENT) spos = 0; /* loop around */
}

/* Circular Queue retrieve function. */
char *qretrieve()
{
  if(rpos==MAX_EVENT) rpos = 0; /* loop back */
  if(rpos==spos) {
    printf("No events to perform.\n");
    return NULL;
  }
  rpos++;
  return p[rpos-1];
}
```

The queue is full when the value of **spos** is one less than **rpos**; otherwise, there is room in the queue for another appointment. When the values of **spos** and **rpos** are equal, the queue is empty. However, this means that when the program starts, the retrieve index **rpos** must not be set to zero, but rather to **MAX—EVENT** so that the first call to **qstore( )** will not produce the **queue full** message. The queue will hold only **MAX—EVENT-1** elements, because **rpos** and **spos** must always be at least one element apart. Otherwise, it would be impossible to know whether the queue was full or empty. The array used for the circular version of the appointment-scheduler program looks like Figure 2-3.

A common use of a circular queue may be for operating systems that buffer the information read from and written to disk files or the console. Another common use of the circular queue is for real-time application programs, which must continue to process information while buffering I/O requests. Many word processors do this when they reformat a paragraph or justify a line. There is a brief period of time during which what is being typed is not displayed until after the other process is completed; the application program must continue to check for keyboard entry during the other process's execution. If a key has been typed, it is quickly placed in the queue and the process continues. When the process is complete, the characters are retrieved from the queue.

To see how this is done, you can study a simple program that contains two processes. The first process prints the numbers 1 to 32,000 on the screen. The second places characters into a circular queue as they are typed, without echoing them to the screen. Typing a semicolon causes the loop to stop. The characters you type will not be displayed as you enter them, because the first process is given priority over the screen at this time. Once the semicolon has been struck, the characters in the queue are retrieved and printed. The proposed ANSI standard does not define library functions to check the keyboard status or read keyboard characters without echoing them to the display, because these functions are dependent on the operating system. However, most compilers supply routines that do these things.

The short program shown here will work with most PC-based C compilers, including Microsoft C and Turbo C. The **kbhit()** function returns TRUE if a key has been struck, and FALSE otherwise. The **getch()** function reads a character from the keyboard but does not echo it to the screen. Refer to your C compiler manual to find out what these functions are called by your compiler.

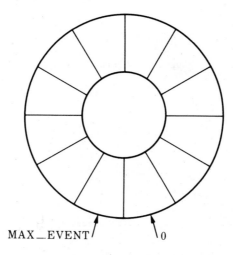

MAX_EVENT   0

Figure 2-3.   The circular array for the appointment-scheduler
program

```
/* A simple circular queue example. */

#include "stdio.h"

#define MAX 80

char buf[MAX+1];
int spos=0;
int rpos=MAX;

void qstore();
char qretrieve();

main() /* circular queue example - keyboard buffer */
{
  register char ch;
  int t;

  buf[80]=NULL;
```

```
    for(ch=' ',t=0; t<32000 && ch!=';'; ++t) {
      if(kbhit()) {
        ch = getch();
        qstore(ch);
      }
      printf("%d ",t);
    }

    while((ch=qretrieve())!=NULL) putchar(ch); /* display buf */
}

/* Store characters in a circular queue. */
void qstore(q)
char q;
{
  if(spos+1==rpos || (spos+1==MAX && !rpos)) {
    printf("list full\n");
    return;
  }
  buf[spos] = q;
  spos++;
  if(spos==MAX) spos = 0; /* loop back */
}

/* Retrieve a character from a circular queue. */
char qretrieve()
{
  if(rpos==MAX) rpos = 0; /* loop back */
  if(rpos==spos) {
    return NULL;
  }
  rpos++;
  return buf[rpos-1];
}
```

STACKS

A *stack* is the opposite of a queue because it uses *last-in, first-out* accessing (sometimes called LIFO). Think of a stack of plates on a table. The first plate on the table is the last to be used, and the last plate placed on the stack is the first to be used. Stacks are used a great deal in system software, including compilers and interpreters. In fact, most C compilers use a stack to pass arguments to functions.

The two basic operations, *store* and *retrieve*, are usually called *push* and *pop*, respectively. To implement a stack you will need two functions: **push()**, which places a value on the stack, and **pop()**, which retrieves a value from the stack. You also need a region of memory to use as the stack; you can either use an array for this purpose or you can allocate a region memory with C's dynamic memory allocation functions. Like the queue, the retrieval function takes a value off the list, and if it is not stored elsewhere, destroys it. The general form for **push()** and **pop()**, using an integer array, is shown here. You may maintain stacks of other data types by changing the base type of the array on which the **push()** and **pop()** functions operate.

```
int stack[MAX];
int tos=0;   /* top of stack */

/* Place an element on the stack. */
void push(i)
int i;
{
  if(tos>=MAX) {
    printf("stack full\n");
    return;
  }
  stack[tos] = i;
  tos++;
}

/* Return the top element from the stack. */
int pop()
{
  tos--;
  if(tos<0) {
    printf("stack underflow\n");
    return NULL;
  }
  return stack[tos];
}
```

The variable **tos** is the index of the next open stack location. When implementing these functions, you must always remember to prevent overflow and underflow. In these routines if **tos** is 0, the stack is empty; if **tos** is greater than the last storage location, the stack is full. The **pop()** function returns **NULL** if an error is encountered, but this will only be useful if **NULL** is not a valid stack value. Figure 2-4 shows how a stack works.

An excellent example of stack usage is a four-function calculator. Most calculators today accept a standard form of expression called *infix notation,* which takes the general form *operand-operator-operand.* For example, to add 100 to 200, you would enter **100**, press the + key, enter **200**, and press the equal-sign key. However, many early calculators, in an effort to save memory (which used to be expensive), used a form of expression evaluation called *postfix notation,* in which both operands are entered before the operator is entered. For example, to add 100 to 200 by using postfix, you would first enter **100**, then enter **200**, and then press the + key. As operands are entered, they are placed on a stack. Each time an operator is entered, two operands are removed from the stack, and the result is pushed back on the stack. The advantage of the postfix form is that very complex expressions can be evaluated easily by the calculator without much code.

Before developing a four-function calculator for postfix expressions, you need to modify the basic **push( )** and **pop( )** functions. The program will use C's dynamic memory allocation routines to provide memory for the stack. The stack functions, as they will be used in the calculator example, are shown here:

```
int *p;    /* will point to a region of free memory */
int *tos; /* points to top of stack */
int *bos; /* points to bottom of stack */

/* Place an element on the stack. */
void push(i)
int i;
{
  if(p>bos) {
    printf("stack full\n");
    return;
  }
  *p = i;
  p++;
}

/* Return the top element from the stack. */
pop()
{
  p--;
```

```
if(p<tos) {
  printf("stack underflow\n");
  return 0;
}
return *p;
}
```

Notice that you must define a pointer to the bottom as well as the top of the stack, because **tos** and **bos** are not indexes into an array—they are pointers into memory.

Before these functions can be used, you must allocate a region of free memory by using **malloc( )**. You must also assign the address of the beginning of that region to **tos** and the address of the end to **bos**.

The entire calculator program is shown here. In addition to the plus, minus, times, and divide operators, you may also enter a

Action	Contents of Stack
push(A)	A
push(B)	B A
push(C)	C B A
pop( ) retrieves C	B A
push(F)	F B A
pop( ) retrieves F	B A
pop( ) retrieves B	A
pop( ) retrieves A	*empty*

Figure 2-4.   A stack in action

period, which causes the current value of the top of the stack to be displayed. Type a "q" to quit the program.

```
/* A simple four-function calculator. */

#include "stdlib.h"  /* "malloc.h" in some compilers */

#define MAX 100

int *p;     /* will point to a region of free memory */
int *tos; /* points to top of stack */
int *bos; /* points to bottom of stack */
void push();

main()
{
  int a, b;
  char s[80];

  p = (int *) malloc(MAX*sizeof(int));  /* get stack memory */
  if(!p) {
    printf("allocation failure\n");
    exit(1);
  }
  tos = p;
  bos = p+MAX-1;

  printf("Four Function Calculator\n");

  do {
    printf(": ");
    gets(s);
    switch(*s) {
      case '+':
        a = pop();
        b = pop();
        printf("%d\n", a+b);
        push(a+b);
        break;
      case '-':
        a = pop();
        b = pop();
        printf("%d\n", b-a);
        push(b-a);
        break;
      case '*':
        a = pop();
        b = pop();
        printf("%d\n", b*a);
        push(b*a);
        break;
      case '/':
        a = pop();
        b = pop();
        if(a==0) {
```

```
                printf("divide by 0\n");
                break;
              }
              printf("%d\n", b/a);
              push(b/a);
              break;
          case '.': /* show  contents of top of stack */
              a = pop();
              push(a);
              printf("Current value on top of stack: %d\n", a);
              break;
          default:
              push(atoi(s));
        }
    } while(*s!='q');
}

/* Place an element on the stack. */
void push(i)
int i;
{
  if(p>bos) {
    printf("stack full\n");
    return;
  }
  *p = i;
  p++;
}

/* Return the top element from the stack. */
pop()
{
  p--;
  if(p<tos) {
    printf("stack underflow\n");
    return 0;
  }
  return *p;
}
```

A sample session at the calculator is shown here:

```
Four Function Calculator
: 10<cr>
: 10<cr>
: +<cr>
20
: 5<cr>
: /<cr>
4
: .<cr>
Current value on top of stack: 4
: q<cr>
```

LINKED LISTS

Queues and stacks share common traits. First, they both have strict rules for referencing the data stored in them. Second, their retrieval operations are by nature *consumptive;* that is, accessing an item in a stack or queue requires its removal and, unless it is stored elsewhere, its destruction. Both stacks and queues also need, at least in concept, a contiguous region of memory to operate.

Unlike a stack or a queue, a *linked list* may access its storage in a random fashion, because each piece of information carries with it a *link* to the next data item in the chain. A linked list requires a complex data structure, whereas a stack or a queue can operate on both simple and complex data items. Also, a linked-list retrieval operation does not remove and destroy an item from the list; in fact, a specific deletion operation must be added to do this.

Linked lists are used for two purposes. The first is to create arrays of unknown size in memory. If you know the amount of storage in advance, you can use a simple array, but if you do not know the actual size of a list, then you must use a linked list. The second use of a linked list is for the disk-file storage of databases. A linked list allows you to insert and delete items quickly and easily without rearranging the entire disk file. For these two reasons, linked lists are used extensively in database-management software.

Linked lists can be either *singly linked* or *doubly linked.* A singly linked list contains a link to the next data item. A doubly linked list contains links to both the next and the previous element in the list. The type you use depends on your application.

Singly Linked Lists

A singly linked list requires that each item of information contain a link to the next element in the list. Each data item usually consists of a structure containing both information fields and a link pointer. The concept of a singly linked list is shown in Figure 2-5.

There are two ways to build a singly linked list. The first is simply to add each new item on the end of the list. The second is to add items at specific places in the list (for example, in ascending sorted order). How you build the list determines how the store function will be coded. Creating a linked list by adding items on the end will demonstrate this.

First, you need need to define a data structure to hold the information and the links. Because mailing lists are common, this example uses one. The data structure for each element in the

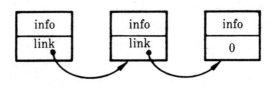

Figure 2-5.   A singly linked list in memory

mailing list is defined here:

```
struct address {
  char name[40];
  char street[40];
  char city[20];
  char state[3];
  char zip[10];
  struct address *next;
} info;
```

The **slstore( )** function builds a singly linked list by placing each new element on the end of the list. A pointer to a structure of type **address** must be pased to **slstore( )**, as shown here:

```
/* Store an element in a list. */
void slstore(i)          .
struct address *i;
{
  static struct address *last=NULL; /* start with null link */

  if(!last) last=i; /* first item in list */
  else last->next=i;
  i->next=NULL;
  last=i;
}
```

Notice the use of the **static** variable **last**. Because initialization of a **static** occurs once at the start of the program, a **static** can be used to start the list-building process. If your C compiler does not support either **static** or initializers, then you must make **last** into a global variable and initialize it explicitly in **main( )**. Also, you may want **last** to be a global variable if the list-building process will be restarted.

Although you can sort the list created with **slstore( )** as a separate operation, it is easier to sort the list while building it by inserting each new item in the proper sequence of the chain. Also, if the list is already sorted, then it is advantageous to keep it sorted by inserting new items in their proper locations. To do this, the program must scan the list sequentially until it finds the proper location, insert the new address at that point, and rearrange the links as necessary.

Three situations can occur when you are inserting an item in a singly linked list. First, the item can become the new first item; second, it can be inserted in the middle, between two other items; third, it can become the last element. Figure 2-6 shows how the links are changed for each case.

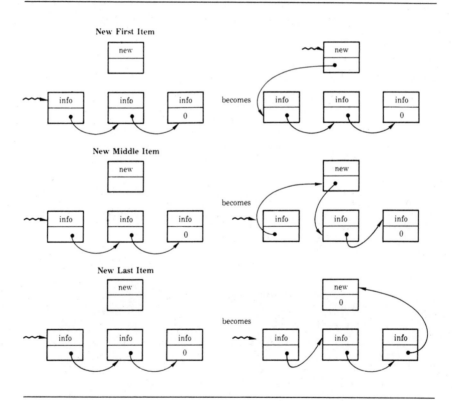

Figure 2-6.   Inserting an item into a singly linked list

If you change the first item in the list, you must update the entry point to the list elsewhere in your program. To avoid this, you can use a *sentinel* as a first item. A sentinel is a special value that will always, under all circumstances, be first in the list. With this method, the entry point to the list will not change; however, one extra storage will be used to hold the sentinel, which may be a drawback.

The **sls_store( )** function shown here inserts addresses into the mailing list in ascending order based on the **name** field. It returns a pointer to the first element in the list and also requires that the pointer to the start of the list be passed to it. When the first element is inserted, both **top** and **i** are the same.

```c
/* Build a list in sorted order. */
struct address *sls_store(i,top)  /* store in sorted order */
struct address *i;      /* new element to store */
struct address *top;    /* start of list */
{
  static struct address *last=0; /* start with null link */
  struct address *old, *start;

  start=top;

  if(!last) { /* first element in list */
    i->next = NULL;
    last = i;
    return i;
  }

  old = NULL;
  while(top) { /* while there are still elements on list */
    /* see if new item is less than current element */
    if(strcmp(top->name, i->name)<0) {
      /* if not, continue searching */
      old = top;
      top = top->next;
    }
    else {
      if(old) { /* goes in middle */
        old->next=i;
        i->next=top;
        return start;
      }
      i->next=top; /* new first element */
      return    i;
    }
  }
  last->next=i; /* goes on end */
  i->next=NULL;
  last=i;
  return start;
}
```

In a linked list you seldom find a specific function dedicated to the retrieve process, which returns item after item in list order. This code is usually so short that it is placed inside another routine (such as a search, delete, or display function). For example, the routine shown here displays all of the names in a mailing list:

```
void display(top)
struct address *top;
{
  while(top) {
    printf(top->name);
    top = top->next;
  }
}
```

Here, **top** is a pointer to the first structure in the list, and it must be initialized to zero elsewhere in the program. Retrieving items from the list is as simple as following a chain. A search routine based on the **name** field could be written like this:

```
struct address *search(top, n)
struct address *top;
char *n;
{
  while(top) {
    if(!strcmp(n, top->name)) return top;
    top = top->next;
  }
  return NULL;  /* no match */
}
```

Because **search( )** returns a pointer to the list item that matches the search name, it must be declared as returning a structure pointer of type **address**. If there is no match, a **NULL** is returned.

The process of deleting an item from a singly linked list is straightforward. As with insertion, there are three cases: deleting the first item, deleting a middle item, and deleting the last item. Figure 2-7 shows each case.

The function shown next deletes a given item from a list of structures of type **address**.

```
struct address *sldelete(p, i, top)
struct address *p; /* previous item */
struct address *i; /* item to delete */
struct address *top; /* start of list */
{
    if(p) p->next = i->next;
    else   top = i->next;

    return top;
}
```

Pointers to the deleted item, to the item before it in the chain, and to the start of the list must be sent to **sldelete( )**. If the first item is to be removed, then the previous pointer must be **NULL**. The function must return a pointer to the start of the list because of the case in which the first item is deleted—the program must know where the new first element is located.

Singly linked lists have one major drawback that prevents their extensive use: the list cannot be followed in reverse order. For this reason, doubly linked lists are generally used.

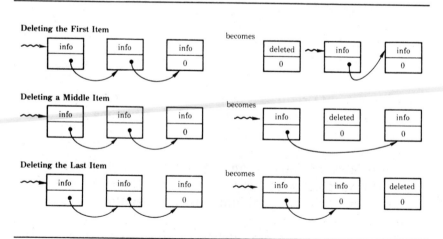

Figure 2-7.   The three cases of item deletion for a singly linked list

Doubly Linked Lists

Doubly linked lists consist of data and links to both the next item and the preceding item. Figure 2-8 shows how these links are arranged. Two links instead of one offers two major advantages. First, the list can be read in either direction. This not only simplifies sorting the list but also, in the case of a database, allows a user to scan the list in either direction. Second, because either a forward link or a backward link can read the entire list, the list can be reconstructed with the other link should one of the links become invalid. This is meaningful only in the case of equipment failure.

Three primary operations can be performed on a doubly linked list: you can insert a new first element, insert a new middle element, and insert a new last element. These operations are shown in Figure 2-9.

Building a doubly linked list is similar to building a singly linked list, except that two links must be maintained. Therefore, the structure needs to have room for both links. Using the mailing-list example again, you can modify the structure **address** as shown here to accommodate this:

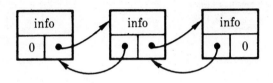

Figure 2-8.   A doubly linked list

```
struct address {
  char name[40];
  char street[40];
  char city[20];
  char state[3];
  char zip[10];
  struct address *next;
  struct address *prior;
} info;
```

With the **address** structure as the basic data item, the function shown here, **dlstore()**, builds a doubly linked list.

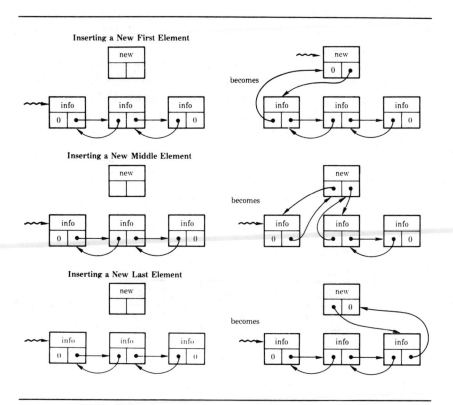

Figure 2-9.   The three primary operations of a doubly linked list

```
/* Build a doubly linked list. */
void dlstore(i)
struct address *i;
{
  static struct address *last=NULL; /* start with null link */

  if(last==NULL) last=i; /* first item in list */
  else last->next=i;
  i->next=NULL;
  i->prior=last;
  last=i;
}
```

This function places each new entry on the end of the list. If your
compiler does not support the **static** type modifier or initializa-
tions, make **last** a global.

Like a singly linked list, a doubly linked list can have a function that stores each element in a specific location in the list as it
is built, instead of always placing each new item on the end. The
function shown here, called **dls—store( )** creates a list that is
sorted in ascending order:

```
/* Create a doubly linked list in sorted order.
   A pointer to the first element is returned because
   it is possible that a new element will be inserted
   at the start of the list.
*/
struct address *dls_store(i,top)  /* store in sorted order */
struct address *i;       /* new element */
struct address *top;   /* first element in list */
{
  struct address *old, *p;

  if(last==NULL) {  /* first element in list */
    i->next = NULL;
    i->prior = NULL;
    last = i;
    return i;
  }

  p = top; /* start at top of list */

  old = NULL;
  while(p) {
    if(strcmp(p->name, i->name)<0){
      old = p;
      p = p->next;
    }
    else {
      if(p->prior) {
        p->prior->next = i;
        i->next = p;
        i->prior = p->prior;
        p->prior = i;
        return top;
      }
```

```
      i->next = p; /* new first element */
      i->prior = NULL;
      p->prior = i;
      return  i;
    }
  }
  old->next = i; /* put on end */
  i->next = NULL;
  i->prior = old;
  last = i;
  return start;
}
```

Because an item can be inserted at the top of the list, this function must return a pointer to the first item in the list so that other parts of the program will know where the list begins.

As with the singly linked list, retrieving a specific data item consists of simply following the links until the proper element is found. There are three cases to consider when deleting an element from a doubly linked list: deleting the first item, deleting an item from the middle, and deleting the last item. Figure 2-10 shows how the links are rearranged.

The following function deletes an item of type **address** from a doubly linked list:

```
/* Delete the specified element from a doubly linked list */
struct address *dldelete(i, top)
struct address *i; /* item to delete */
struct address *top;  /* first item in list */
{
  if(i->prior) i->prior->next = i->next;
  else { /* new first item */
    top = i->next;
    if(top) top->prior = 0;
  }
  if(i->next) i->next->prior = i->prior;
  return top;
}
```

This function requires one less pointer to be passed to it than does the singly linked list. This is because the data item being deleted already carries with it a link to the previous element and the next element. Again, because the first element in the list might change, the pointer to the top element is returned to the calling routine.

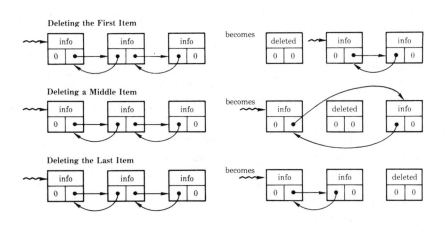

Figure 2-10.   Deletion in a doubly linked list

A Mailing-List Example

A simple but complete mailing-list program finishes this discussion of doubly linked lists. The entire list is kept in memory while in use; however, the list can be stored in a disk file and loaded for later use. Except for a few support functions, this program uses the doubly linked list routines developed earlier.

```
/* A simple mailing list program. */

#include "stdio.h" /* "malloc.h" for some compilers */

struct address {
  char name[30];
  char street[40];
  char city[20];
  char state[3];
  char zip[10]; /* hold US and Canadian zips */
  struct address *next;  /* pointer to next entry */
  struct address *prior;  /* pointer to previous record */
} list_entry;
```

```
struct address *start;  /* pointer to first entry in list */
struct address *last;   /* pointer to last entry */

void enter(), display(), search(), save(), load();

main()
{
  char s[80], choice;
  struct address *info;

  start = last = NULL;  /* zero length list */

  for(;;) {
    switch(menu_select()) {
      case 1: enter();  /* enter addresses */
        break;
      case 2: delete();  /* remove an address */
        break;
      case 3: list();   /* list the addresses */
        break;
      case 4: search();  /* find an address */
        break;
      case 5: save();   /* save list to disk */
        break;
      case 6: load();   /* read from disk */
        break;
      case 7: exit(0);
    }
  }
}

/* Select an operation. */
menu_select()
{
  char s[80];
  int c;

  printf("1. Enter a name\n");
  printf("2. Delete a name\n");
  printf("3. List the file\n");
  printf("4. Search\n");
  printf("5. Save the file\n");
  printf("6. Load the file\n");
  printf("7. Quit\n");
  do {
    printf("\nEnter your choice: ");
    gets(s);
    c = atoi(s);
  } while(c<0 || c>7);
  return c;
}

/* Enter names and addresses. */
void enter()
{
  struct address *info, *dls_store();
```

```
  for(;;) {
    info=(struct address *) malloc(sizeof(list_entry));
    if(!info) {
      printf("\nout of memory");
      return;
    }

    inputs("enter name: ", info->name, 30);
    if(!info->name[0]) break;  /* stop entering */
    inputs("enter street: ", info->street, 40);
    inputs("enter city: ", info->city, 20);
    inputs("enter state: ", info->state, 3);
    inputs("enter zip: ", info->zip, 10);

    start=dls_store(info, start);
  } /* entry loop */
}

/* This function prompts for input and accepts
   a string up to the length in count.  This prevents
   the string from overrunning its array.
*/
inputs(prompt, s, count)
char *prompt;
char *s;
int count;
{
  char p[255];

  do {
    printf(prompt);
    gets(p);
    if(strlen(p)>count) printf("\ntoo long\n");
  } while(strlen(p)>count);
  strcpy(s, p);
}

/* Create a doubly linked list in sorted order.
   A pointer to the first element is returned because
   it is possible that a new element will be inserted
   at the start of the list.
*/
struct address *dls_store(i, top)  /* store in sorted order */
struct address *i;    /* new element */
struct address *top;  /* first element in list */
{
  struct address *old, *p;

  if(last==NULL) {  /* first element in list */
    i->next = NULL;
    i->prior = NULL;
    last = i;
    return i;
  }

  p = top; /* start at top of list */
```

```
    old = NULL;
    while(p) {
      if(strcmp(p->name,i->name)<0){
        old = p;
        p = p->next;
      }
      else {
        if(p->prior) {
          p->prior->next = i;
          i->next = p;
          i->prior = p->prior;
          p->prior = i;
          return top;
        }
        i->next = p; /* new first element */
        i->prior = NULL;
        p->prior = i;
        return    i;
      }
    }
    old->next = i; /* put on end */
    i->next = NULL;
    i->prior = old;
    last = i;
    return start;
}

/* Remove an element from the list. */
delete()
{
    struct address *info, *find();
    char s[80];

    printf("enter name: ");
    gets(s);
    info=find(s);
    if(info) {
      if(start==info) {
        start = info->next;
        if(start) start->prior = NULL;
        else last = NULL;
      }
      else {
        info->prior->next = info->next;
        if(info!=last)
            info->next->prior = info->prior;
        else
          last = info->prior;
      }
      free(info);  /* return memory to system */
    }
}

/* Find the address given the name. */
struct address *find(name)
char *name;
{
    struct address *info;
```

```
    info = start;
    while(info) {
      if(!strcmp(name,info->name)) return info;
      info = info->next;  /* get next address */
    }
    printf("name not found\n");
    return NULL;  /* not found */
  }

/* List the mailing list on the screen. */
list()
{
  register int t;
  struct address *info;

  info = start;
  while(info) {
    display(info);
    info = info->next;  /* get next address */
  }
  printf("\n\n");
}

/* Display an address. */
void display(info)
struct address *info;
{
    printf("%s\n", info->name);
    printf("%s\n", info->street);
    printf("%s\n", info->city);
    printf("%s\n", info->state);
    printf("%s\n", info->zip);
    printf("\n\n");
}

/* Search for an address given the name. */
void search()
{
  char name[40];
  struct address *info,*find();

  printf("enter name to find: ");
  gets(name);
  if(!(info=find(name))) printf("not found\n");
  else display(info);
}

/* Save the mailing list to a disk file. */
void save()
{
  register int t;
  struct address *info;

  FILE *fp;
  if((fp=fopen("mlist","wb"))==NULL) {
    printf("cannot open file\n");
    exit(1);
  }
  printf("\nsaving file\n");
```

```
  info = start;
  while(info) {
    fwrite(info, sizeof(struct address), 1, fp);
    info = info->next;  /* get next address */
  }
  fclose(fp);
}

/* Load an address file from disk. */
void load()
{
  register int t;
  struct address *info, *temp=NULL;
  FILE *fp;

  if((fp=fopen("mlist","rb"))==NULL) {
    printf("cannot open file\n");
    exit(1);
  }

  while(start) {
    info = start->next;
    free(info);
    start = info;
  }

  printf("\nloading file\n");

  start = (struct address *) malloc(sizeof(struct address));
  if(!start) {
    printf("out of memory\n");
    return;
  }
  info = start;
  while(!feof(fp)) {
    if(1!=fread(info, sizeof(struct address), 1, fp)) break;
    /* get memory for next */
    info->next=(struct address *) malloc(sizeof(struct address));
    if(!info->next) {
      printf("out of memory\n");
      return;
    }
    info->prior = temp;
    temp = info;
    info = info->next;
  }
  temp->next = NULL;  /* last entry */
  last = temp;

  start->prior = NULL;
  fclose(fp);
}
```

BINARY TREES

The final data structure is the *binary tree*. Although there can be many types of trees, binary trees are special because, when they are sorted, they lend themselves to rapid searches, insertions, and deletions. Each item in a binary tree consists of information along with a link to the left member and a link to the right member. Figure 2-11 shows a small tree.

Computer scientists are not known for their grammar, and the terminology used to discuss trees is a classic case of mixed metaphors. The *root* is the first item in the tree. Each data item is called a *node* (or sometimes a *leaf*) of the tree, and any piece of the tree is called a *subtree*. A node that does not have subtrees attached to it is called a *terminal node*. The *height* of the tree is equal to the number of layers deep that its roots grow. Throughout this discussion, think of binary trees as appearing in memory the way they do on paper, but remember that a tree is only a way to structure data in memory, and memory is linear in form.

The binary tree is a special form of linked list. Items can be inserted, deleted, and accessed in any order. In addition, the retrieval operation is not destructive. Although trees are easy to visualize, they present some very difficult programming problems, which this section will only introduce.

Most functions that use trees are recursive, because the tree itself is a recursive data structure—that is, each subtree is, itself, a tree. Therefore, the routines that developed here will be recursive as well. Nonrecursive versions of these functions exist, but their code is much more difficult to understand.

The order of a tree depends on how the tree will be referenced. The process of accessing each node in a tree is called a *tree traver-*

sal, which is shown by this tree diagram:

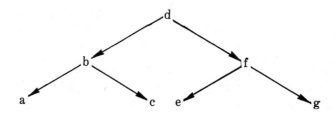

There are three ways to traverse a tree: *inorder, preorder,* and *postorder.* Using inorder, you visit the left subtree, visit the root, and then visit the right subtree. In preorder, you visit the root, the left subtree, and then the right subtree. With postorder, you visit the left subtree, the right subtree, and then the root. The order of access for the tree just shown, using each method, is as follows:

Inorder	a b c d e f g
Preorder	d b a c f e g
Postorder	a c b e g f d

Although a tree need not be sorted, most uses require it. Of course, what constitutes a sorted tree depends on how you will be traversing the tree. The examples in the rest of this chapter access the tree in inorder fashion. Therefore, a sorted binary tree is one in which the subtree on the left contains nodes that are less than or equal to the root, while those on the right are greater than the root.

The following function, **stree( )**, will build a sorted binary tree:

```
/* Build a sorted binary tree. */
struct tree *stree(root, r, info)
struct tree *root; /* pointer to the root */
struct tree *r; /* pointer to subroot */
char info; /* information to place in the tree */
{
  if(!r) {
    r=(struct tree *) malloc(sizeof(struct tree));
    if(!r) {
      printf("out of memory\n");
      exit(0);
    }
}
```

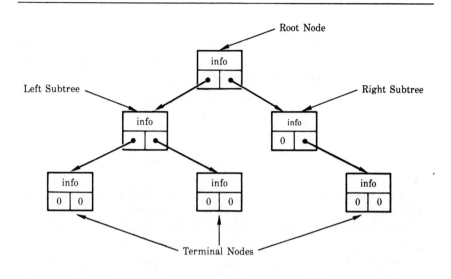

Figure 2-11.   A sample binary tree with a height of 3

```
    r->left = NULL;
    r->right = NULL;
    r->info = info;
    if(!root) return r; /* first entry */
    if(info<root->info) root->left = r;
    else root->right = r;
    return r;
}

/* if new info less than current root, go left */
if(info<r->info) stree(r, r->left, info);
else
/* go right */
if(info>r->info) stree(r, r->right, info);
return root;
}
```

This algorithm simply follows the links through the tree, going left or right based on the **info** field, until a terminal node is reached. At this point, a new element is acquired and linked into the tree.

To use this function, you need a variable that will hold the pointer to the root of the tree. This variable must initially be set to **NULL**, so that a pointer to the root must be assigned on the first call to **stree( )**. If you assume that the name of this variable is **rt**, then to call the **stree( )** function, you would use

```
/* call stree()  */
rt = stree(rt, rt, info);
```

In this way, both the first element and subsequent elements can be inserted correctly.

The **stree( )** function is a recursive algorithm, as are most tree routines. The same routine would be several times longer if straight iterative methods were employed. The function must be called with a pointer to the root, to the left or right node, and to information. For the sake of clarity, a single character is used here as the information; however, you could substitute any simple or complex data type you like.

To traverse the tree built by using **stree( )** inorder and to print the **info** field of each node, you could use the **inorder( )** function:

```
/* Traverse a tree in order. */
void inorder(root)
struct tree *root;
{
  if(!root) return;

  inorder(root->left);
  printf("%c ", root->info);
  inorder(root->right);
}
```

This recursive function returns when a terminal node (a **NULL** pointer) is encountered. The functions to traverse the tree in preorder and in postorder are shown here:

```
/* Traverse a tree in preorder. */
void preorder(root)
struct tree *root;
{
  if(!root) return;

  printf("%c ", root->info);
  preorder(root->left);
  preorder(root->right);
}

/* Traverse a tree in postorder */
void postorder(root)
struct tree *root;
{
  if(!root) return;

  postorder(root->left);
  postorder(root->right);
  printf("%c ", root->info);
}
```

You can write a short program that builds a sorted binary tree and prints the tree sideways on the screen of your computer. To accomplish this, you need only a small modification to the **inorder()** function. The new function, called **print—tree()**, prints a tree in inorder fashion:

```
/* Print a tree in order */
void print_tree(r,l)
struct tree *r;
int l;
{
  int i;

  if(r==NULL) return; /* end of the tree */

  print_tree(r->left, l+1);
  for(i=0; i<l; ++i) printf("   ");
  printf("%c\n", r->info);
  print_tree(r->right, l+1);
}
```

The entire tree-printing program is given here. You should try entering various trees to see how each one is built.

```
/* This program allows you to enter a tree and then prints
   the tree in order sideways on the screen.
*/

#include "stdlib.h"   /* "malloc.h" for some compilers */
#include "stdio.h"

struct tree {
  char info;
  struct tree *left;
  struct tree *right;
};

struct tree *root;   /* first node in tree */
void print_tree();

main()
{
  char s[80];
  struct tree *stree();

  root = NULL;   /* initialize the root */

  do {
    printf("enter a letter: ");
    gets(s);
    root = stree(root, root, *s);
  } while(*s);

  print_tree(root, NULL);

}

/* Build a sorted binary tree. */
struct tree *stree(root, r, info)
struct tree *root;
struct tree *r;
char info;
{

  if(!r) {
    r=(struct tree *) malloc(sizeof(struct tree));
    if(!r) {
      printf("out of memory\n");
      exit(0);
    }
    r->left = NULL;
    r->right = NULL;
    r->info = info;
    if(!root) return r; /* first entry */
    if(info<root->info) root->left = r;
    else root->right = r;
    return r;
  }

  if(info<r->info) stree(r, r->left, info);
  else
  if(info>r->info) stree(r, r->right, info);
  return root;
}
```

```
/* Print a tree in order */
void print_tree(r, l)
struct tree *r;
int l;
{
  int i;

  if(!r) return; /* end of the tree */

  print_tree(r->left, l+1);
  for(i=0; i<l; ++i) printf("    ");
  printf("%c\n", r->info);
  print_tree(r->right, l+1);
}
```

You may not have thought about it, but this program actually sorts the information you are giving it. This is a variation on the Insertion sort that you saw in the previous chapter. For the average case its performance can be quite good, but the Quicksort is still a better general-purpose sorting method—it uses less memory and has lower processing overhead. However, if you have to build a tree from scratch, or if you have to maintain an already sorted tree, you should always insert new entries in sorted order by using the **stree( )** function.

If you run this tree-printing program, you will probably notice that some trees are balanced—each subtree is the same or nearly the same height as any other—and that other trees are far out of balance. In fact, if you entered the tree **abcd**, it would be built like this:

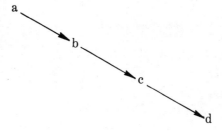

As you can see, there would be no left subtrees. This is called a *degenerate tree* because it has degenerated into a linear list. In general, if the data you are using as input for a binary tree is fairly random, the tree produced will approximate a balanced tree. However, if the information is already sorted, a degenerate tree will result. (It is possible to readjust the tree with each insertion to keep the tree in balance. The algorithms to do this are fairly complex; if you are interested, refer to books on advanced programming algorithms.)

Search functions are easy to implement for binary trees. The following function returns a pointer to the node in the tree that matches the key; otherwise, it returns **NULL**:

```
/* Search for a node. */
struct tree *search_tree(root, key)
struct tree *root;
char key;
{
  if(!root) return root;  /* empty tree */
  while(root->info!=key) {
    if(key<root->info) root = root->left;
    else root = root->right;
    if(root==NULL) break;
  }
  return root;
}
```

Unfortunately, deleting a node from a tree is not as simple as searching the tree. The deleted node may be either the root, a left node, or a right node. Also, the node may have from zero to two subtrees attached to it. The process of rearranging the pointers lends itself to a recursive algorithm, as shown here:

```
/* Delete the specified node from the tree. */
struct tree *dtree(root, key)
struct tree *root;
char key;
{
  struct tree *p, *p2;

  if(root->info==key) { /* delete root */
    /* this means an empty tree */
    if(root->left==root->right){
      free(root);
      return NULL;
    }
```

```
/* or if one subtree is null */
else if(root->left==NULL) {
  p = root->right;
  free(root);
  return p;
}
else if(root->right==NULL) {
  p = root->left;
  free(root);
  return p;
}
/* or both tree present */
else {
  p2 = root->right;
  p = root->right;
  while(p->left) p = p->left;
  p->left = root->left;
  free(root);
  return p2;
}
}
if(root->info<key) root->right = dtree(root->right, key);
else root->left = dtree(root->left, key);
return root;
}
```

You must remember to update the pointer to the root in the rest of your program, because the deleted node could be the root of the tree.

Binary trees offer tremendous power, flexibility, and efficiency when they are used with database-management programs. This is because the information for these databases must reside on disk, and access times are important. Because a balanced binary tree has as a worst case $\log_2 n$ comparisons in searching, it is far better than a linked list, which must rely on a sequential search.

3

DYNAMIC ALLOCATION

C's dynamic allocation system has many uses. It can be used to create variable-length lists of information, as in the database application described in Chapter 2. A second use is for supporting *sparse arrays*. In a sparse array, not all the array's elements are actually present—or necessary. You will need to create a sparse array when the array dimensions required by the application are larger than will fit in the memory of the machine, but not all array locations will actually be used.

You should recall that arrays, especially multidimensional arrays, can consume vast quantities of memory because their storage needs are exponentially related to their size. For example, a character array of 10×10 needs only 100 bytes of memory. A 100×100 array needs 10,000 bytes; a 1000×1000 array needs 1,000,000 bytes of memory. Dynamically allocated variables can also help you squeeze more performance out of a computer with limited RAM. Before you explore the ways in which dynamic allocation can be used in your C programs, however, you will find that a brief review of the dynamic allocation system will be helpful.

THE C DYNAMIC ALLOCATION SYSTEM

Before you can understand C's allocation system, you should visualize how a program compiled by C organizes memory. Figure 3-1 illustrates the concept of how a program compiled by a C compiler appears in memory. (Compiling with different memory models will cause this organization to change somewhat, but it will still be essentially correct.) The stack grows downward as it is used, so the amount of memory needed by the stack is determined by how your program is designed. For example, a program with many recursive functions makes much greater demands on stack memory than does a program without recursive functions, because local variables are stored on the stack. The memory required for the program code and global data is fixed during the execution of the program. Memory to satisfy an allocation request is taken from the free memory area, starting just above the global variables and growing towards the stack. As you might guess, in fairly extreme cases it is possible for the stack to run into allocated memory. (Indeed, if the program has been compiled with a large data model, the entire 64K segment used for the heap could become exhausted.)

C's dynamic allocation system contains several functions, but the most important of these are **malloc( )** and **free( )**. Let's examine these now.

malloc( ) and free( )

The functions **malloc( )** and **free( )** form the core of C's dynamic allocation system and are part of its standard library. They work together, using the heap to establish and maintain a list of available storage. Each time a memory request is made by using **malloc( )**, a portion of the remaining free memory is allocated. Each time **free( )** is called, memory is returned to the system.

In C, **malloc( )** is declared as

void *malloc(*unsigned int size*)

System Memory

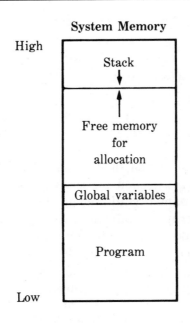

Figure 3-1.   A conceptual view of a C program's memory usage

Here, *size* is the number of bytes you wish to allocate. If *size* bytes can be allocated, then a pointer will be returned to the first byte. You must use an explicit type cast to make the **void** pointer returned by **malloc( )** compatible with the type of the pointer that it is being assigned to. If there is not enough available memory to satisfy the **malloc( )** request, an allocation failure will occur and **malloc( )** will return a null value. It is very important that you confirm that a valid pointer has been returned by **malloc( )** prior to using it. Using a null pointer on the left side of an assignment statement will probably cause your system to crash, because you will be overwriting some important memory locations.

The following fragment shows the proper way to allocate memory, in this case for data of type **float**:

```
float *f;

f = (float *) malloc(sizeof(float));

if(!f) {
  printf("memory allocation error");
  exit(1);  /* or call error handling routine */
}
```

As this fragment shows, you should use **sizeof** to determine the exact number of bytes needed for the type of data you will be storing, instead of manually adding up the bytes. Not only does this make your program portable to a variety of systems, but the use of **sizeof** also makes it easier to maintain when changes to the dynamically allocated object occur. This is especially important when you are using dynamic allocation to store structure variables. Because many computers require that data be aligned on even word boundaries, it is possible that the actual size of a structure will be one or more bytes larger that the sum of the sizes of the individual fields.

The **free()** function is the opposite of **malloc()** — it returns previously allocated memory to the system. Once the memory has been released, it can be reused by a subsequent call to **malloc()**. The **free()** function is declared as

    void free(*void *p*);

Remember that you must *never* call **free()** with an invalid argument. If you do, the free list may be destroyed, causing the allocation system to stop working.

It is good programming practice to include the header file STDLIB.H in any program that uses C's allocation system, because it declares the allocation functions and ensures proper type checking. (In some non-ANSI standard compilers, this file is called MALLOC.H.) Many of the routines presented in this chapter will require that the file STDIO.H be included.

The following short program provides a simple example of how **malloc( )** and **free( )** work together by allocating enough storage for 40 integers, assigning them some values, and then releasing them back to the system. Here **sizeof** is used to ensure portability to other computer types.

```
#include "stdlib.h"

main()  /* short allocation example */
{
  int *p, t;

  p = (int *) malloc(40*sizeof(int));
  if(!p) {
    printf("out of memory\n");
    exit(0);
  }

  for(t=0; t<40; ++t) *(p+t)=t;
  for(t=0; t<40; ++t) printf("%d ",*(p+t));
  free(p);
}
```

SPARSE-ARRAY PROCESSING

There are many applications that require sparse-array processing. Some of these deal with scientific and engineering problems that are only easily understood by specialists in these fields. However, there is one very familiar application that commonly uses sparse arrays: a spreadsheet program.

Even though the matrix of the average spreadsheet is very large—say, 999 by 999—only a portion of the matrix may actually be in use at any one time. Spreadsheets use the matrix to hold formulas, values, and strings associated with each location. With a sparse array, storage for each element is allocated from the pool of free memory as it is needed. Although only a small portion of the elements are actually in use, the array may appear very large—larger than would normally fit in the memory of the computer.

Two terms can be used to describe this: *logical array* and *physical array*. The logical array is the array that you think of as existing in the system. For example, the spreadsheet matrix is a logical array. The physical array is the array that actually exists inside the computer. It is the job of the sparse-array support routines to link these two arrays together.

Four distinct techniques for creating a sparse array will be examined in this chapter: the linked list, the binary tree, a pointer array, and hashing. All examples assume that the spreadsheet matrix is organized as shown in Figure 3-2, with X located in cell B2.

The Linked-List Approach to Sparse Arrays

When you implement a sparse array that uses a linked list, a structure is used to hold the cell information, including its logical position in the array and links to both the previous element and the next element. Each structure is placed in the list with the elements in a sorted order that is based on the array index. The array is accessed by following the links.

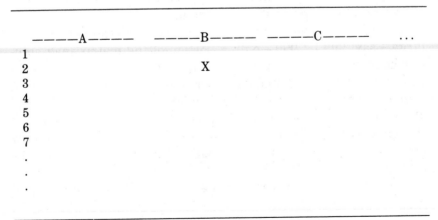

Figure 3-2. The organization of a sample spreadsheet

For example, you could use the following structure to create a sparse array for use in a spreadsheet program:

```
struct cell {
  char cell_name[9];   /* cell name e.g., A1, B34 */
  char formula[128];   /* info e.g.,. 10/B2 */
  struct cell *next;   /* pointer to next entry */
  struct cell *prior;  /* pointer to previous record */
} ;
```

The **cell_name** field holds a string that contains the cell name (such as A1, B34, or Z19). The **formula** string holds the formula that is assigned to each spreadsheet location.

While an entire spreadsheet program would be far too large to use as an example here, the key functions that support linked-list sparse arrays will be examined next. Remember that there are many ways to implement a spreadsheet program. The data structures and routines used here should serve only as examples of sparse-array techniques. The following global variables will point to the beginning and the end of the linked array list:

```
struct cell *start;  /* first element in list */
struct cell *last;   /* last element in list */
```

In most spreadsheets, when you enter a formula into a cell, you are in effect creating a new element in the sparse array. If the spreadsheet uses a linked list, the new cell is inserted by using a function similar to **dls_store( )**, which was developed in Chapter 2. Remember, the list is sorted by cell name; that is, A12 precedes A13, and so on.

```
/* Store a cell in sorted order based upon the cell's
   name. */
struct cell *dls_store(i)
struct cell *i;
{
  struct cell *old, *p;

  if(last==NULL) {  /* first element in list */
    i->next = NULL;
    i->prior = NULL;
    last = i;
    return i;
  }

  p = start; /* start at top of list */
```

```
  old = NULL;
  while(p) {
    if(strcmp(p->cell_name, i->cell_name)<0){
      old = p;
      p = p->next;
    }
    else { /* is a middle element */
      if(p->prior) {
        p->prior->next = i;
        i->next = p;
        i->prior = p->prior;
        p->prior = i;
        return start;
      }
      i->next = p; /* new first element */
      i->prior = NULL;
      p->prior = i;
      return   i;
    }
  }
  old->next = i; /* put on end */
  i->next = NULL;
  i->prior = old;
  last = i;
  return start;
}
```

To remove a cell from the spreadsheet, you must remove the proper structure from the list and allow the memory it occupies to be returned to the system by using **free( )**. The **delete( )** function shown here will remove a cell from the list when given the cell name:

```
/* Delete a cell from the list given its name and
   free the memory for later use.
*/
void delete(cell_name)
char *cell_name;
{
  struct cell *info, *find();

  /* get a pointer to the cell to delete */
  info = find(cell_name);

  if(info) {
    /* delete first element */
    if(start==info) {
      start = info->next;
      if(start) start->prior = NULL;
      else last = NULL;
    }
    else { /* element in middle or end */
      if(info->prior)
      info->prior->next = info->next;
      if(info!=last) /* is in middle */
        info->next->prior = info->prior;
      else /* is on end */
        last = info->prior;
    }
    free(info);  /* return memory to system */
  }
}
```

The final function needed to support a linked-list sparse array is **find( )**, which locates any specific cell. It returns a pointer to the proper cell if it exists or a null value if it does not. The **find( )** function requires the use of a linear search to locate each item. As you saw in Chapter 1, the average number of comparisons in a linear search is $n/2$, where n is the number of elements in the list. A significant loss of performance also occurs because each cell may contain references to other cells in the formula, and each of these cells must be found. Here is an example of **find( )**:

```
/* Return a pointer to the cell given its name.
   Return null value if cell does not exist.
*/
struct cell *find(cell_name)
char *cell_name;
{
  struct cell *info;

  info = start;
  while(info) {
    if(!strcmp(cell_name, info->cell_name)) return info;
    info = info->next;  /* get next cell */
  }
  printf("cell not found\n");
  return NULL;  /* not found */
}
```

The following **main( )** function can be used to demonstrate the linked-list approach to sparse arrays. Be sure to include the sparse-array functions developed above. Note that the validity of the input is not checked.

```
#include "stdio.h"
#include "stdlib.h"  /* "malloc.h" for some compilers */

struct cell {
  char cell_name[9];  /* cell name e.g., A1, B34 */
  char  formula[128]; /* info e.g.,. 10/B2 */
  struct cell *next;  /* pointer to next entry */
  struct cell *prior; /* pointer to previous record */
} list_entry;

struct cell *start; /* first element in list */
struct cell *last;  /* last element in list */

void delete();
struct cell *dls_store(), *find();

/* A simple main() that illustrates the linked list approach
   to sparse arrays.
*/

main()
```

```
{
  struct cell *i;
  char name[80];

  start = last = NULL;

  for(;;) {
    i = (struct cell *) malloc(sizeof(struct cell));
    if(!i) {
      printf("allocation failure");
      exit(1);
    }

    printf("name? ");
    gets(i->cell_name);
    if(*i->cell_name)
      start = dls_store(i);
    else break; /* stop entry on blank line */
  }

  /* display the entire array */
  i = start;
  printf("current list is: ");
  while(i) {
    printf("%s ", i->cell_name);
    i = i->next;
  }
  printf("\n");

  /* Demonstrate the find() function */
  printf("cell to find: ");
  gets(name);
  i = find(name);
  if(i) printf("cell found\n");
  else printf("cell not in array\n");

  /* demonstrate the delete() function */
  printf("cell to delete: ");
  gets(name);
  i = find(name); /* make sure cell is in list */
  if(i) delete(name); /* if in list, delete */
  else printf("cell not in array\n");

  /* redisplay the list after the deletion */
  i = start;
  printf("current list is: ");
  while(i) {
    printf("%s ", i->cell_name);
    i = i->next;
  }
  printf("\n");
}
```

To use this program, first enter a few cell names, such as A3, B14, and D27. Then enter a blank line. Next, you will see the current contents of the list displayed. You will be prompted to enter a cell to find. If the cell you enter is in the array, it will be reported as such; otherwise, you will be told that the cell is not in the array. Finally, enter the cell you want deleted. When the cell has been deleted, the contents of the array will be redisplayed.

Analysis of the Linked-List Approach

The principal advantage of the linked-list method is that it is very memory efficient. However, it has one major drawback — it must use a linear search to access each cell in the list. Without using additional information, which requires additional memory overhead, you cannot perform a binary search to locate a cell. Even the store routine uses a linear search to find the proper location to insert a new cell into the list. You can solve these problems by using a binary tree to support the sparse array.

The Binary Tree Approach to Sparse Arrays

In essence, the binary tree is simply a modified doubly linked list. Its major advantage over a list is that it can be searched quickly, which means that insertions, deletions, and lookups can be very fast. For applications in which you want a linked-list structure but need fast search times, the binary tree is the preferred solution.

To use a binary tree to support the spreadsheet example, you must change the **cell** structure as shown here:

```
struct cell {
    char cell_name[9];  /* cell name e.g., A1, B34 */
    char  formula[128]; /* info e.g., 10/B2 */
    struct cell *left;  /* pointer to left subtree */
    struct cell *right; /* pointer to right subtree */
} ;
```

You can modify the **stree( )** function from Chapter 2 so that it builds a tree based on the cell name. Notice that it assumes that the parameter **new** is a pointer to a new entry in the tree.

```
/* Store a cell in a tree using its name. */
struct cell *stree(root,r,new)
struct cell *root;
struct cell *r;
struct cell *new;
{
    if(r==NULL) {      /* first node in subtree */
        new->left = NULL;
        new->right = NULL;
        if(root) {
```

```
      if(strcmp(new->cell_name, root->cell_name)<NULL)
         root->left = new;
      else root->right = new;
   }
   else {  /* first node in tree */
     new->right = NULL;
     new->left = NULL;
   }
   return new;  /* root of tree */
 }

 if(strcmp(new->cell_name, r->cell_name)<=NULL)
   stree(r,r->left, new);
 if(strcmp(new->cell_name, r->cell_name)>NULL)
   stree(r,r->right, new);

 return root;
}
```

The **stree( )** function must be called with a pointer to the root
node for the first two parameters, and a pointer to the new cell for
the third. It returns a pointer to the root.

To delete a cell from the spreadsheet, you can modify the
dtree( ) function as shown here to accept the name of the cell as a
key:

```
/* Delete a cell. */
struct cell *dtree(root, key)
struct cell *root;
char *key;
{
  struct cell *p,*p2;

  if(!strcmp(root->cell_name, key)) { /* delete root */
    /* this means an empty tree */
    if(root->left==root->right){
      free(root);
      return NULL;
    }
    /* or if one subtree is null */
    else if(root->left==NULL) {
      p = root->right;
      free(root);
      return p;
    }
    else if(root->right==NULL) {
      p = root->left;
      free(root);
      return p;
    }
    /* or both trees present */
    else {
      p2 = root->right;
      p = root->right;
      while(p->left) p = p->left;
      p->left = root->left;
      free(root);
      return p2;
    }
```

```
    }
    if(strcmp(root->cell_name, key)<NULL)
      root->right = dtree(root->right, key);
    else root->left = dtree(root->left, key);
    return root;
}
```

Finally, you can use a modified **search( )** function to quickly locate any cell in the spreadsheet, given its cell name:

```
/* Search for a specific cell. */
struct cell *search_tree(root, key)
struct cell *root;
char *key;
{
  /* If root is null then either the tree
     is empty or the cell is not in the tree.
  */
  if(!root) return root;
  while(strcmp(root->cell_name, key)) {
    if(strcmp(root->cell_name, key)>NULL)
      root = root->left;
    else root = root->right;
    if(root==NULL) break;
  }
  return root;
}
```

The following **main( )** function demonstrates the binary tree approach to sparse arrays. Notice that it uses a slightly modified version of **print—tree( )**, developed in Chapter 2, to display the tree. Don't forget to link the previously discussed tree functions.

```
#include "stdio.h"
#include "stdlib.h" /* use "malloc.h" for some compilers */

struct cell {
  char cell_name[9];  /* cell name e.g., A1, B34 */
  char  formula[128]; /* info e.g., 10/B2 */
  struct cell *left;  /* pointer to left subtree */
  struct cell *right; /* pointer to right subtree */
} list_entry;

struct cell *root;  /* root of the tree */

struct cell *stree(), *search_tree(), *dtree();
void print_tree();

/* A simple main() that illustrates the binary tree approach
   to sparse arrays.
*/

main()
{
```

```
    struct cell *i;
    char name[80];

    root = NULL;

    for(;;) {
      i = (struct cell *) malloc(sizeof(struct cell));
      if(!i) {
        printf("allocation failure");
        exit(1);
      }

      printf("name? ");
      gets(i->cell_name);
      if(*i->cell_name)
        root = stree(root, root, i);
      else break; /* stop entry on blank line */
    }

    /* display the entire array */
    printf("current tree is:\n");
    print_tree(root, 0);
    printf("\n");

    /* Demonstrate the search_tree() function */
    printf("cell to find: ");
    gets(name);
    i = search_tree(root, name);
    if(i) printf("cell found\n");
    else printf("cell not in array\n");

    /* demonstrate the dtree() function */
    printf("cell to delete: ");
    gets(name);
    i = search_tree(root, name); /* make sure cell is in tree */
    if(i) root = dtree(root, name); /* if in tree, delete */
    else printf("cell not in array\n");

    /* redisplay the tree after the deletion */
    printf("current tree is:\n");
    print_tree(root, 0);
    printf("\n");

}

/* Print a tree in order */
void print_tree(r, l)
struct cell *r;
int l;
{
  int i;

  if(!r) return; /* end of the tree */

  print_tree(r->left, l+1);
  for(i=0; i<l; ++i) printf("    ");
  printf("%s\n", r->cell_name);
  print_tree(r->right, l+1);
}
```

Analysis of the Binary Tree Approach

The most important advantage of a binary tree over a linked list is that it results in much faster insertion and search times. Remember, a sequential search requires, on average, $n/2$ comparisons, where n is the number of elements in the list, whereas a binary search requires only $\log_2 n$ comparisons. Also, the binary tree is as memory efficient as a doubly linked list. However, there is still a better method in some situations: using a pointer array.

The Pointer-Array Approach to Sparse Arrays

Suppose that a spreadsheet's dimensions were 26×100 (A1 through Z100, for a total of 2600 elements. In theory, then, the following array of structures could be used to hold the spreadsheet entries:

```
struct cell {
  char cell_name[9];
  char   formula[128];
} list_entry[2600];    /* 2,600 cells */
```

The raw size of each structure is 137 bytes. (Some machines will require slightly more memory for each structure to be aligned on a word boundary.) However, 2600 structures, each of 137 bytes, requires 356,200 bytes of memory. This is too large for many systems and compilers, especially compilers that do not support the huge data model. In addition, on processors that use a segment architecture, such as the 8086, memory access to such a large array will be very slow, because 32-bit points will be required. Therefore, this approach is obviously not practical in all situations.

Instead, you could create an array of pointers to structures. This method would require significantly less permanent storage than would the creation of an entire array, and it would offer performance far superior to that of the linked-list and binary tree methods. The declaration would be as follows:

```
struct cell {
  char cell_name[9];
  char  formula[128];
} ;

struct cell *sheet[2600]; /* array of 2,600 pointers */
```

You can use this smaller array to hold pointers to the information that is actually entered into the spreadsheet. As each entry is made, a pointer to the cell information is stored in the proper location in the array. Figure 3-3 shows how this process might appear in memory, with the pointer array providing support for the sparse array.

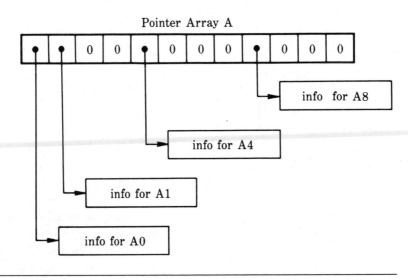

Figure 3-3.   A pointer array as support for a sparse array

Before you can use the pointer array, you must first initialize each element to null, indicating that there is no entry in that location. Use the following function for this purpose:

```
/* Initialize the pointer array. */
void init_sheet()
{
  register int t;

  for(t=0; t<2600; ++t) sheet[t] = NULL;
}
```

When the user enters a formula for a cell in the spreadsheet, the cell location, defined by its name, is used to produce an index for the pointer array **sheet**. The index is derived from the cell name by converting the name into a number, as shown here in **store()**. When computing the index, **store()** assumes that all cell names begin with a capital letter followed by an integer—for example, B34 or C19.

```
/* Store an entry. */
void store(i)
struct cell *i;
{
  int loc;
  char *p;

  /* compute location given point name */

  /* rows * 26 * /
  loc = (*(i->cell_name)-'A');
  p = &(i->cell_name[1]);
  loc += (atoi(p)-1) * 26; /* plus columns */

  if(loc>=2600) {
    printf("cell out of bounds\n");
    return;
  }
  sheet[loc] = i; /* place pointer in the array */
}
```

Because each cell name is unique, each index is also unique; and because the ASCII collating sequence is used, the pointer to each entry is stored in the proper array element. If you compare this procedure to the linked-list or binary tree version, you will see how much shorter and simpler it is.

The **delete( )** function also becomes short. When called with the index of the cell to be removed, **delete( )** simply zeros the pointer to the element and returns the memory to the system:

```
/* Delete an entry given its index. */
void delete(cell_index)
int cell_index;
{
   free(sheet[cell_index]);  /* return memory to system */
   sheet[cell_index] = NULL;
}
```

Once again, compared to the linked-list version, this code is much faster and simpler. In addition, the process of locating a cell by its name is trivial, because the name itself directly produces the array index; therefore, the **find( )** function changes, as shown here:

```
/* Return a pointer to a cell if it exists; otherwise
   return null.
*/
struct cell *find(cell_name)
char *cell_name;
{
   int loc;
   char *p;

   /* compute location given name */

   /* rows * 26 */
   loc = (*(cell_name)-'A');
   p = &(cell_name[1]);
   loc += (atoi(p)-1) * 26; /* plus columns */

   if(loc>=2600 || !sheet[loc]) {  /* no entry in that cell */
     printf("cell not found\n");
     return NULL;  /* not found */
   }
   else return sheet[loc];
}
```

The following **main( )** function demonstrates the pointer-array approach to sparse arrays:

```
#include "stdio.h"
#include "stdlib.h" /* "malloc.h" for some compilers */

struct cell {
```

```
    char cell_name[9];
    char formula[128];
} list_entry;

struct cell *sheet[2600]; /* array of 2,600 pointers */

void store(), delete();
struct cell * find();

/* A simple main() that illustrates the linked list approach
   to sparse arrays.
*/

main()
{
  struct cell *i;
  char name[80];
  int t;

  for(;;) {
    i = (struct cell *) malloc(sizeof(struct cell));
    if(!i) {
      printf("allocation failure");
      exit(1);
    }

    printf("name? ");
    gets(i->cell_name);
    if(*i->cell_name) {
      *i->cell_name = toupper(*i->cell_name);
      store(i);
    }
    else break; /* stop entry on blank line */
  }

  /* display the entire array */
  printf("current list is: ");
  for(t=0; t<2600; t++)
    if(sheet[t]) printf("%s ", sheet[t]->cell_name);
  printf("\n");

  /* Demonstrate the find() function */
  printf("cell to find: ");
  gets(name);
  *name = toupper(*name);
  i = find(name);
  if(i) printf("cell found\n");
  else printf("cell not in array\n");

  /* demonstrate the delete() function */
  printf("cell index to delete: ");
  scanf("%d", &t);
  delete(t);

  /* redisplay the list after the deletion*/
  printf("current list is: ");
  for(t=0; t<2600; t++)
    if(sheet[t]) printf("%s ", sheet[t]->cell_name);
  printf("\n");
}
```

Analysis of the Pointer-Array Approach

The pointer-array method of sparse-array handling provides much faster access to array elements than does either the linked-list or the binary tree method. Unless the array is very sparse, the memory used by the pointer array is usually not a significant drain on the free memory of the system. However, keep in mind that the pointer array itself uses some memory for every location, whether or not the pointers are pointing to actual information. This may be a serious limitation for some applications, but it is usually not a problem.

The Hashing Approach to Sparse Arrays

Hashing is the process of extracting the index of an array element directly from the information that will be stored there; the *hash* itself is the index generated by this method. Traditionally, hashing has been applied to disk files as a means of decreasing access time. However, the same methods can be used to implement sparse arrays. The procedure in the previous pointer-array example used a special form of hashing called *direct indexing*, in which each key maps onto one—and only one— array location. Each hashed index is unique. (The pointer-array approach does not *require* a direct indexing hash; it is simply an obvious approach given the spreadsheet problem.) In actual practice, such direct hashing schemes are few, and a more flexible method is required. In this section, you will see how hashing can be generalized to allow greater power and flexibility.

If you think about the spreadsheet example, you will realize that even in the most rigorous environments, not every cell in the sheet will be used. Suppose that for most cases no more than 10% of the potential cells will be occupied by actual entries. This means that if the spreadsheet's dimensions are 26×100 (2600 cells), then only about 260 will be used at any one time. Therefore, the largest array necessary to hold all the entries will be only 260 cells in size. The problem then becomes this: how do the logical array locations get mapped onto and accessed from this smaller physical array, and what happens when this array is full? The solution is that a *hash chain* can be used.

When a user enters a formula for a cell in the spreadsheet (the logical array), the cell location, defined by its name, is used to produce an index (a hash) into the smaller physical array, sometimes called the primary array. Assume that the physical array is called **primary**. The index is derived from the cell name by converting the name into a number as in the pointer-array example. However, the number is then divided by 10 to produce an initial entry point into the array. (Remember, in this example, the physical array's size is only 10% of the logical array's size.) If the location that is referenced by this index is free, then the logical index and the value are stored there. However, since 10 physical locations actually map onto one logical location, hash *collisions* can occur. When this happens, a second array, sometimes called the collision array, is used to hold the entry, and a linked list of indexes is generated. This situation is depicted in Figure 3-4.

To find an element in the physical array, given its logical array index, the program first transforms the logical index into its hash value. It then checks the physical array at the index generated by the hash to see if the logical index stored there matches the one that you are searching for. If it does match, the function returns the information. Otherwise, the function follows the hash chain until it finds the proper index or it reaches the end of the chain.

To see how this procedure applies to the spreadsheet program, you must first define two arrays of structures. The array called **primary** is the one indexed by the hash algorithm. The array called **collision** is used to hold the hash chain generated when collisions occur.

```
#define MAX 260

struct htype {
  int index; /* actual index */
  int val; /* actual value of the array element */
  int next; /* index of next value with same hash */
} primary[MAX];

struct htype collision[MAX];
```

	Primary Array		
	index	val	next
0	A1	100	0
1	B10	19	1
2			
3			
4			
5	G11	21	−1
6			
7			
8			
9			
10			

	Collision Array		
	index	val	next
0	A2	10	3
1	B11	20	2
2	B121	−18	−1
3	A5	20	−1
4			
5			
6			
7			
8			
9			
10			

given entries in this order: A1, 100
A2, 10
B10, 19
B11, 20
B121, −18
A5, 20
G11, 21

Figure 3-4.   A hashing example

Before these arrays can be used, they must be initialized. The following function initializes the **index** field to −1 (a value that, by definition, cannot be generated) to indicate an empty element.

The −1 in the **next** field indicates the end of a hash chain.

```
/* Initialize the hash array. */
void init()
{
  register int i;

  for (i=0; i<MAX; i++) {
    primary[i].index = -1;
    primary[i].next = -1;   /* null chain */
    primary[i].val = 0;
    collision[i].index = -1;
    collision[i].next = -1;
    collision[i].val = 0;
  }
}
```

The **store( )** procedure converts a cell name into a hashed index into the **primary** array. If the location directly pointed to by the hashed value is occupied, **store( )** searches for the first free location in the **collision** array. When it finds a free location, it stores the value of the logical index as well as the value of the array element in the location. The logical index must be stored because it will be needed when that element is accessed again.

```
/* Compute hash and store the value. */
void store(cell_name, v)
char *cell_name;
int v;
{
  int h, c, prior, loc;

  /* produce the hash value */
  loc = *cell_name-'A';
  loc += (atoi(&cell_name[1])-1) * 26; /* WIDTH columns*num rows*/
  h = loc/10;

  /* store in the location unless full or
     store there if logical indexes agree - i.e., update.
  */
  if(primary[h].index==-1 || primary[h].index==loc) {
    primary[h].index = loc;
    primary[h].val = v;
    return;
  }

  /* otherwise, place in collision array */
  c = primary[h].next; /* see if chain started */
  if(c==-1) {
    c = 0; /* start new chain */
    while(collision[c].index!=-1 && c < MAX) c++;
    if(c==MAX) {
      printf("collision array full");
      return;
```

```
    }
    primary[h].next = c;
  }
  else { /* follow existing chain */
    prior = c;
    while(c<MAX) {  /* find a free loc */
      if(collision[c].index == loc || c == -1) break;
      prior = c;
      c = collision[c].next;
    }
    if(c==MAX) {
      printf("hash error or primary array full\n");
      return;
    }
  }
  if(c==-1) {  /* not in hash chain so find
                   a free spot to put it */
    c = 0;
    while(collision[c].index!=-1 && c<MAX) c++;
    if(c==MAX) {
      printf("hash error or primary array full\n");
      return;
    }
  }
  /* store and update hash chain */
  collision[c].val = v;
  collision[c].index = loc;
  collision[c].next = -1;
  collision[prior].next = c;
}
```

Finding the value of an element requires that you first compute the physical address, and then check to see if the logical index stored in the physical array matches that of the index of the logical array that is requested. If it does, then that value is returned; otherwise, the chain is followed. The **find( )** function, which does this, is shown here:

```
/* Compute hash and return the value. */
int find(cell_name)
char *cell_name;
{
  int h, c, loc;

  /* produce the hash value */
  loc = *cell_name-'A';
  loc += (atoi(&cell_name[1])-1) * 26;/* WIDTH columns * num rows */
  h = loc/10;

  /* return the value if found */
  if(primary[h].index==loc)  return(primary[h].val);
  else { /* look in collision array */
    c = primary[h].next;
    while(c != -1 && c<MAX) {  /* find a loc */
      if(collision[c].index == loc) return collision[c].val;
      c = collision[c].next;
```

```
    }
    printf("not in array\n");
    return -1;
  }
}
```

The hashing alogrithm used here is very simple. You would usually use a more complex method to make the distribution of indexes in the primary array more even, thus avoiding the creation of long hash chains. However, the basic principle is the same. As a challenge, try modifying one of the other example **main( )** functions in this chapter so that it works with the hashing functions.

For the purpose of clarity, the hashing examples you have seen so far used fixed-length arrays for both the primary and collision storage. However, a better approach is to make the collision storage a linked list by using dynamically allocated storage for each entry. In this way, the **collision** array can shrink or grow as necessary to meet the demands of the situation.

Analysis of Hashing

In a best-case scenario, which is always quite rare, each physical index created by the hashing method is unique, and access times approximate that of direct indexing. This means that no hash chains are created and all lookups are essentially direct accesses. However, this is seldom the case; the logical indexes would have to be distributed evenly throughout the logical index space. In a worst-case scenario, also quite rare, a hashed scheme degenerates into a linked list. This can happen when the hashed value of the logical indexes are all the same. In the average (and most likely) case, the hash method can access any specific element in a time equal to that of using a direct index divided by some constant that is proportional to the average length of the hash chains. The most critical task in using hashing to support a sparse array is to make sure that the hashing algorithm spreads the physical index evenly, so that you can avoid long hash chains. Also, hashing is best applied to situations in which you know that there is a limit to the number of array locations actually required.

CHOOSING AN APPROACH

When deciding whether to use a linked-list, binary tree, pointer-array, or hashing approach to implement a sparse array, you must have two main considerations. The first is memory efficiency and the second is speed.

When an array is very sparse, the most memory efficient approaches are the linked-list and binary tree implementations, because only those array elements that are actually in use have memory allocated to them. The links themselves require very little additional memory and generally have a negligible effect. The pointer-array design requires that the entire pointer array exist, even if some of its elements are not used. Not only must the entire pointer array fit in memory, but there must be enough memory left over for the application to use. This could be a serious problem for certain applications, whereas it may not be a problem at all for others. You can usually decide this issue by calculating the approximate amount of free memory and determining whether that is sufficient for your program.

The hashing method lies somewhere in between the pointer-array, linked-list, and binary tree approaches. Although it does require all of the physical array to exist, even if it is not all used, it might still be smaller than a pointer array, which needs at least one pointer for each logical array location.

When the array is fairly full, the situation changes—the pointer array then makes better use of memory. The binary tree and linked-list implementations need two pointers for each element, whereas the pointer array needs only one pointer. For example, if a 1000-element array was full, and if pointers were 2 bytes long, then both the binary tree and linked list would use 4000 bytes for pointers. The pointer array would only need 2000 bytes, saving you 2000 bytes. With the hashing method, even more memory would be "wasted" to support the array.

By far the fastest approach, in terms of execution speed, is the pointer array. As in the spreadsheet example, there is often an easy way to index the pointer array and link it with the sparse-array elements. This makes accessing the sparse array's elements nearly as fast as it would be if it were a normal array. The linked-list version is very slow by comparison, because it must use a linear search to locate each element. Even if extra information were added to the linked list to allow faster accessing, it would still be slower than the pointer array's direct accessing capability. The binary tree certainly speeds up the search time, but when compared with the pointer array's direct indexing capability, it still seems sluggish. If the hashing algorithm is chosen properly, the hashing method can often beat the binary tree in access times, but it will never be faster than the pointer-array approach.

A good rule of thumb is to use a pointer-array implementation when possible—it allows the fastest access time. If memory usage is critical, however, you have no choice but to use the linked-list or binary tree approach.

REUSABLE BUFFERS

When memory is scarce, dynamic allocation can be used in place of normal variables. As an example, consider two processes, **A( )** and **B( )**, inside one program. Assume that **A( )** requires 60% of free memory and that **B( )** needs 55% of free memory. If both **A( )** and **B( )** derive their storage needs from local variables, then **A( )** cannot call **B( )**, and **B( )** cannot call **A( )**, because more than 100% of memory would be required. If **A( )** never calls **B( )**, then there is no trouble. The problem arises when you want **A( )** to be able to call **B( )**. The only way this can work successfully is for both to use dynamic storage and to free that memory prior to calling the other. In other words, if both **A( )** and **B( )** require more than one-half of available free memory while executing, and if **A( )** must call **B( )**, then they *must* use dynamic allocation. In this way, both **A( )** and **B( )** will have the memory they need, when they need it.

Imagine that there are 10,000 bytes of free memory left in a computer that is running a program with the following two functions in it:

```
A()
{
    char a[6000];
    .
    .
    .
    B();
    .
    .
    .
}
B()
{
    char b[5500];
    .
    .
    .
}
```

Here, **A()** and **B()** both have local variables requiring more than one-half of free memory. In this case, there is no way that **B()** can execute, because there is not enough memory available to allocate the 5500 bytes needed for the local array **b**.

A situation like this is sometimes insurmountable, but in certain instances you can work around it. If **A()** did not need to preserve the contents of array **a** while **B()** was executing, then both **A()** and **B()** could share the memory. The way to do this is to allocate **A()**'s arrays and **B()**'s arrays dynamically. Then **A()** could free the memory prior to the call to **B()** and reallocate it later if necessary. The code would look like this:

```
A()
{
    char *a;
    a = (char *) malloc(6000);
    .
    .
    .
    free(a); /* free memory for B() */
```

```
    B();
    a=(char *) malloc (6000);
    .

    .

    .

    free(a); /* all done */
}

B()
{
    char *b;
    b= malloc(5500);
    .

    .

    .

    free(5500);
}
```

Only the pointer **a** is in existence while **B( )** is executing.

Although there are few times when you will need to do something like this, you should master the technique. It is often the only way around this type of problem.

THE "UNKNOWN MEMORY" DILEMMA

If you are a professional programmer, you probably have faced the "unknown memory" dilemma. This occurs when you write a program that has some aspect of its performance based on the amount of memory inside the computer that is running it. Examples of programs that exhibit this problem are spreadsheets, in-RAM mailing-list programs, and sorts. For example, an in-memory sort that can handle 10,000 addresses in a 256K machine may be able to sort only 5000 addresses in a 128K computer. If this program were to be used on computers of unkonwn memory sizes, you could not use a fixed-size array to hold the sort information. Either the program would not work because the machine had too little memory and the array would not fit, or you would have to create an array for the worst case and not allow users who had more memory to use it. The solution is to use dynamic allocation to hold the information.

A text editor illustrates the memory dilemma and its solution quite well. Many text editors do not have a fixed number of characters that they can hold, but rather use all of the computer's available memory to store the text that you enter. For example, as each line is entered, storage is allocated and a linked list is maintained. When a line is deleted, memory is returned to the system. One way to implement such a text editor would be to use the following structure for each line:

```
struct line {
   char text[81];
   int num;  /* line number of line */
   struct line *next;  /* pointer to next entry */
   struct line *prior;  /* pointer to previous record */
} ;

struct line *start;  /* pointer to first entry in list */
struct line *last;  /* pointer to last entry */
```

For simplicity, this editor always allocates enough memory for each line to be 80 characters long with a null terminator. (In reality, only the exact length of the line would be allocated, and additional overhead would be incurred when the line was altered.) The element **num** holds the line number for each line of text. This allows you to use the standard sorted, doubly linked list-storage function **dls_store()** to create and maintain the text file as a linked list.

The entire program for a simple text editor, shown next, supports the insertion of lines at any point based on the line number specified and supports the deletion of any line. You may also list the text and store it in a disk file.

This editor operates by means of a sorted, linked list of lines of text. The sort key is the line number of each line. In this way, not only can you insert text easily at any point by specifying the starting line number, but you can also delete text easily. The only function whose purpose may not be obvious to you is **patchup ()**. It renumbers the element **num** for each line of text as needed when insertions or deletions cause the line number to be changed.

The key point of this example is that the amount of text that the editor can hold is based directly on the amount of free memory in the user's system. Thus, the editor automatically uses additional memory without having to be reprogrammed. This is the most important reason for using dynamic allocation when you are faced with the memory dilemma.

The program as shown is limited, but the basic-text editing support is solid. You might enjoy enhancing it to create a customized text editor for your own use.

```c
/* A very simple editor that uses dynamic allocation. */

#include "stdio.h"
#include "stdlib.h" /* "malloc.h" for some compilers */

struct line {
  char text[81];
  int num;  /* line number of line */
  struct line *next;  /* pointer to next entry */
  struct line *prior;  /* pointer to previous record */
} ;

struct line *start;  /* pointer to first entry in list */
struct line *last;  /* pointer to last entry */
struct line *dls_store(), *find();

void patchup(), delete(), list(), save(), load();

main(argc, argv)
int argc;
char *argv[];
{
  char s[80], choice, fname[80];
  struct line *info;
  int linenum=1;

  start = NULL; last = NULL; /* zero length list */

  if(argc==2) load(argv[1]); /* read file on command line */

  do {
      choice = menu_select();
      switch(choice) {
        case 1: printf("Enter line number: ");
          gets(s);
          linenum = atoi(s);
          enter(linenum);
          break;
        case 2: delete();
          break;
        case 3: list();
          break;
        case 4: printf("enter filename: ");
          gets(fname);
          save(fname);  /* write to disk */
          break;
        case 5: printf("enter filename: ");
```

```
            gets(fname);
            load(fname);  /* read from disk */
            break;
          case 6: exit(0);
        }
  } while(1);
}

/* Select a menu option. */
menu_select()
{
  char s[80];
  int c;

  printf("1. Enter text\n");
  printf("2. Delete a line\n");
  printf("3. List the file\n");
  printf("4. Save the file\n");
  printf("5. Load the file\n");
  printf("6. Quit\n");
  do {
    printf("\nEnter your choice: ");
    gets(s);
    c = atoi(s);
  } while(c<0 || c>6);
  return c;
}

/* Insert text beginning at specified line number. */
enter(linenum)
int linenum;
{
  struct line *info;
  char t[81];

  for(;;) {
    /* get memory to hold new line */
    info = (struct line *) malloc(sizeof(struct line));
    if(!info) {
      printf("\nout of memory");
      return NULL;
    }

    printf("%d : ", linenum);
    gets(info->text); /* read line of text */
    info->num = linenum;

    /* Enter a blank line to stop entry; otherwise
       insert into the list and fix up the line
       numbers using patchup.
    */
    if(*info->text) {
      if(find(linenum)) patchup(linenum, 1); /* fix up
                                                old line nums */
      if(*info->text) start = dls_store(info);
    }
    else break;
    linenum++;

  } /* entry loop */
  return linenum;
}
```

```
/* When text is inserted into middle of file
   line numbers below it must be increased by one
   and those after deleted lines must be decreased
   by 1.
*/
void patchup(n, incr)
int n;
int incr;
{
  struct line *i;

  i = find(n);

  while(i) {
    i->num = i->num+incr;
    i = i->next;
  }
}

/* store in sorted order by line number */
struct line *dls_store(i)
struct line *i;
{
  struct line *old, *p;

  if(last==NULL) {  /* first element in list */
    i->next = NULL;
    i->prior = NULL;
    last = i;
    return i;
  }

  p = start; /* start at top of list */

  old = NULL;
  while(p) {
    if(p->num < i->num){
      old = p;
      p = p->next;
    }
    else {
      if(p->prior) {
        p->prior->next = i;
        i->next = p;
        p->prior = i;
        return start;
      }
      i->next = p; /* new first element */
      i->prior = NULL;
      p->prior = i;
      return   i;
    }
  }
  old->next = i; /* put on end */
  i->next = NULL;
  i->prior = old;
  last = i;
  return start;
}

/* delete a line */
void delete()
```

```
{
  struct line *info;
  char s[80];
  int linenum;

  printf("enter line number ");
  gets(s);
  linenum = atoi(s);
  info = find(linenum);
  if(info) {
    if(start==info) {
      start = info->next;
      if(start) start->prior = NULL;
      else last = NULL;
    }
    else {
      info->prior->next = info->next;
      if(info!= last)
          info->next->prior = info->prior;
      else
        last = info->prior;
    }
    free(info);  /* return memory to system */
    patchup(linenum+1, -1); /* decrement line numbers */
  }
}

/* find a line of text */
struct line *find(linenum)
int linenum;
{
  struct line *info;

  info = start;
  while(info) {
    if(linenum==info->num) return info;
    info = info->next;  /* get next address */
  }
  return NULL;  /* not found */
}

/* list the text */
void list()
{
  struct line *info;

  info = start;

  while(info) {
    printf("%d: %s\n", info->num, info->text);
    info = info->next;  /* get next address */
  }
  printf("\n\n");
}

/* save the file */
void save(fname)
char *fname;
{
  register int t;
  struct line *info;
  char *p;
```

```
      FILE *fp;

      if((fp=fopen(fname, "wb"))==NULL) {
        printf("cannot open file\n");
        exit(0);
      }
      printf("\nsaving file\n");

      info = start;
      while(info) {
        p = info->text;  /* convert to char pointer */
        while(*p) putc(*p++, fp);  /* save byte at a time */
        putc('\r', fp);  /* terminator */
        putc('\n', fp);  /* terminator */
        info = info->next;  /* get next line */
      }
      fclose(fp);
    }

    /* load the file */
    void load(fname)
    char *fname;
    {
      register int t, size, lnct;
      struct line *info, *temp;
      char *p;
      FILE *fp;

      if((fp=fopen(fname, "rb"))==NULL) {
        printf("cannot open file\n");
        return;
      }
      while(start) {   /* free any previous edit */
        temp = start;
        start = start->next;
        free(temp);
      }

      printf("\nloading file\n");

      size = sizeof(struct line);
      start = (struct line *) malloc(size);
      if(!start) {
        printf("out of memory\n");
        return;
      }
      info = start;
      p = info->text;  /* convert to char pointer */
      lnct = 1;
      while((*p=getc(fp))!=EOF) {
        p++;
        while((*p=getc(fp))!='\r') p++;
        getc(fp); /* through away the \n */
        *p = '\0';
        info->num = lnct++;
        info->next = (struct line *) malloc(size);
        if(!info->next) {
          printf("out of memory\n");
          return;
        }
        info->prior = temp;
        temp = info;
```

```
    info = info->next;
    p = info->text;
  }
  temp->next = NULL;  /* last entry */
  last = temp;
  free(info);
  start->prior = NULL;
  fclose(fp);
}
```

FRAGMENTATION

Because **malloc( )** and **free( )** are not technically part of the C language but are part of the C library, their exact implementation varies from compiler to compiler. Most compiler developers have put a great deal of effort into their dynamic allocation routines. However, under all implementations of **malloc( )** and **free( )**, *fragmentation* of memory can occur, which over time can cause allocation requests to fail even though enough free memory actually exists.

Fragmentation occurs when pieces of free memory lie between blocks of allocated memory. Although this is often acceptable when the free memory is large enough to fill allocation requests, it becomes a problem when the pieces are too small, by themselves, to fill a request, even though there would be sufficient memory if they were added together. Figure 3-5 shows how a sequence of calls to **malloc( )** and **free( )** can produce this situation. You can avoid some types of fragmentation if the dynamic allocation functions combine adjacent regions of memory. For example, if memory regions A, B, C, and D in the following example were allocated, and then regions B and C were freed, B and C could in theory be combined because they are next to each other. However, if B and D were freed, there would be no way to combine them, because C would lie between them and would still be in use.

| A | B | C | D |

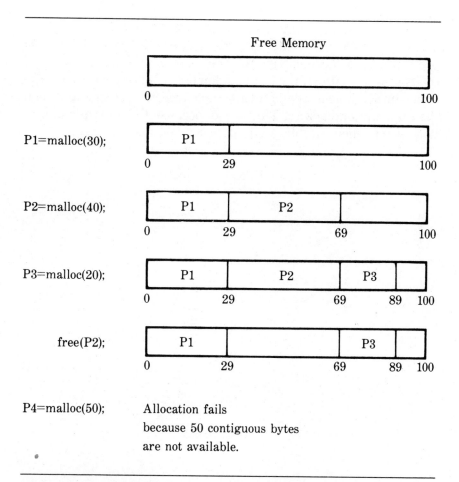

Figure 3-5.   Fragmentation in dynamic allocation

At first you might wonder why, if B and D were free while C was allocated, you couldn't just move C's contents to D and combine B and C. The problem is that your program would have no way of knowing that what was in C had been moved to D.

Fragmentation is difficult to eliminate. Sometimes it is possible to pack several small requests into one large request, thus preventing the development of very small fragments. Another solution is to write all the information out to a temporary disk file from time to time as the program runs, free all memory, and read the information back in. This works because the dynamic allocation system then combines all adjacent free memory regions.

4

C's MEMORY
MODELS

If your programming environment uses a processor that is based on the 8086 family, then one of C's most confusing aspects is not really its fault. You can compile a C program using one of the six different memory models defined by the the 8086 family of processors. (For other types of processors, the information in this chapter may not be applicable.) Each of these models organizes the memory of the computer differently and governs the size of the code, the data, or both. Because the model you use has a profound effect on your program's execution speed and on the way it accesses the system resources (especially memory), this chapter begins with an overview of the various memory models. It then develops a program that lets you inspect and change any part of the RAM in your system.

This chapter is specifically for C on the 8086 family of processors. The discussion of the C memory models assumes that you understand a little about how the 8086 CPU operates. However, even if you don't, you will still understand the difference between the various memory models in a practical sense, even if you don't technically understand the underlying principles.

THE 8086 FAMILY OF PROCESSORS

It will be easier to understand the way the various memory models work if you know something about how the 8086 family of processors addresses memory. (For the rest of this chapter, the CPU will be referred to as the 8086, but the information presented here applies to all processors in this family, including the 8088, 80186, 80286, and 80386.)

The 8086 contains 14 registers into which information is placed for processing or program control. The registers fall into the following categories:

- General-purpose registers
- Base-pointer and index registers
- Segment registers
- Special-purpose registers

All registers in the 8086 CPU are 16 bits (2 bytes) wide.

The *general-purpose registers* are the "workhorse" registers of the CPU. Values are placed in these registers for arithmetic operations, such as adding or multiplying; comparisons, including equality, less-than, greater-than, and the like; and branch (jump) instructions. Each general-purpose register may be accessed in two ways: either as a 16-bit register, or as two 8-bit registers.

The *base-pointer and index registers* are used to provide support for such things as relative addressing, the stack pointer, and block-move instructions. The *segment registers* support the 8086's segmented memory scheme. The **CS** register holds the current code segment, the **DS** register holds the current data segment, the **ES** register holds the extra segment, and the **SS** register holds the stack segment. These segments will be discussed in depth later in this chapter.

Finally, the *special-purpose registers* include the flag register, which holds the state of the CPU, and the instruction pointer, which points to the next instruction for the CPU to execute. Figure 4-1 shows the layout of the 8086 registers.

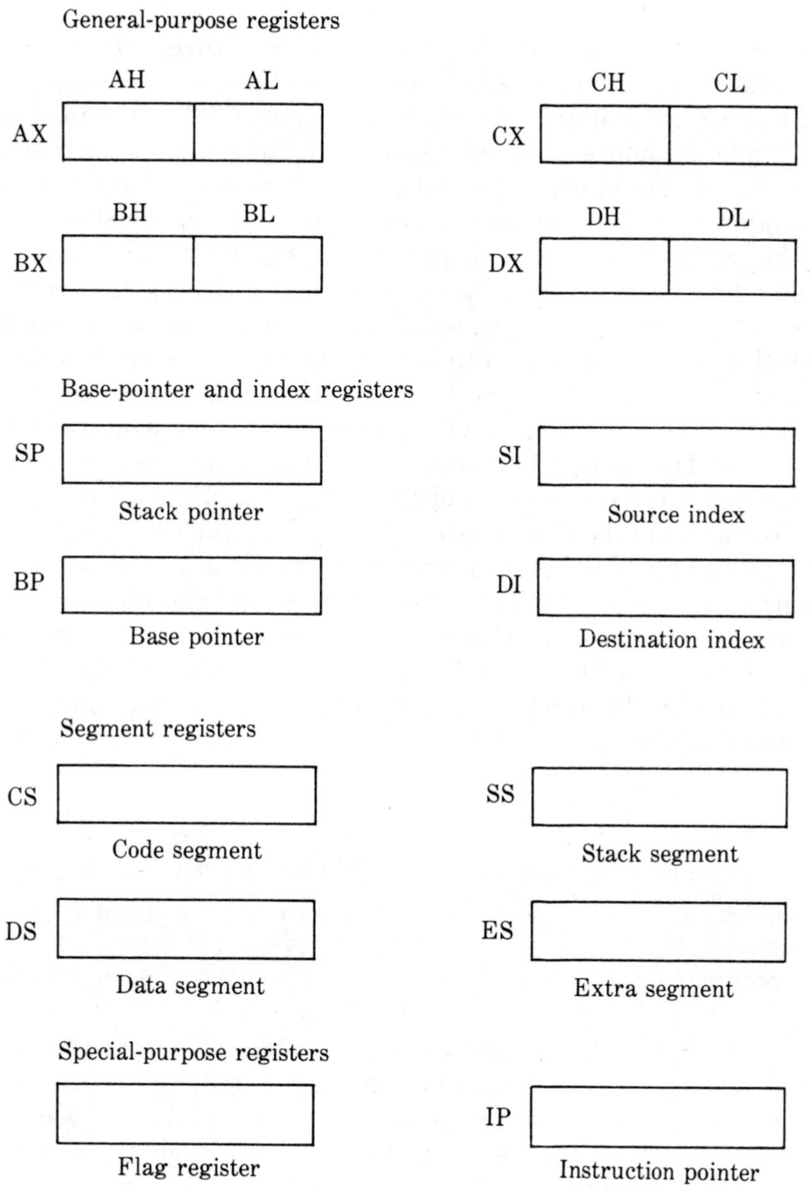

General-purpose registers

	AH	AL			CH	CL
AX				CX		

	BH	BL			DH	DL
BX				DX		

Base-pointer and index registers

SP [   ]   SI [   ]

Stack pointer   Source index

BP [   ]   DI [   ]

Base pointer   Destination index

Segment registers

CS [   ]   SS [   ]

Code segment   Stack segment

DS [   ]   ES [   ]

Data segment   Extra segment

Special-purpose registers

[   ]   IP [   ]

Flag register   Instruction pointer

Figure 4-1.   Layout of the 8086 registers

Address Calculation

The 8086 uses a segmented memory architecture with a total address space of one megabyte (or more, for the more powerful CPUs in the family). To access a megabyte of RAM requires at least a 20-bit address. For the 8086 family of processors, a 20-bit address is represented internally by two words (32 bits), even though only 20 bits are actually used. However, on the 8086, this 20-bit address is divided between two registers. One register holds the *segment* address and must be one of the segment registers. A segment is a 64K region of RAM that must start a boundary that is on an even multiple of 16 bytes. The 8086 uses four segments: one for code, one for data, one for the stack, and one extra segment. The location of any byte within a segment is called the *offset*. The actual 20-bit address of any specific byte within the computer is the combination of the segment and the offset.

To calculate the actual byte referred to by the combination of the segment and offset, you first shift the value in the segment register to the left by four bits and then add the offset to the shifted segment value. This makes a 20-bit address. For example, if the segment register holds the value 10H and the offset 100H, then the following sequence shows how the actual (physical) address is derived:

Segment register:		0 0 0 0	0 0 0 0	0 0 0 1	0 0 0 0
Segment shifted:	0 0 0 0	0 0 0 0	0 0 0 1	0 0 0 0	
Offset:		0 0 0 0	0 0 0 1	0 0 0 0	0 0 0 0
Segment+offset:	0 0 0 0	0 0 0 0	0 0 1 0	0 0 0 0	0 0 0 0 (200H)

As long as you are only accessing addresses within the segment that is currently loaded in a segment register, you only need to load the offsets of the various addresses. However, if you want to access an address that is not in the current segment, you must load both the segment and the offset of the desired address.

Addresses are most commonly referred to in the 8086 in *segment:offset* form. In this form the outcome of the previous example is 0010:0100H. The same byte can be described by many segment: offset values, because the segments may overlap each other. For example, 0000:0010 is the same as 0001:0000.

16 - Versus 20-bit Addresses

As you just learned, you need to load only a 16-bit address to access memory within a segment that has already been loaded into one of the segment registers. However, if you wish to access memory outside of such a segment, both the segment register and the offset must be loaded with the proper values. This means that a 20-bit address is required. The difference between the two is that it takes twice as long to load two 16-bit registers as it does to load one. Hence, your programs run much more slowly when you use 20-bit addresses, but they allow you to use larger programs and more data. The way in which compiling with different memory models affects your program is the subject of the next section of this chapter.

MEMORY MODELS

Most C compilers for the 8086 family of processors can compile your program in six different ways. Each way organizes the memory in the computer differently. The six models are called tiny, small, medium, compact, large, and huge. Let's look at how these differ.

The Tiny Model

The tiny model compiles a C program so that all of the segment registers are set to the same value, and all addressing is done using 16-bits. This means that the code, data, and stack must all be within the same 64K segment. The tiny model's method of compilation produces the smallest, fastest code. Programs compiled with this model can usually be converted into .COM files with the DOS command EXE2BIN. The tiny model produces the fastest run times.

The Small Model

The small model is the most common default mode of compilation. It is useful for a wide variety of tasks. Although all addressing is done with only the 16-bit offset, the code segment is separate from the data, stack, and extra segments, which are in their own segment. This means that the total size of a program compiled by this model is 128K, split between code and data. The addressing time is the same for the tiny model, but the program can be twice as big. Most programs that you will write will fall into this model. The small model produces run times that equal or nearly equal those of the tiny model.

The Medium Model

The medium model is for large programs in which the code exceeds the one-segment restriction of the small model. Here, the code can use multiple segments and requires 20-bit addresses, but the code, data, and extra segments are in their own segment and use 16-bit addresses. This is good for large programs that use little data. Your programs will run more slowly as far as function calls are concerned, but references to data will be as fast as those with the small model.

The Compact Model

The complement of the medium model is the compact model. In this model, program code is restricted to one segment, but data can occupy several segments. This means that all accesses to data require 20-bit addressing, but the code uses 16-bit addressing.

The compact model is good for programs that require large amounts of data but little code. Your program will run as fast as it would with the small model except when it is referencing data, which will be slower.

The Large Model

The large model allows both code and data to use multiple segments. However, the largest single item of data (such as an array) is limited to 64K. This model is used when you have both large code and large data requirements. It runs much more slowly than any of the other models.

The Huge Model

The huge model is the same as the large model, with one exception: individual data items can exceed 64K in size. This degrades run times further.

Selecting a Model

You should usually use the small model unless you have a reason to do otherwise. Select the medium model if you have a lot of code but not much data; use the compact model if you have a lot of data but not much code. If you have both a large amount of code and a large amount of data, use the large model—unless you will have single data items that are larger than 64K, in which case you should use the huge model. Remember, both the large and huge models run substantially more slowly than the other models.

OVERRIDING A MEMORY MODEL

You may have thought during the preceding discussion how unfortunate it is that even a single reference to data in another segment requires the use of the compact rather than small model. This slows down the execution of the entire program, even if only an isolated part of it actually needs a 20-bit address. For example, you must use 20-bit addressing to enable the graphics functions to write directly to the video RAM. *Segment-override* type modifiers, which are enhancements provided with most 8086-based C compilers, can solve this problem and related ones. These modifiers are called **near**, **far**, and **huge**. They can be applied only to pointers or to functions. When they are applied to pointers, they affect the way data is accessed; when applied to functions, they affect the way the functions are called and returned.

These modifiers follow the base type and precede the variable name. For example, this declares a **far** pointer called **f_pointer**:

```
char far *f_pointer;
```

Let's look at segment overrides further.

far

The most common model override is the **far** pointer. A common problem is that a program needs to access a region of memory that is (or may be) outside the data segment. However, if the program has been compiled for one of the large data models, all access to data is very slow —not just access to the region outside the data segment. The solution to this problem is to use **far**. If you explicitly declare **far** pointers to the memory that is outside the current data segment, only references to objects that are actually far away will incur the additional overhead.

The use of **far** functions is less common and is generally restricted to specialized programming situations in which a function may lie outside the current code segment (for example, in ROM). In such a case, the use of **far** ensures that the proper calling and returning sequences are used.

Because of the way **far** pointers are implemented in many 8086-based C compilers, pointer arithmetic only affects the offset.

This means that when a **far** pointer with the value 0000:FFFF is incremented, its new value will be 0000:0000, not 0001:FFF1. Therefore, even though the pointer can access objects that are not in its own data segment, it cannot access objects larger than 64K.

Two **far** pointers, as implemented by many C compilers, should not be used in a relational expression—only their offsets will be checked. As stated earlier, it is possible for two different pointers to contain the same physical address but have different segments and offsets. If you need to compare 20-bit pointers, you must use **huge** pointers.

near

A **near** pointer is a 16-bit offset that uses the value of the appropriate segment to determine the actual memory location. The **near** modifier forces C to treat the pointer as a 16-bit offset to the segment contained in DS register. You will use a **near** pointer when you have compiled a program using the medium, large, or huge memory model.

Using **near** on a function causes the function to be treated as if it had been compiled with the small model. When a function is compiled with the tiny, small, or compact model, all calls to the function place a 16-bit return address on the stack. Compiling with a large model causes a 32-bit address to be pushed on the stack. Therefore, in programs that are compiled with the large model, a highly recursive function should be declared as **near** to conserve stack space and speed execution time.

huge

The **huge** pointer is like the **far** pointer with two additions. First, its segment is normalized, so that comparisons between **huge** pointers are meaningful. Second, a **huge** pointer can be incremented any number of times—it does not suffer from the "wraparound" problem that afflicts **far** pointers.

A MEMORY DISPLAY AND CHANGE PROGRAM

Now that you understand how memory models work in C, it's time to put your knowledge to use. The simple memory display and change program presented here allows you to examine any byte in RAM and, if desired, alter its value. The program uses the segment override **far** so that any address in memory may be accessed.

The display—mem( ) Function

The first function needed for this program is **display—mem( )**, which displays the memory contents of the address requested by the user. This function first asks for a 20-bit address in hexadecimal form and then displays the contents of 256 bytes, beginning with the specified address. The output is arranged with 16 values to a line, 16 lines at a time. The address of each line is shown on the left. The **display—mem( )** function is shown here:

```
/* Displays 256 bytes of memory starting at specified
   address.
*/
void display_mem()
{
  register int i;
  unsigned char ch;
  unsigned char far *p;

  /* get a 20 bit address */
  printf("beginning address (in hex): ");
  scanf("%p%*c", &p);

  printf("%p: ", p); /* print address */
  for(i=1; i<=256; i++) {
    ch = *p;
    printf("%02x ", ch); /* display in hex */
    p++;
    if(!(i%16)) { /* every 16 bytes use new line */
      printf("\n");
      if(i!=256) printf("%p: ", p); /* print address */
    }
  }
}
```

The change—mem( ) Function

The second function required by the program, **change—mem( )**, changes the contents of a specified byte. It first requests a 20-bit address and then prompts the user for a new value for that address. The **change—mem( )** function is shown here:

```
/*  Change the contents of a byte of memory. */
void change_mem()
{
  unsigned char far *p;
  char value;

  /* get a 20-bit address */
  printf("Enter address to change (in hex): ");
  scanf("%p%*c", &p);
  printf("Enter new value (in hex): ");
  scanf("%x", &value);

  /* change the value */
  *p = (unsigned char) value;
}
```

The Entire Program

The entire memory display and change program is shown here. This program prompts for input by using the ¦ < symbol. Press D to display memory, C to change it, and Q to exit the program.

```
/* Display and/or change memory program. */

#include "stdlib.h"

void display_mem(), change_mem();

main()
{
  char ch;
  for(;;) {
    printf("|< "); /* display the prompt symbol */
    ch = getche(); /* read command */
    printf("\n");
    switch(tolower(ch)) {
      case 'd': display_mem();
        break;
      case 'c': change_mem();
        break;
      case 'q': exit(0);
    }
  }
}
```

```
/* Displays 256 bytes' of memory starting at specified
   address.
*/
void display_mem()
{
  register int i;
  unsigned char ch;
  unsigned char far *p;

  /* get a 20 bit address */
  printf("beginning address (in hex): ");
  scanf("%p%*c", &p);

  printf("%p: ", p); /* print address */
  for(i=1; i<=256; i++) {
    ch =  *p;
    printf("%02x ", ch); /* display in hex */
    p++;

    if(!(i%16)) { /* every 16 bytes use new line */
      printf("\n");
      if(i!=256) printf("%p: ", p); /* print address */
    }
  }
}

/*  Change the contents of a byte of memory. */
void change_mem()
{
  unsigned char far *p;
  char value;

  /* get a 20-bit address */
  printf("Enter address to change (in hex): ");
  scanf("%p%*c", &p);
  printf("Enter new value (in hex): ");
  scanf("%x", &value);

  /* change the value */
  *p = (unsigned char) value;
}
```

A sample of the program's output is shown here. (The exact output will vary from computer to computer.)

```
!< d
beginning address (in hex): e001a
000E:001A: 70 02 45 14 70 02 59 ec 00 f0 3d 04 00 e0 0d 21
000E:002A: 00 f0 66 52 00 e0 0d 21 00 f0 0d 21 00 f0 5d 02
000E:003A: 00 e0 0d 21 00 f0 0d 21 00 f0 0d 21 00 f0 0d 21
000E:004A: 00 f0 0d 21 00 f0 0d 21 00 f0 0d 21 00 f0 0d 21
000E:005A: 00 f0 0d 21 00 f0 0d 21 00 f0 0d 21 00 f0 0d 21
000E:006A: 00 f0 0d 21 00 f0 0d 21 00 f0 0d 21 00 f0 0d 21
000E:007A: 00 f0 0d 21 00 f0 0d 21 00 f0 0d 21 00 f0 0d 21
000E:008A: 00 f0 0d 21 00 f0 0d 21 00 f0 0d 21 00 f0 0d 21
000E:009A: 00 f0 0d 21 00 f0 00 00 00 00 00 00 00 00 00 00
000E:00AA: 00 00 00 00 00 00 00 00 00 00 00 00 00 00 00 00
000E:00BA: 00 00 00 00 00 00 0d 21 00 f0 0d 21 00 f0 0d 21
000E:00CA: 00 f0 0d 21 00 f0 0d 21 00 f0 0d 21 00 f0 0d 21
000E:00DA: 00 f0 0d 21 00 f0 a3 01 7a 0e 5c 21 00 f0 0d 21
000E:00EA: 00 f0 0d 21 00 f0 d1 05 7a 0e 65 21 00 f0 59 06
000E:00FA: 7a 0e 0d 21 00 f0 00 00 00 00 00 00 00 00 00 00
000E:010A: 00 00 00 00 00 00 00 00 00 00 00 00 00 00 00 00
```

```
!< c
Enter address to change (in hex): e001b
Enter new value (in hex): 00
!< d
beginning address (in hex): e001a
000E:001A: 70 00 45 14 70 02 59 ec 00 f0 3d 04 00 e0 0d 21
000E:002A: 00 f0 66 52 00 e0 0d 21 00 f0 0d 21 00 f0 5d 02
000E:003A: 00 e0 0d 21 00 f0 0d 21 00 f0 0d 21 00 f0 0d 21
000E:004A: 00 f0 0d 21 00 f0 0d 21 00 f0 0d 21 00 f0 0d 21
000E:005A: 00 f0 0d 21 00 f0 0d 21 00 f0 0d 21 00 f0 0d 21
000E:006A: 00 f0 0d 21 00 f0 0d 21 00 f0 0d 21 00 f0 0d 21
000E:007A: 00 f0 0d 21 00 f0 0d 21 00 f0 0d 21 00 f0 0d 21
000E:008A: 00 f0 0d 21 00 f0 0d 21 00 f0 0d 21 00 f0 0d 21
000E:009A: 00 f0 0d 21 00 f0 00 00 00 00 00 00 00 00 00 00
000E:00AA: 00 00 00 00 00 00 00 00 00 00 00 00 00 00 00 00
000E:00BA: 00 00 00 00 00 00 00 00 00 00 0d 21 00 f0 0d 21
000E:00CA: 00 f0 0d 21 00 f0 0d 21 00 f0 0d 21 00 f0 0d 21
000E:00DA: 00 f0 0d 21 00 f0 a3 01 7a 0e 5c 21 00 f0 0d 21
000E:00EA: 00 f0 0d 21 00 f0 d1 05 7a 0e 65 21 00 f0 59 06
000E:00FA: 7a 0e 0d 21 00 f0 00 00 00 00 00 00 00 00 00 00
000E:010A: 00 00 00 00 00 00 00 00 00 00 00 00 00 00 00 00
```

5

INTERFACING TO ASSEMBLY LANGUAGE ROUTINES AND THE OPERATING SYSTEM

As powerful as C is, there are times when you must either write a routine using assembly language or use a function call into the operating system. The way to do both of these varies among compilers, but the general procedures described in this chapter will apply to most compilers.

Each processor has a different assembly language, and each operating system has a different interface structure. Also, various C compilers have different "calling conventions," which define how information is passed to and from a function. In this chapter we will be using the IBM PC-DOS operating system and the 8086 assembly language. Many of the assembly language interfacing examples use Microsoft C, but the information is generally applicable to other C compilers. Even if you have a different computer or compiler, you can use the following discussions as a guide.

ASSEMBLY LANGUAGE INTERFACING

There are three reasons you might want to use a routine written in assembly language:

- Speed and efficiency
- To perform some machine-specific function that is unavailable in C
- To use a third-party assembly language routine

Although C compilers tend to produce extremely fast, compact object code, no compiler will consistently create code that is as fast or compact as that written by an excellent programmer using assembly language. Most of the time the small difference does not matter, nor does it warrant the extra time needed to write in assembly language. There can be special cases, however, where a specific function must be coded in assembly language so that it runs very quickly. This is true if a function is used frequently and has great effect on the execution speed of a program. A floating-point math package is a good example. Also, special hardware devices sometimes need exact timing, which means that you must code in assembly language so that this strict timing requirement is met.

Many computers, including 8086-based machines, have certain instructions that cannot be executed by most C compilers. For example, it is not possible to change data segments with any ANSI standard C instruction. It is also not possible to issue a software interrupt or to control the contents of specific registers by using a standard C statement.

It is very common in professional programming environments to purchase subroutine libraries for graphics, floating-point math, and the like. Sometimes you must take these in object format because the developer will not sell the source code. Occasionally, you can simply link these routines with code compiled by your compiler; at other times, you must write an interface module to correct any differences in the interface used by your compiler and the routines you purchased.

There are basically two ways to integrate assembly code modules into your C programs. The first is to code the routine separately and link it with the rest of your program. The second is to use the in-line assembly code capabilities of many C compilers. Both methods will be explored here.

This chapter will not teach you how to code in assembly language—it assumes that you know how. If you do not know how, please don't try the examples. It is very, very easy to do something slightly wrong, thereby creating a disaster—such as erasing your hard disk.

Calling Conventions
of a C Compiler

A *calling convention* is the method by which a C compiler passes information to functions and returns values from functions. The usual solutions use either the internal register of the CPU or the system stack to pass information between independent functions. Generally, C compilers use the stack to pass arguments to functions. If the arguments are one of the seven built-in data types **(char, short int, int, long int, unsigned int, float, or double)** or a structure, then the actual value is placed on the stack. If the argument is an array, then its address is placed on the stack. When a C function begins execution, it gets its parameter's values from the stack. When a C function terminates, it passes a return value back to the calling routine. This return value usually is placed in a register, although it could, in theory, be passed on the stack.

Another aspect of the calling convention concerns exactly which registers must be preserved and which ones can be used freely. Often a compiler will produce object code that needs only a portion of the registers available in the processor. You must preserve the contents of the register used by your compiler, usually by pushing their contents onto the stack prior to use. Any other registers are generally free for your use.

When you write an assembly language module that must interface to the code compiled by your C compiler, you must follow all of the conventions that are defined and used by your compiler. Only by doing so can you hope to have assembly language routines correctly interface to your C code.

The Calling Conventions of Microsoft C

Like most C compilers, Microsoft C passes arguments to functions on the stack. The arguments are pushed onto the stack from right to left. That is, given the call

    func(a, b, c);

c is pushed first, followed by b and a. The number of bytes occupied on the stack by each type is shown in Table 5-1.

Upon entry into an assembly code procedure, the contents of the BP register must be saved on the stack and the current value of the stack pointer (SP) must be placed into BP. The only other registers that you must preserve are SI and DI, if your routine uses them. Prior to returning from your assembly language function, you must restore the value of BP, SI, and DI and reset the stack pointer.

If your assembly language function returns a value, it is placed into the AX register if it is a 16-bit value. Otherwise, it is returned according to Table 5-2.

CREATING AN ASSEMBLY CODE FUNCTION

Without a doubt, the easiest way to learn to create assembly language functions that are compatible with your compiler's calling convention is to see how your compiler generates code. Virtually

Table 5-1.   The Number of Bytes on the Stack Required for Each Data Type When Passed to a Function for Microsoft C

Type	Number of Bytes
char	2
short	2
signed char	2
signed short	2
unsigned char	2
unsigned short	2
int	2
signed int	2
unsigned int	2
long	4
unsigned long	4
float	8
double	8
(near) pointer	2 (offset)
(far) pointer	4 (segment and offset)

Table 5-2.   Register Usage for Return Values Using Microsoft C

Type	Register(s) and Meaning
char	AX
unsigned char	AX
short	AX
unsigned short	AX
int	AX
unsigned int	AX
long	Low-order word in AX High-order word in DX
unsigned long	Low-order word in AX High-order word in DX
float & double	Address (offset only) to value
struct & union	Address (offset only) to value
(near) pointer	AX
(far) pointer	Offset in AX, segment in DX

all C compilers have a compile-time option that causes the compiler to output an assembly language listing of the code that it generates. By examining this file you can learn a great deal not only about interfacing to the compiler, but also about how the compiler actually works.

The Microsoft C compiler option −**FA** causes an assembly language file to be created. −**FC** creates a file that contains the assembly language instructions, the actual hexadecimal codes for the instructions, and the lines of C code that generated those instructions. These two files have the extensions .ASM and .COD, respectively. Let's use this feature to see how Microsoft C generates code for two short programs.

A Simple Assembly Code Function

The first program illustrates how code will be generated for a function call with arguments:

```
int sum;
main()
{
   sum = add(10,12);
}

add(a,b)
int a,b;
{
   int t;

   t = a+b;
   return t;
}
```

The variable **sum** is intentionally declared as global so that you can see examples of both local and global data. If this program is called TEST, then this command line will cause TEST.COD to be created.

>msc TEST−FC;

The contents of TEST.COD are shown here:

```
;       Static Name Aliases
;
        TITLE   test
;       NAME    test.C

        .287
_TEXT   SEGMENT  BYTE PUBLIC 'CODE'
_TEXT   ENDS
_DATA   SEGMENT  WORD PUBLIC 'DATA'
_DATA   ENDS
CONST   SEGMENT  WORD PUBLIC 'CONST'
CONST   ENDS
_BSS    SEGMENT  WORD PUBLIC 'BSS'
_BSS    ENDS
DGROUP  GROUP    CONST, _BSS, _DATA
        ASSUME  CS: _TEXT, DS: DGROUP, SS: DGROUP, ES: DGROUP
EXTRN   __chkstk:NEAR
EXTRN   _sum:WORD
_DATA       SEGMENT
;       .comm _sum,02H
_DATA       ENDS
_TEXT       SEGMENT
;|*** int sum;
;|*** main()
;|*** {
; Line 3
        PUBLIC  _main
_main   PROC NEAR
        *** 000000    55              push    bp
        *** 000001    8b ec           mov     bp,sp
        *** 000003    33 c0           xor     ax,ax
        *** 000005    e8 00 00        call    __chkstk
;|***   sum=add(10,12);
; Line 4
        *** 000008    b8 0c 00        mov     ax,12
        *** 00000b    50              push    ax
        *** 00000c    b8 0a 00        mov     ax,10
        *** 00000f    50              push    ax
        *** 000010    e8 00 00        call    _add
        *** 000013    83 c4 04        add     sp,4
        *** 000016    a3 00 00        mov     _sum,ax
;|*** }
; Line 5
        *** 000019    8b e5           mov     sp,bp
        *** 00001b    5d              pop     bp
        *** 00001c    c3              ret

_main   ENDP
;|***
;|*** add(a,b)
;|*** int a,b;
; Line 8
        PUBLIC  _add
_add    PROC NEAR
        *** 00001d    55              push    bp
        *** 00001e    8b ec           mov     bp,sp
        *** 000020    b8 02 00        mov     ax,2
        *** 000023    e8 00 00        call    __chkstk
```

```
;|***  {
; Line 9
;         a = 4
;         b = 6
;         t = -2
;|***     int t;
;|***     t=a+b;
; Line 11
          ***  000026      8b 46 04          mov      ax,[bp+4] ;a
          ***  000029      03 46 06          add      ax,[bp+6] ;b
          ***  00002c      89 46 fe          mov      [bp-2],ax ;t
;|***     return t;
; Line 12
          ***  00002f      8b e5             mov      sp,bp
          ***  000031      5d                pop      bp
          ***  000032      c3                ret

 _add      ENDP
 _TEXT     ENDS
 END
;|***  }
```

The program begins by establishing the various segments required by a C program. These will vary among the different memory models. (This file was produced by the small model compiler.) For the exact names, meaning, and usage of these segments, refer to your compiler's user manual.

Next, two bytes are allocated in the DATA segment for the global variable **sum**. The underscore in front of "sum" is added by the compiler to avoid confusion with any internal compiler names; it is added to the front of all function and variable names. After this, the code to the program begins. In Microsoft C, the code segment is called **_TEXT**.

The first thing that **main( )** does is save the BP register and place the current value of the stack pointer into it. This is to be expected, because C treats **main( )** like any other function. (The **main( )** function is called at startup by a small piece of code, added automatically by the linker, that performs certain actions dependent on the operating system.) The next two instructions are used to call the compiler-supplied routine named **___chkstk**, which checks to see if the stack has enough space in it to allocate the number of bytes contained in the AX register. Here, that value is 0 because there are no local variables. Next, the two arguments to **add( )** are pushed onto the stack and **_add** is called. Finally, the stack pointer is reset, BP is restored, and **main( )** returns.

The **add( )** function begins by saving BP, placing the value of SP into BP, checking the stack, and allocating two bytes. The next three lines of code add the numbers together and place their sum in **t**'s location on the stack. Notice, however, that the compiler is smart enough to know that AX already has the value of **t** in it, so it is not reloaded from memory prior to returning. This type of manipulation is called a *compiler optimization*. It is used to increase the efficiency of the code.

The same program, in its assembly language listing file, is shown here:

```
;       Static Name Aliases
;
        TITLE    test
;       NAME     test.C

        .287
_TEXT   SEGMENT  BYTE PUBLIC 'CODE'
_TEXT   ENDS
_DATA   SEGMENT  WORD PUBLIC 'DATA'
_DATA   ENDS
CONST   SEGMENT  WORD PUBLIC 'CONST'
CONST   ENDS
_BSS    SEGMENT  WORD PUBLIC 'BSS'
_BSS    ENDS
DGROUP  GROUP    CONST, _BSS, _DATA
        ASSUME   CS: _TEXT, DS: DGROUP, SS: DGROUP, ES: DGROUP
EXTRN      __chkstk:NEAR
EXTRN      _sum:WORD
_DATA       SEGMENT
;       .comm _sum,02H
_DATA  .    ENDS
_TEXT       SEGMENT
; Line 3
        PUBLIC   _main
_main   PROC NEAR
        push     bp
        mov      bp,sp
        xor      ax,ax
        call     __chkstk
; Line 4
        mov      ax,12
        push     ax
        mov      ax,10
        push     ax
        call     _add
        add      sp,4
        mov      _sum,ax
; Line 5
        mov      sp,bp
        pop      bp
        ret

_main   ENDP
; Line 8
        PUBLIC   _add
```

```
_add      PROC NEAR
          push      bp
          mov       bp,sp
          mov       ax,2
          call      __chkstk
; Line 9
;         a = 4
;         b = 6
;         t = -2
; Line 11
          mov       ax,[bp+4]        ;a
          add       ax,[bp+6]        ;b
          mov       [bp-2],ax        ;t
; Line 12
          mov       sp,bp
          pop       bp
          ret

_add      ENDP
_TEXT     ENDS
END
```

You can literally assemble this file by using the Microsoft macro
assembler **masm**, link it by using the standard **link** utility, and
run it. You can also modify it to make it run faster and still leave
the C source code untouched. For example, you could remove the
instructions that related to the local variable **t** — it's not actually
needed — and assemble the file. Doing this is called *hand
optimization.*

A Call-By-Reference
Example

In this program, the **get_val( )** function is called by using the
address of **a** to illustrate the code produced when pointers are
used:

```
main()
{
  int a;

  get_val(&a);
  printf("%d", a);
}


get_val(x)
int *x;
{
  *x = 100;
}
```

The assembly language file is shown here.

```
;        Static Name Aliases
;
         TITLE    test
;        NAME     test.C

         .287
_TEXT    SEGMENT  BYTE PUBLIC 'CODE'
_TEXT    ENDS
_DATA    SEGMENT  WORD PUBLIC 'DATA'
_DATA    ENDS
CONST    SEGMENT  WORD PUBLIC 'CONST'
CONST    ENDS
_BSS     SEGMENT  WORD PUBLIC 'BSS'
_BSS     ENDS
DGROUP   GROUP    CONST, _BSS,   _DATA
         ASSUME   CS: _TEXT, DS: DGROUP, SS: DGROUP, ES: DGROUP
EXTRN    _printf:NEAR
EXTRN    __chkstk:NEAR
_DATA       SEGMENT
$SG12    DB          '%d', 00H
_DATA    ENDS
_TEXT       SEGMENT
; Line 2
         PUBLIC  _main
_main    PROC NEAR
         push    bp
         mov     bp,sp
         mov     ax,2
         call    __chkstk
;        a = -2
; Line 5
         lea     ax,[bp-2]        ;a
         push    ax
         call    _get_val
         add     sp,2
; Line 6
         push    WORD PTR [bp-2] ;a
         mov     ax,OFFSET DGROUP:$SG12
         push    ax
         call    _printf
; Line 7
         mov     sp,bp
         pop     bp
         ret

_main    ENDP
; Line 11
         PUBLIC  _get_val
_get_val          PROC NEAR
         push    bp
         mov     bp,sp
         xor     ax,ax
         call    __chkstk
; Line 12
;        x = 4
; Line 13
         mov     bx,[bp+4]        ;x
         mov     WORD PTR [bx],100
; Line 14
         mov     sp,bp
         pop     bp
         ret
```

```
_get_val        ENDP
_TEXT   ENDS
END
```

The address of **a** is found by using the LEA (load effective
address) assembly language instruction. Inside **get_val( )**, this
address is used to load the value 100 into **a**, using the indirect
addressing mode of the 8086.

Using the Large-Code and Data Memory Model

As a final example of the way in which a C compiler generates
code, let's compile the same test program used by the previous
section, only this time use the huge memory model. To do this
with the Microsoft compiler, specify the −AH compiler option.
The following assembly code module is produced:

```
;       Static Name Aliases
;
        TITLE   test
;       NAME    test.C

        .287
TEST_TEXT       SEGMENT BYTE PUBLIC 'CODE'
TEST_TEXT       ENDS
_DATA   SEGMENT WORD PUBLIC 'DATA'
_DATA   ENDS
CONST   SEGMENT WORD PUBLIC 'CONST'
CONST   ENDS
_BSS    SEGMENT WORD PUBLIC 'BSS'
_BSS    ENDS
DGROUP  GROUP   CONST,  _BSS,   _DATA
        ASSUME  CS: TEST_TEXT, DS: DGROUP, SS: DGROUP, ES: DGROUP
EXTRN   _printf:FAR
EXTRN   __chkstk:FAR
_DATA       SEGMENT
$SG12   DB      '%d',   00H
_DATA       ENDS
TEST_TEXT       SEGMENT
; Line 2
        PUBLIC  _main
_main   PROC FAR
        push    bp
        mov     bp,sp
        mov     ax,2
        call    FAR PTR __chkstk
;       a = -2
; Line 5
        lea     ax,[bp-2]       ;a
        push    ss
        push    ax
```

```
        call    FAR PTR _get_val
        add     sp,4
; Line 6
        push    WORD PTR [bp-2] ;a
        mov     ax,OFFSET DGROUP:$SG12
        push    ds
        push    ax
        call    FAR PTR _printf
; Line 7
        mov     sp,bp
        pop     bp
        ret
_main   ENDP
; Line 11
        PUBLIC  _get_val
_get_val        PROC FAR
        push    bp
        mov     bp,sp
        xor     ax,ax
        call    FAR PTR __chkstk
; Line 12
;       x = 6
; Line 13
        les     bx,[bp+6]       ;x
        mov     WORD PTR es:[bx],100
; Line 14
        mov     sp,bp
        pop     bp
        ret

_get_val        ENDP
TEST_TEXT       ENDS
END
```

Notice that all calls are now **FAR**. This means that if you are
going to be linking your own assembly language routines with C
code compiled for a large code and data model, you must be sure
to generate compatible return code when you return from a **FAR**
call. When a procedure is called as **FAR**, both the segment and
offset are placed on the stack. In the small-code models, only the
offset is placed on the stack. Confusing the two models will cause
the stack to become corrupted, and the program will crash.

Creating an Assembly Code Skeleton

Now that you have seen two examples of how C compilers call
functions, it is just a short step to writing your own. One of the
easist ways to do this is to let the compiler generate an assembly
language skeleton for you. Once you have the skeleton, all you have
to do is fill in the details.

As an example, let's say that it is necessary to create an assembly routine that multiplies two integers together. To have the compiler generate a skeleton for this function, first create a file containing only this function:

```
mul(a,b)
int a,b;
{
}
```

Next, compile it with the proper option so that an assembly language file is produced. This is the file produced by using the −**FA** option of the Microsoft compiler:

```
;        Static Name Aliases
;
         TITLE    funcfile
;        NAME     funcfile.C

         .287
_TEXT    SEGMENT  BYTE PUBLIC 'CODE'
_TEXT    ENDS
_DATA    SEGMENT  WORD PUBLIC 'DATA'
_DATA    ENDS
CONST    SEGMENT  WORD PUBLIC 'CONST'
CONST    ENDS
_BSS     SEGMENT  WORD PUBLIC 'BSS'
_BSS     ENDS
DGROUP   GROUP    CONST, _BSS, _DATA
         ASSUME   CS: _TEXT, DS: DGROUP, SS: DGROUP, ES: DGROUP
EXTRN    __chkstk:NEAR
_TEXT         SEGMENT
; Line 2
         PUBLIC   _mul
_mul     PROC NEAR
         push     bp
         mov      bp,sp
         xor      ax,ax
         call     __chkstk
;        a = 4
;        b = 6
; Line 3
         mov      sp,bp
         pop      bp
         ret

_mul     ENDP
_TEXT    ENDS
END
```

In this skeleton, the compiler has done all the work of defining the proper segments and setting up the stack and registers. All you have to do is fill in the details. The finished **mul( )** function is shown here:

```
;          Static Name Aliases
;
           TITLE    funcfile
;          NAME     funcfile.C

           .287
_TEXT      SEGMENT  BYTE PUBLIC 'CODE'
_TEXT      ENDS
_DATA      SEGMENT  WORD PUBLIC 'DATA'
_DATA      ENDS
CONST      SEGMENT  WORD PUBLIC 'CONST'
CONST      ENDS
_BSS       SEGMENT  WORD PUBLIC 'BSS'
_BSS       ENDS
DGROUP     GROUP    CONST,  _BSS,   _DATA
           ASSUME   CS: _TEXT, DS: DGROUP, SS: DGROUP, ES: DGROUP
EXTRN      __chkstk:NEAR
_TEXT         SEGMENT
; Line 2
           PUBLIC   _mul
_mul       PROC NEAR
           push     bp
           mov      bp,sp
           xor      ax,ax
           call     __chkstk
;          a = 4
;          b = 6
; Line 3
;
;
; here is where the actual multiplication takes place
           mov      ax,[bp+4]        ;a
           imul     [bp+6]           ;b
;
;
           mov      sp,bp
           pop      bp
           ret

_mul       ENDP
_TEXT      ENDS
END
```

Once this file has been assembled, it can be linked to any C program that requires it. For example, the following program will print the number 10 on the screen. Remember to link in **mul( )**.

```
main()
{
  printf("%d ",mul(2,5));
}
```

Also remember that every compiler is different, and that every processor is different. The exact calling conventions may differ from the ones seen here. You must study your user manuals to find out how the calling convention works in your compiler.

The best way to learn more about interfacing assembly language code with your C programs is to write short functions in C that do something similar to what you want the assembly language version to do. Then, using the assembly language compiler option, create an assembly language file. Most of the time, you only need to hand-optimize this code, instead of having to actually create an assembly language routine from the ground up.

Using #asm and #endasm

Many C compilers, such as Aztec C, have added an extension to the C preprocessor directives that allow in-line assembly code to be made part of a C program, instead of using a completely separate module. (This is not supported by some compilers.) There are two advantages to this: first, the programmer is not required to write all the interface code, and second, all the code is in one place, making support a little easier.

The two preprocessor directives that make this possible are **#asm** and **#endasm**. The **#asm** directive is used to begin a block of assembly code; **#endasm** is used to end the block. All code inside of an **#asm** block must be correct assembly code for your computer. The C compiler simply passes this code, untouched, through to the assembly language phase of the compiler.

For example, the following short function, called **init—port1()**, sends 255 and then 0 to port 26 using 8086 assembly code:

```
init_port1()
{
  printf("Initializing Port\n");
  #asm
        out 26,255
        out 26,0
  #endasm
}
```

Here, the C compiler automatically provides the code to save registers and to return from the function. When the compiler compiles this code, it will fill in the code to preserve all registers and set up the return value.

You could use in-line assembly code to create a function that multiplies two numbers together without actually creating a separate assembly language file. Using this approach, the code for the **mul( )** function (which is compatible with Aztec C) is shown here:

```
mul(a, b)
int a, b;
{
  #asm
        mov ax,word ptr 8[bp]
        imul ax,word ptr 10[bp]
  #endasm
}
```

Remember that the C compiler provides all customary support for setting up and returning from a function call. You only need to provide the body of the function and follow the calling conventions to access the arguments.

Whatever method you use, you are creating machine dependencies that will make your program difficult to port to a new machine. For demanding situations that require assembly code, however, it is usually worth the effort.

Using the asm Statement

Turbo C supports the general concept of in-line assembly code in a somewhat different manner: it uses the **asm** keyword. The **asm** command is not part of the ANSI standard, however. It takes this general form:

asm <assembly code statement>

Whatever follows **asm** is passed directly to the assembler. The **asm** keyword must appear on each line of assembly code. For example, here is the **mul( )** function using the **asm** statement:

```
mul(a ,b)
int a, b;
{
asm      mov ax,word ptr 8[bp]
asm      imul ax,word ptr 10[bp]
}
```

When to Code in Assembly Language

Because of the difficulty of coding in assembly language, most programmers only do it when absolutely necessary. The general rule is don't do it—it creates too many problems. However, there are two cases in which coding in assembly language makes sense. The first case is when there is absolutely no other way to do it. This could be the case if you are performing some machine-specific function unavailable in C, or if you are using a third party language routine. It also could be the case if you have to interface directly to a hardware device that cannot be handled using C.

The second case is when a C program's execution time must be reduced. When it is necessary to speed up a program, you should carefully choose the functions you code in assembly language. If you code the wrong ones, you will see very little increase in speed. If you choose the right one, your program will fly! You can determine which functions need recoding simply by reviewing how your program runs. The functions used inside loops are generally the ones you should program in assembly language because they are executed repeatedly. Using assembly language to code a function that is used only once or twice will not speed up your program, but using it to code a function that is used several times will.

For example, consider the following **main( )** function:

```
main()
{
  register int t;

    init();

    for(t=0;t<1000;++t) {
      phase1();
      phase2();
      if(t==10) phase3();
    }

    byebye();
}
```

Recoding **init( )** and **byebye( )** will not measurably affect the speed of this program, because they execute only once. Both **phase1( )** and **phase2( )** are executed 1000 times, and definitely have a major effect on the runtime of this program. Even though it is inside the loop, **phase3( )** is only executed once, so this function also does not need to be recoded into assembly language.

With careful thought you can improve the speed of your program by recoding only a few functions in assembly language.

OPERATING-SYSTEM INTERFACING

Because many C programs fall into the category of system programs, it is often necessary to interface directly to the operating system, bypassing C's normal interface, to perform I/O operations. There may also be operating-system functions that cannot be accessed by your C compiler, although you would like to make use of them. For these reasons (and others), using the low-level resources of the operating system is common in C programming.

There are several operating systems in wide use today on microcomputers. They include the following:

- PC-DOS and its variant MS-DOS
- CP/M
- UNIX
- Apple DOS

All operating systems have a set of functions that programs use to perform such tasks as opening disk files, reading and writing characters to and from the console, and allocating memory for the program to run in. The way in which these functions are accessed varies from system to system, but they all use the concept of a *jump table* to access these functions. In an operating system like CP/M, system calls are executed by using a CALL instruction to a specific region of memory, with the desired function code in a register. In PC-DOS, a software interrupt is used. In either case, the

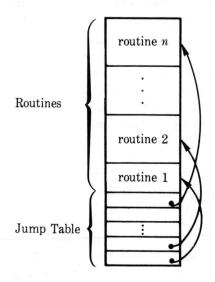

Figure 5-1.   Operating system jump table

jump table routes your program to the proper functions. Figure 5-1 shows how an operating system and its jump table might appear in memory.

It is not possible to discuss all operating systems here. This chapter focuses only on PC-DOS because it is in the widest use. You should remember, however, that the general techniques applied here will be applicable to all operating systems.

8086 INTERRUPTS AND PC-DOS

An interrupt is a special type of instruction that halts the execution of the current program, saves the current state of the system on the stack, and then jumps to an interrupt-handling routine that is determined by the number of the interrupt. When the interrupt routine has finished, it performs an *interrupt return*, which causes the previously executing program to resume. There are two basic types of interrupts: those generated by hardware, and those caused by software. It is the latter type of interrupt that is of interest here.

The 8086 CPU allows a program to execute a *software interrupt* via the **INT** instruction. The number that follows the instruction determines the number of the interrupt; for example, **INT 21h** causes the execution of interrupt 21h. The number of the interrupt is used to find the proper interrupt handler. The 8086 reserves the first 1K in memory for use as an *interrupt vector table*. This table contains the addresses (in segment: offset form) of the interrupt handlers, which means that each address requires four bytes. Thus, the 8086 supports 256 interrupt vectors. For example, the instruction **INT 5** tells the CPU to use the address found at the 5*4=20 byte in memory as the location of the interrupt routine. (Incidentally, **INT 5** calls the print screen utility.) This situation is depicted in Figure 5-2.

The PC-DOS operating system has allocated a number of these vectors as a means of accessing various functions that are part of the operating system. Operating-system functions are accessed in PC-DOS through the use of software interrupts. Each interrupt has its own category of functions that it accesses, and these functions are determined by the value of the AH register. If additional information is needed, it is passed in the AL, BX, CX, and DX registers. The PC-DOS operating system is divided into ROM-BIOS (Basic I/O System) and DOS (Disk Operating System). The ROM-BIOS provides the lowest-level routines, which DOS uses to provide the higher-level functions. The two overlap, however. Fortunately, for our purposes, they are accessed in basically the same way: through software interrupts. Let's begin with the ROM-BIOS routines, and end with a discussion of some of the more important DOS services.

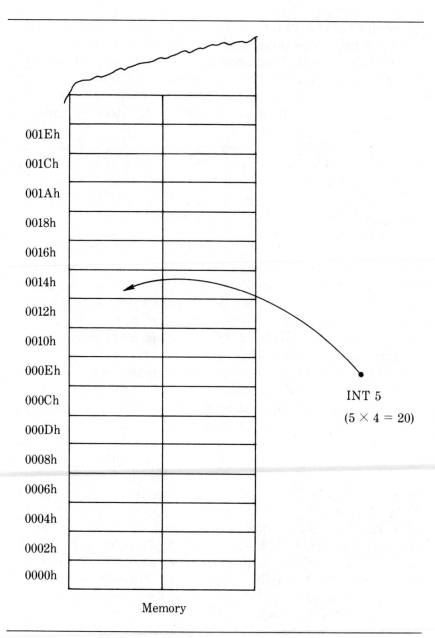

Figure 5-2.   The interrupt vector table for the 8086

Table 5-3.   ROM-BIOS Interrupts

Interrupt	Function
5h	Print screen utility
10h	Video I/O
11h	Equipment list
12h	Memory size
13h	Disk I/O
14h	Serial port I/O
15h	Cassette control
16h	Keyboard I/O
17h	Printer I/O
18h	Execute ROM BASIC
19h	Execute bootstrap loader
1Ah	Time and date

ACCESSING SYSTEM RESOURCES IN ROM-BIOS

There are twelve ROM-BIOS interrupts, as shown in Table 5-3. Most of these interrupts are associated with a number of options that can be accessed depending upon the value of the AH register when called. Table 5-4 shows a partial list of the options available for several of these interrupts. For a complete list and explanation, refer to the IBM *Technical Reference* Manual or *DOS: The Complete Reference* by Kris Jamsa (Berkeley, Calif.: Osborne/McGraw-Hill, 1987).

There are basically two ways you can access the functions found in Table 5-3. The first is through the use of a system-call function, often called **int86( )**, which is supplied with most compilers. The second is through the use of assembly language interfacing. In this section, the **int86( )** approach is explored.

Using int86( ) to Access
System Functions

Many C compilers, including Microsoft C and Turbo C, supply the
library routine called **int86( )**, which is used to execute a software
interrupt. (Other compilers may call it a different name.) The
function's general form is

```
#include "dos.h"
int int86(intnum, in, out)
int intnum;
union REGS *in, *out;
```

Here, *intnum* is the number of the interrupt; *in* is a union that
contains the registers that will be used to pass information to the
interrupt handlers; and *out* is the union that will hold the values,

Table 5-4.   Options Available for Some Interrupts

AH register	Function
ROM-BIOS Video I/O Functions — Interrupt 10h	
0	Set video mode
	if AL=0: 40×25 BW
	1: 40×25 color
	2: 80×25 BW
	3: 80×25 color
	4: 320×200 color graphics
	5: 320×200 BW graphics
	6: 340×200 BW graphics
1	Set cursor lines
	CH bits 0-4 contain start of line
	bits 5-7 are 0
	CL bits 0-4 contain end of line
	bits 5-7 are 0

Table 5-4.   Options Available for Some Interrupts (*continued*)

AH register	Function

2	Set cursor position
	    DH: row
	    DL: column
	    BH: video page number

3	Read cursor position
	    BH: video page number
	Returns:
	    DH: row
	    DL: column
	    CX: mode

4	Read light-pen position
	Returns:
	    if AH=0 pen not triggered
	    if AH=1 pen triggered
	    DH: row
	    DL: column
	    CH: raster line (0-199)
	    BX: pixel column (0-319 or 0-639)

5	Set active video page AL may be 0-7

6	Scroll page up
	    AL: number of lines to scroll, 0 for all
	    CH: row of upper-left corner of scroll
	    CL: column of upper-left corner of scroll
	    DH: row of lower-right corner of scroll
	    DL: column of lower-right corner of scroll
	    BH: attribute to be used on blank line

7	Scroll page down same as 6

8	Read character at cursor position
	    BH: video page
	Returns
	    AL: character read
	    AH: attribute

Table 5-4.   Options Available for Some Interrupts (*continued*)

AH register	Function
9	Write character and attribute at cursor position BH: video page BL: attribute CX: number of characters to write AL: character
10	Write character at current cursor position BH: video page CX: number of characters to write AL: character
11	Set color palette BH: palette number BL: color
12	Write a dot DX: row number CX: column number AL: color
13	Read a dot DX: row number CX: column number Returns AL: dot read
14	Write character to screen and advance cursor AL: character BL: foreground color BH: video page
15	Read video state Returns AL: current mode AH: number of columns on screen BH: current active video page

BIOS Disk I/O Functions—Interrupt 13h

AH register	Function
0	Reset disk system
1	Read disk status Returns AL: status (see IBM *Technical Reference* manual)

Table 5-4.   Options Available for Some Interrupts (*continued*)

AH register	Function

2	Read sectors into memory
	    DL: drive number
	    DH: head number
	    CH: track number
	    CL: sector number
	    AL: number of sectors to read
	    ES:BX: address of buffer
	Returns
	    AL: number of sectors read
	    AH: 0 on success, otherwise status

3	Write sectors to disk (same as Read above)
4	Verify (same as Read above)

5	Format a track
	    DL: drive number
	    DH: head number
	    CH: track number
	    ES:BX: sector information

BIOS Keyboard I/O Functions—Interrupt 16h

AH register	Function

0	Read scan code
	Returns
	    AH: scan code
	    AL: character code

1	Get status of buffer
	Returns
	    ZF: 1 then buffer empty
	        0 then characters waiting with next char
	        in AX as described above

2	Get status of keyboard (see IBM *Technical Reference* manual)

BIOS Printer I/O Functions—Interrupt 17h

AH register	Function

0	Print a character
	    AL: character
	    DX: printer number
	Returns
	    AH: status

Table 5-4. Options Available for Some Interrupts (*continued*)

AH register	Function

1	Initialize printer
	    DX: printer number
	Returns
	    AH: status

2	Read status
	    DX: printer number
	Returns
	    AH: status

High-Level DOS Functions Calls—Interrupt 21h (Partial List)

1	Read character from the keyboard Returns AL: character
2	Display a character on the screen DL: character
3	Read a character from async port Returns AL: character
4	Write a character to async port DL: character
5	Print a character to list device DL: character
7	Read character from keyboard but do not display it Returns AL: character
B	Check keyboard status Returns AL: 0FFH if key struck; 0 otherwise
D	Reset disk
E	Set default drive DL: Drive number (0=A, 1=B,...)

11
(4E under 2.X)
	Search for file name
	    DX: Address of FCB
	Returns
	    AL: 0 if found, FFh if not with name in disk
	        transfer address

12 (4F under 2.X)	Find next occurrence of file name same as 11

Table 5-4.   Options Available for Some Interrupts (*continued*)

AH register	Function
1A	Set disk transfer address DX: disk transfer address

2A	Get system date
	Returns
	    CX: year (1980-2099)
	    DH: month (1-12)
	    DL: day (1-31)

2B	Set system date
	    CX: year (1980-2099)
	    DH: month (1-12)
	    DL: day (1-31)

2C	Get system time
	Returns
	    CH: hours (0-23)
	    CL: minutes (0-59)
	    DH: seconds (0-59)
	    DL: hundredths of seconds (0-99)

2D	Set system time
	    CH: hours (0-23)
	    CL: minutes (0-59)
	    DH: seconds (0-59)
	    DL: hundredths of seconds (0-99)

if any, returned by the interrupt routine. However, the value of the AX register will also be returned by **int86( )**. The type **REGS** is supplied in the header **DOS.H**. The Microsoft version shown here is very similar to the versions supplied by other compilers.

```
/* word registers */

struct WORDREGS {
        unsigned int ax;
        unsigned int bx;
        unsigned int cx;
        unsigned int dx;
        unsigned int si;
```

```
        unsigned int di;
        unsigned int cflag;
        };

/* byte registers */

struct BYTEREGS {
        unsigned char al, ah;
        unsigned char bl, bh;
        unsigned char cl, ch;
        unsigned char dl, dh;
        };

/* general purpose registers union - overlays the
   corresponding word and byte registers.
 */

union REGS {
        struct WORDREGS x;
        struct BYTEREGS h;
        };
```

The **int86()** function will be used in the examples in this section to access the various ROM-BIOS functions. Although it will not be possible to look at examples of all the ROM-BIOS functions, a few of the more interesting ones will be examined.

Changing the Mode of the Screen

Suppose that you wish to change the screen mode during the execution of a program. With PC-DOS, the screen can have 16 modes; they are shown in Table 5-5. Using the **int86()** function, you can create the following function, called **mode()**, to change the mode of the screen to the specified type:

```
#include "dos.h"

void mode(mode_code)
int mode_code;
{
  union REGS r;

  r.h.al = mode_code;
  r.h.ah = 0;
  int86(0x10, &r, &r);
}
```

Table 5-5.　The Screen Modes Available for the Various IBM PCs

Mode	Type	Dimensions	Adapters
0	Text, B/W	40×25	CGA,EGA
1	Text, 16 colors	40×25	CGA,EGA
2	Text, B/W	80×25	CGA,EGA
3	Text, 16 colors	80×25	CGA,EGA
4	Graphics, 4 colors	320×200	CGA,EGA
5	Graphics, 4 gray tones	320×200	CGA,EGA
6	Graphics, B/W	640×200	CGA,EGA
7	Text, B/W	80×25	Monochrome
8	Graphics, 16 colors	160×200	PCjr
9	Graphics, 16 colors	320×200	PCjr
10	Graphics, PCjr, 4 colors		
	EGA, 16 colors	640×200	PCjr, EGA
13	Graphics, 16 colors	320×200	EGA
14	Graphics, 16 colors	640×200	EGA
15	Graphics, 4 colors	640×350	EGA

Clearing the Screen

It is easy to create a clear-screen function by calling the ROM-BIOS interrupt 10h function 6, as shown here:

```
#include "dos.h"

/* clear the screen */
void cls()
{
  union REGS r;

  r.h.ah=6; /* screen scroll code */
  r.h.al=0; /* clear screen code */
  r.h.ch=0; /* start row */
  r.h.cl=0; /* start column */
  r.h.dh=24; /* end row */
  r.h.dl=79; /* end column */
  r.h.bh=7;  /* blank line is blank */
  int86(0x10, &r, &r);
}
```

The value placed in AL determines the number of lines the screen will be scrolled, given the starting and ending coordinates. However, if AL is 0, then the entire screen is erased. The BH register is used to determined the attribute of a blank line. In this case, 7 is used, which means that blank lines will be black.

Cursor Positioning

Another useful function is **goto—xy( )**, which locates the cursor at the specified x and y coordinates. This function uses the ROM-BIOS interrupt 0x10, function 2, which places the cursor at the location specified by the DL and DH registers. The **goto—xy( )** function is shown here:

```
#include "dos.h"
/* send cursor to x,y */

/* send the cursor to x,y */
.void goto_xy(x,y)
int x,y;
{
  union REGS r;

  r.h.ah=2; /* cursor addressing function */
  r.h.dl=y; /* column coordinate */
  r.h.dh=x; /* row coordinate */
  r.h.bh=0; /* video page */
  int86(0x10, &r, &r);
}
```

For the IBM PC, 0,0 is the upper-left corner of the screen.

To see how this function works, try the following short program. It first clears the screen and then prints X characters diagonally across the screen.

```
#include "dos.h"

void cls(), goto_xy();

/* clear the screen and print Xs */
main()
{
  register int x,y;

  cls();
```

```
for(x=0, y=0; x<25; x++, y+=3) {
   goto_xy(x,y);
   printf("X");
 }
}

/* clear the screen */
void cls()
{
  union REGS r;

  r.h.ah=6; /* screen scroll code */
  r.h.al=0; /* clear screen code */
  r.h.ch=0; /* start row */
  r.h.cl=0; /* start column */
  r.h.dh=24; /* end row */
  r.h.dl=79; /* end column */
  r.h.bh=7; /* blank line is blank */
  int86(0x10, &r, &r);
}

/* send the cursor to x,y */
void goto_xy(x,y)
int x,y;
{
  union REGS r;

  r.h.ah=2; /* cursor addressing function */
  r.h.dl=y; /* column coordinate */
  r.h.dh=x; /* row coordinate */
  r.h.bh=0; /* video page */
  int86(0x10, &r, &r);
}
```

Using the Scan Codes
from the PC Keyboard

One of the most frustrating experiences you can encounter while
programming for the IBM PC and its clones is trying to use the
arrow keys (as well as INS, DEL, PGUP, PGDN, END, and HOME) and
the function keys. These keys do not return the normal 8-bit (1-
byte) characters in the way that the rest of the keys do. When you
press a key on the IBM PC, you are actually generating a 2-byte
(16-bit) value called a *scan code*. The scan code consists of the low-
order byte that contains the ASCII code for the key (if it is a normal key) and a high-order byte that contains the key's position on
the keyboard. For most keys on the keyboard, these scan codes are
converted into 8-bit ASCII values by the operating system, but for
function keys, arrow keys, and the like, this is not done. The char-

acter code for a special key is 0, which means that you must use the position code to determine which key was pressed. (The standard character input routine to read a character from the keyboard supported by DOS function call number 1 will not allow you to read the special keys.) Although a few C compilers have built-in routines to read these special keys, most do not. The problem occurs when you want to use these keys in a program.

The easiest way to access the special keys is to write a small function that calls interrupt 16h to read the scan code. After a call to interrupt 16h function 0, the position code is in AH and the character code is in AL. The **get_key()** function, shown here, returns these codes as an integer:

```
#include "dos.h"

/* read the 16-bit scan code of a key */
get_key()
{
  union REGS r;

  r.h.ah = 0;
  return int86(0x16, &r, &r);
}
```

The trick to using **get_key()** is that when a special key is struck, the character code is 0. In this case, you then decode the position code to determine which key was actually typed. Using **get_key()** to do all keyboard input requires that the calling routine make decisions based on the contents of AH and AL. Here is a short program that illustrates one way to do this:

```
#include "dos.h"

main()  /* scan code example */
{
  union scan {
    int c;
    char ch[2];
  } sc;

  do { /* read the keyboard */
    sc.c=get_key();
    if(sc.ch[0]==0)   /* is special key */
      printf("special key number %d",sc.ch[1]);
    else /* regular key */
      printf("%c/n",sc.ch[0]);
  } while(sc.ch[0]!='q');
}
```

The use of **union** allows the two halves of the scan code returned by **get_key( )** to be decoded easily.

There are basically two ways to decode a scan code. The first is to look in the IBM PC *Technical Reference* Manual; the other is to use the short program just shown, and determine the values experimentally. The latter method is more fun. To help you get started, here are the scan codes for the arrow keys:

left : arrow	75
right : arrow	77
up : arrow	72
down : arrow	80

Fully integrating the special keys with the normal keys requires that you write special input functions and bypass the normal **gets( )**, **scanf( )**, and **getche( )** type of functions found in the library. This is unfortunate, but it is the only way. However, the reward is that your program will appear very professional, and it will be much easier to use.

USING DOS TO ACCESS SYSTEM FUNCTIONS

The part of the PC-DOS operating system that is loaded and executed by the ROM-BIOS bootstrap loader is called DOS. It contains various higher-level functions that are not found, for the most part, in the ROM-BIOS routines (although there is some overlap). All of the DOS functions are accessed through interrupt 21h by using the AH register to pass the specific DOS function number requested. Table 5-6 shows a partial list of the DOS functions.

Although it is possible to access the DOS functions using **int86( )** as you did for the ROM-BIOS functions, many C compilers, including Microsoft C, Aztec C, and Turbo C, include a specific function for this purpose. The function is called **bdos( )**. It is used to perform an interrupt 21h call to access one of the higher-

Table 5-6. High-Level DOS Functions Calls—Interrupt 21h (partial list)

AH Register	Function
1	Reads a character from keyboard
	Returns:
	AL: character
2	Displays a character on screen
	DL: character
3	Reads a character from async port
	Returns:
	AL: character
4	Writes a character to async port
	DL: character
5	Prints a character to list device
	DL: character
7	Reads a character from keyboard but does not display it
	Returns:
	AL: character
8	Checks keyboard status
	Returns:
	AL: OFFH if key struck; otherwise, returns 0
D	Resets disk
E	Sets default drive
	DL: drive number (0 = A, 1 = B,...)
11	Searches for file name
(4E under 2.x)	DX: Address of FCB
	Returns:
	AL: 0 if found, FFh if not
	with name in disk-transfer address
12	Finds next occurrence of file name
(4F under 2.x)	same as 11
1A	Sets disk-transfer address
	DX: disk transfer address
2A	Gets system date
	Returns:
	CX: year (1980-2099)
	DH: month (1-12)
	DL: day (1-31)
2B	Sets system date
	CX: year (1980-2099)
	DH: month (1-12)
	DL: day (1-31)
2C	Gets system time

level functions in the operating system. The **bdos( )** function is declared as

    int bdos(int fnum, unsigned Reg—DX, unsigned Reg—AL)

where *fnum* is the number of the DOS function. The values of *Reg—DX* and *Reg—AL* are assigned to the DX and AL registers, respectively. Upon return, **bdos( )** returns the value of the AX register.

Checking Keyboard Status

A useful function that uses DOS and the **bdos( )** function is **kbhit( )**, which returns TRUE if a key has been struck and FALSE otherwise. It uses interrupt 21h number Bh:

```
#include "dos.h"

/* return 0 if no key struck, non-zero otherwise */
kbhit()
{
   return((char) bdos(0xB,0,0));
}
```

Notice that zeros were used for all but the first argument, because no other information was needed. This is the case in general as well. When a specific register is not used in the call, it can have any value assigned to it as a place holder. The cast to **char** is necessary because the status is returned in AL and AH is not defined.

A very common use of **kbhit( )** is to allow a routine to be interrupted by a user command. For example, a database may be doing a very long search that the user wants to stop. The following fragment will give you an idea of how this can be done:

```
        .
        .
        .
/* look up something */
while(!found) {
   if(kbhit())
      if(getchar()=='q') return; /* abort the search */
        .
        .
        .
}
        .
        .
        .
```

Using the Printer

By using the DOS function number 5, you can easily create a function that sends characters to the printer. The short function **prints()**, shown here, will print a null-terminated string to the printer:

```
#include "dos.h"

/* send a string to the printer */
prints(s)
char *s;
{
  while(*s) bdos(0x5,*s++,0);
}
```

It is important to keep in mind that many printers buffer a full line of text before printing it. If this is the case with your printer, be sure to send a carriage return as the last character.

Reading from and Writing to the Serial Port

Another function commonly absent from the standard library is one that reads or writes characters from or to the asynchronous serial port. (You would use this port if, for example, you wanted to write a modem program.) It is easy to write two functions that access the serial port using DOS function 3 to read a character and function 4 to write a character. They are shown here:

```
#include "dos.h"

/* send a character out the port */
put_async(ch)
char ch;
{
  bdos(0x4,ch,0);
}

/* return a character read from the port */
get_async()
{
  return((char) bdos(0x3,0,0));
}
```

Again, **char** is cast to ensure that any value in AH does not confuse any calling routine.

FINAL THOUGHTS ON
USING SYSTEM RESOURCES

This chapter has only scratched the surface of what can be done with the creative use of system resources. To fully integrate your program with the operating system, you will need to have access to information that describes all the functions in detail.

There are several things that you should remember before you use operating system functions. They can make your programs look and feel very professional. Bypassing some of C's built-in functions in favor of the operating system's functions can create programs that run faster and use less memory. Also, you will have access to functions that are not available in C's library. However, you are creating more trouble for yourself when you use the operating-system functions instead of C's standard functions—your code will no longer be portable. You may also become dependent on specific versions of a given operating system, creating compatibility problems for distributing your program. However, only you can decide when—and if—you should introduce machine and operating-system dependencies into your programs.

6

STATISTICS

Everyone who owns or has frequent access to a computer uses it at some point to perform *statistical analysis*. This analysis could take the form of monitoring or trying to predict the movement of stock prices in a portfolio, performing clinical testing to establish safe limits for a new drug, or even providing batting averages for the Little League team. The branch of mathematics that deals with the condensation, manipulation, and extrapolation of data is called *statistics*.

As a discipline, statistical analysis is quite young. It was born in the 1700s out of studies of games of chance. Indeed, probability and statistics are closely related. Modern statistical analysis began around the turn of this century when it became possible to sample and work with large sets of data. The computer made it possible to correlate and manipulate even larger amounts of data rapidly and to convert this data into a readily usable form. Today, because of the ever-increasing amount of information created and used by the government and the media, every aspect of life is adorned with reams of statistical information. It is difficult to listen to the radio or TV news, or to read a newspaper article, without being informed of some statistic.

Although C was not designed specifically for statistical programming, it adapts to the task quite well. It even offers some flexibility not found in more common business languages such as COBOL or BASIC. One advantage of C over COBOL is the speed and ease with which C programs can interface to the graphics functions of the system to produce charts and graphs of data. Also, depending on the compiler you have, C's math routines can be much faster than those commonly found in interpretive BASIC.

This chapter focuses on various concepts of statistics, including

- Mean
- Median
- Mode
- Standard deviation
- Regression equation (line of best fit)
- Coefficient of correlation

It also explores some simple graphing techniques.

SAMPLES, POPULATIONS, DISTRIBUTIONS, AND VARIABLES

Before you use statistics, you must understand a few key concepts. Statistical information is derived first by taking a *sample* of specific data points and then drawing generalizations about them. Each sample comes from the *population*, which consists of all of the possible outcomes for the situation under study. For example, if you wished to measure the output of a box factory over a year by using only the Wednesday output figures and generalizing from them, then your sample would consist of a year's worth of Wednesday figures taken from the larger population of each day's output in a year.

It is possible for the sample to equal the population if the sample is exhaustive. In the case of the box factory, your sample would equal the population if you used the actual output figures — five days a week for the entire year. When the sample is less than the population, there is always room for error; however, in many cases you can determine the probability for this error. This chapter assumes that the sample is the same as the population, and hence does not cover the problem of sample error.

For election projections and opinion polls, a proportionately small sample is used to project information about the population as a whole. For example, you might use statistical information about the Dow Jones stocks to make an inference about the stock market in general. Of course, the validity of these conclusions varies widely. In other uses of statistics, a sample that equals or nearly equals the population is used to summarize a large set of numbers for easier handling. For example, a board of education usually reports on the *average grade point* for a class, rather than on each student's individual grade.

Statistics are affected by the way that events are distributed in the population. Of the several common distributions in nature, the most important (and the only one used in this chapter) is the *normal distribution curve*, or the familiar "bell-shaped curve" as shown in Figure 6-1. As suggested by the graph in Figure 6-1, the elements in a normal distribution curve are found mostly in the middle. In fact, the curve is completely symmetrical around its peak—which is also the average for all the elements. The further from the middle in either direction on the curve, the fewer elements there are.

In any statistical process there is always an *independent variable*, which is the number under study, and a *dependent variable*, which is the factor that determines the independent variable. This chapter uses *time*—the stepwise incremental passage of events— for the dependent variable. For example, when watching a stock portfolio you may wish to see the movement of the stock on a daily basis. You would therefore be concerned with the movement of stock prices over a given period of time, not with the actual calendar date of each price.

Throughout this chapter, individual statistical functions will be developed and then assembled into a single menu-driven program. You can use this program to perform a wide variety of statistical analyses, as well as to plot information on the screen.

Whenever the elements of a sample are discussed, they will be called D and indexed from 1 to N, where N is the number of the last element.

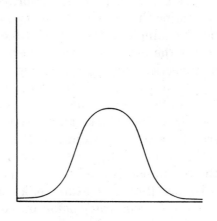

Figure 6-1.   The normal distribution curve

THE BASIC STATISTICS

Three important values form the basis of many statistical analyses and are also useful individually. They are the *mean*, the *median*, and the *mode*.

The Mean

The mean, or arithmetic average, is the most common of all statistics. This single value can be used to represent a set of data—the mean can be called the set's "center of gravity." To compute the mean, all elements in the sample are added together and the result is divided by the total number of elements. For example, the sum of the set

    1 2 3 4 5 6 7 8 9 10

equals 55. When that number is divided by the number of elements in the sample, which is 10, the mean is 5.5.

The general formula for finding the mean is

$$M = \frac{D_1 + D_2 + D_3 + \ldots + D_N}{N}$$

or

$$M = \frac{1}{N} \sum_{i=1}^{N} D_i$$

The symbol Σ indicates the summation of all elements between 1 and N.

As the statistical functions are developed in C, you should assume that all data is stored in an **array of floating-point numbers** and that the number of sample elements is known. The following function computes the mean of an array of **num** floating-point numbers and returns the floating-point average:

```
/* Compute the average. */
float mean(data, num)
float *data;
int num;
{
  int t;
  float avg;

  avg = 0;
  for(t=0; t<num; ++t)
    avg += data[t];

  avg /= num;

  return avg;
}
```

For example, if you called **mean()** with a 10-element array that contained the numbers 1 through 10, then **mean()** would return the result 5.5.

The Median

The median of a sample is the middle value based on order of magnitude. For example, in the sample set

1 2 3 4 5 6 7 8 9

5 is the median because it is in the middle. In the set

   1 2 3 4 5 6 7 8 9 10

you could use either 5 or 6 as the median. In a well-ordered sample that has a normal distribution, the median and the mean are very similar. However, as the sample moves further from the normal distribution curve, the difference between the median and the mean increases. Calculating the median of a sample is as simple as sorting the sample into ascending order and then selecting the middle element, which is indexed as $N/2$.

The function **median( )** shown here returns the value of the middle element in a sample. A modified version of Quicksort, developed in Chapter 1, is used to sort the data array.

```
/* Find the median. */
float median(data, num)
float *data;
int num;
{
  register int t;
  float dtemp[MAX];

  /* copy data for sorting */
  for(t=0; t<num; ++t) dtemp[t] = data[t];

  quick(dtemp, num);  /* sort data into ascending order */
  return dtemp[num/2]; /* return the middle value */
}

/* Quicksort setup routine */
void quick(item, count)
float *item;
int count;
{
  qs(item, 0, count-1);
}

void qs(item, left, right)  /* quick sort */
float *item;
int left, right;
{
 register int i, j;
 float x, y;

 i = left; j = right;
 x = item[(left+right)/2];

 do {
   while(item[i]<x && i<right) i++;
   while(x<item[j] && j>left) j--;

   if(i<=j) {
     y=item[i];
```

```
      item[i]=item[j];
      item[j]=y;
      i++; j--;
   }
} while(i<=j);

if(left<j)  qs(item, left, j);
if(i<right) qs(item, i, right);
}
```

The Mode

The mode of a sample is the value of the most frequently occurring element. For example, in the set

1 2 3 3 4 5 6 6 6 7 8 9

the mode would be 6 because it occurs three times. There may be more than one mode; for example, the sample

10 20 30 30 40 50 60 60 70

has two modes—30 and 60—because they both occur twice.

The following function, **find_mode( )**, returns the mode of a sample. (Be careful; *mode* is a common function name in many C libraries.) If there is more than one mode, then it returns the last one found.

```
/* Find the mode. */
float find_mode(data, num)
float *data;
int num;
{
  register int t, w;
  float md, oldmode;
  int count, oldcount;

  oldmode = 0; oldcount = 0;
  for(t=0; t<num; ++t) {
    md = data[t];
    count = 1;
    for(w=t+1; w<num; ++w)
      if(md==data[w]) count++;
    if(count>oldcount) {
      oldmode = md;
      oldcount = count;
    }
  }
  return oldmode;
}
```

Using the Mean, the Median, and the Mode

The mean, the median, and the mode share the same purpose: to provide one value that is the condensation of all the values in the sample. However, each represents the sample in a different way. The mean of the sample is generally the most useful value. Because it uses all values in its computation, the mean reflects all elements of the sample. The main disadvantage to the mean is its sensitivity to one extreme value. For example, in an imaginary business called Widget, Incorporated, the owner's salary is $100,000 per year, while the salary of each of the nine employees is $10,000. The average wage at Widget is $19,000, but this figure does not fairly represent the actual situation.

In samples like the salary dispersion at Widget, the mode is sometimes used instead of the mean. The mode of the salaries at Widget is $10,000—a figure that reflects more accurately the actual situation. However, the mode can be misleading. Consider a car company that makes cars in five different colors. In a given week, they made

    100 green cars
    100 orange cars
    150 blue cars
    200 black cars
    190 white cars

Here, the mode of the sample is black, because 200 black cars were made, more than any other color. However, it would be misleading to suggest that the car company primarily makes black cars.

The median is interesting because its validity is based on the *hope* that the sample will reflect a normal distribution. For example, if the sample is

    1 2 3 4 5 6 7 8 9 10

then the median is 5 or 6, and the mean is 5.5. Hence, in this case the median and mean are similar. However, in the sample

1 1 1 1 5 100 100 100 100

the median is still 5, but the mean is about 46.

In certain circumstances, neither the mean, the mode, nor the median can be counted on to give a meaningful value. This leads to two of the most important values in statistics—the *variance* and the *standard deviation*.

Variance and Standard Deviation

Although the one-number summary (such as the mean or median) is convenient, it can easily be misleading. Giving a little thought to this problem, you can see that the cause of the difficulty is not in the number itself, but rather in the fact that it does not convey any information about the variations of the data. For example, in the sample

1 1 1 1 9 9 9 9

the mean is 5; however, there is no element in the sample that is close to 5. What you would probably like to know is how close each element in the sample is to the average. If you know how much the data varies, you can better interpret the mean, median, and mode. You can find the variability of a sample by computing its variance and its standard deviation.

The variance and its square root, the standard deviation, are numbers that tell you the average deviation from the sample mean. Of the two, the standard deviation is the most important. It can be thought of as the average of the distances between the elements and the mean of the sample. The variance is computed as

$$V = \frac{1}{N} \sum_{i=1}^{N} (D_i - M)^2$$

where N is the number of elements in the sample and M is the sample mean. It is necessary to square the difference of the mean and each element in order to produce only positive numbers. If the numbers were not squared, they would by default always sum to 0.

The variance produced by this formula, V, is of limited value because it is difficult to understand. However, its square root, the standard deviation, is the number you are really looking for. The standard deviation is derived by first finding the variance and then taking its square root:

$$std = \sqrt{\frac{1}{N} \sum_{i=1}^{N} (D_i - M)^2}$$

where N is the number of elements in the sample and M is the sample mean.

As an example, for the following sample

11 20 40 30 99 30 50

you compute the variance as follows:

	D	D−M	(D−M)²
	11	−29	841
	20	−20	400
	40	0	0
	30	−10	100
	99	59	3481
	30	−10	100
	50	10	100
sum	280	0	5022
mean(M)	40	0	717.42

Here the average of the squared differences is 717.42. To derive the standard deviation, you simply take the square root of that number; the result is approximately 26.78. To interpret the standard deviation, remember that it is the *average distance that the elements are from the mean of the sample.*

The standard deviation tells you how nearly the mean represents the entire sample. For example, if you owned a candy bar factory and your plant foreman reported that daily output averaged 2500 bars last month but that the standard deviation was 2000, you would know that the production line needed better supervision!

If your sample follows a standard normal distribution, then about 68% of the sample will be within one standard deviation from the mean, and about 95% will be within two standard deviations.

The following function computes and returns the standard deviation of a given sample. Notice that **sqrt( )** requires a **double** type argument and returns **double** explicit type conversions. Although it would have been possible to use a cast instead, a few C compilers do not evaluate a cast correctly in a function call, so the safer option was chosen.

```c
/* Compute the standard deviation. */
float std_dev(data, num)
float *data;
int num;
{
  register int t;
  float std, avg;
  double temp, sqrt();

  avg = mean(data, num);  /* get average */
  std = 0;
  for(t=0; t<num; ++t)
  {
    std += ((data[t]-avg) * (data[t]-avg));
  }
  std /= num;
  temp = std;
  temp = sqrt(temp);
  std = temp;
  return std;
}
```

SIMPLE PLOTTING ON
THE SCREEN

The advantage of using graphs with statistics is that together they can convey the meaning clearly and accurately. A graph also shows at a glance how the sample was actually distributed and how variable the data is. This discussion is limited to two-dimensional graphs, which use the X-Y coordinate system. (Creating three-dimensional graphs is a discipline unto itself and beyond the scope of this book.)

There are two basic forms of two-dimensional graphs: the *bar graph* and the *scatter graph*. The bar graph uses solid bars to represent the magnitude of each element, while the scatter graph uses a single point per element, located at its X and Y coordinates. Figure 6-2 shows an example of each.

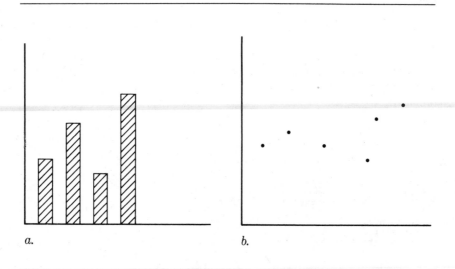

a. *b.*

Figure 6-2.   Samples of a bar graph (*a*) and a scatter graph (*b*)

The bar chart is usually used with a relatively small set of information, such as the Gross National Product for the last ten years or the percentage output of a factory on a monthly basis. The scatter graph is generally used to display a large number of data points, such as the daily stock price of a company over a year. Also, a modification of the scatter graph that connects the data points with a solid line is useful for plotting projections.

Two Important Functions

To construct a function that plots either a bar or a scatter graph, you need two support functions. The first of these, **point( )**, is used to write a specified color to the specified point. Many compilers include such a function in their libraries (although it might be called something else). However, if your compiler does not come with a function like this, you can use the version shown here, which uses BIOS interrupt 12:

```
/* Write a point to the CGA. */
void point(x, y, color_code)
int x, y, color_code;
{
  union REGS r;

  /* check range for mode 4 */
  if(x<0 || x>199 || y<0 || y>319) return;

  r.h.ah = 12; /* write a pixel */
  r.h.al = color_code; /* color to write */
  r.x.dx = x; /* row */
  r.x.cx = y; /* column */
  int86(0x10, &r, &r);  /* call BIOS */

}
```

The graphing functions will use video graphics mode 4, which allows four different colors. Therefore, the valid values for **color_code** are 0 through 3.

The second function you need, **line( )**, is used to draw a line of a specified color, given its starting and ending coordinates. If your compiler does not include a **line( )** function, you will have to create your own. The best way to draw a line is to use Bresenham's line-drawing algorithm. While it is beyond the scope of this chapter to explain its operation, you may use the one shown here, if none is provided with your compiler. (For an in-depth look at Bresenham's line-drawing algorithm and other graphics-related functions, refer to *C: The Complete Reference* by Herbert Schildt (Berkeley, Calif.: Osborne/McGraw-Hill, 1987).

```
/* Draw a line in specified color
   using Bresenham's integer-based algorithm.
*/
void line(startx, starty, endx, endy, color)
int startx, starty, endx, endy, color;
{
  register int t, distance;
  int x=0, y=0, delta_x, delta_y;
  int incx, incy;

  /* compute the distances in both directions */
  delta_x=endx-startx;
  delta_y = endy-starty;

  /* Compute the direction of the increment,
     an increment of 0 means either a vertical or horizontal
     line.
  */
  if(delta_x>0) incx = 1;
  else if(delta_x==0) incx = 0;
  else incx=-1;

  if(delta_y>0) incy = 1;
  else if(delta_y==0) incy = 0;
  else incy=-1;

  /* determine which distance is greater */
  delta_x = abs(delta_x);
  delta_y = abs(delta_y);
  if(delta_x>delta_y) distance = delta_x;
  else distance = delta_y;

  /* draw the line */
  for(t=0; t<=distance+1; t++) {
    point(startx, starty, color);
    x+=delta_x;
    y+=delta_y;
    if(x>distance) {
      x-=distance;
      startx+=incx;
    }
    if(y>distance) {
      y-=distance;
      starty+=incy;
    }
  }
}
```

Bar Plotting

Here is a simple plotting function that creates a bar graph on the IBM PC. It makes use of the **goto_xy( )** and **mode( )** functions developed in Chapter 5.

```
void simple_plot(data, num)   /* bar chart of info */
float *data;
int num;
{
  int a, t;
  mode(4); /* 320x200 graphics mode */

  goto_xy(24, 0); printf("%d", 0);
  goto_xy(0, 0); printf("%d", 200);
  goto_xy(24, 76); printf("%d", 280);
  for(t=0; t<num; ++t) {
    a = data[t];
    if(a<0) a = 0; /* can't display negative values */
    line((t*10)+20, 0, (t*10)+20, a);
  }
  getchar();    /* wait before returning to 25x80
                          character mode */

  mode(3);
}
```

This simple plotting routine has a serious limitation—it assumes that all data will be between 0 and 199 because the only valid numbers that can be used to call **line( )** are within the range 0 to 199. This assumption is fine in the unlikely event that your data elements consistently fit in that range. To make the plotting routine handle other values, you must *normalize* the data before plotting it in order to scale the data values to fit the required range. The process of normalization involves finding a ratio between the actual range of the data and the physical range of the screen resolution. Each data element can be multiplied by this ratio to produce a number that fits the range of the screen. The formula to do this for the Y-axis on the PC is

$$Y' = Y * \frac{200}{(max-min)}$$

where Y' is the value used when calling the plotting function. The same function can be used to spread the scale when the data range is very small.

The following function **barplot( )** scales the X- and Y-axes and plots a bar graph of as many as 280 elements. The X-axis is assumed to be time and is in increments of 1 unit. Generally, the normalizing procedure finds the greatest value and the smallest value in the sample and then calculates their difference. This number, which represents the spread between the minimum and maximum, is used to divide the resolution of the screen. In the case of the IBM PC, the numbers are 200 for the Y-axis and 280 for the X-axis (to create a little room for the border). The ratio is then used to convert the sample data into the proper scale.

```
/* Plot a bar chart of num items of data. */
void barplot(data, num)
float *data;
int num;
{
  int y, t, max, min, incr;
  float a, norm, spread;
  char s[80];

  mode(4); /* 320x200  graphics mode */
  palette(0);

  /* first find max value to enable normalization */
  max = getmax(data, num);
  min = getmin(data, num);
  if(min>0) min = 0;
  spread = max-min;
  norm = 200/spread;   /* absolute increment/spread */

  /* display the grid and range values */
  goto_xy(23, 0); printf("%d", min);
  goto_xy(0, 0); printf("%d", max);
  goto_xy(23, 38) printf("%d", num);

  /* print hash marks */
  for(t=1; t<23; ++t) {
    goto_xy(t, 0);
    printf("-");
  }

  /* plot the data */
  for(t=0; t<num; ++t) {
    a = data[t];
    a = a-min;
    a*=norm; /* normalize */
    y=a; /* type conversion */
    incr = 280/num;
    line(189, ((t*incr)+20), 189-y, ((t*incr)+20), 1);
  }
  gets(s);
  mode(3);
}
```

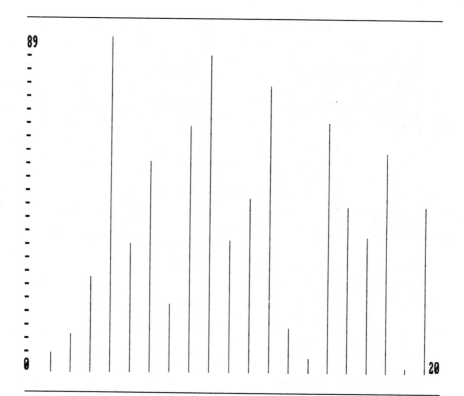

Figure 6-3.   A sample bar graph produced by **barplot( )**

This version also prints hash marks along the Y-axis that represent 1/24th of the difference between the minimum and maximum values. Figure 6-3 gives a sample of the output of **barplot( )** with 20 elements. By no means does **barplot( )** provide all the features you may desire, but it will do a good job of displaying a single sample.

Scatter Graphs

Only a slight modification to **barplot( )** is required to make a function that plots a scatter graph. The major alteration changes the call to **line( )** into a call to **point( )**.

Here is the new function **scatterplot( )**:

```
/* Display scatter chart of num items of data.
   Call with minimum value for Y and max values
   for Y and X.  Also specify color.
*/
void scatterplot(data, num, ymin, ymax, xmax, color)
float *data;
int num, ymin, ymax, xmax, color;
{
  int y, ·t, incr;
  float norm, a, spread;

  if(ymin>0) ymin = 0;
  spread = ymax-ymin;
  norm = 200/spread;   /* absolute increment/spread */

  /* display the grid and range */
  goto_xy(23, 0); printf("%d", ymin);
  goto_xy(0, 0); printf("%d", ymax);
  goto_xy(23, 38); printf("%d", xmax);

  /* hash marks */
  for(t=1; t<23; ++t) {
    goto_xy(t, 0);
    printf("-");
  }

  incr = 280/xmax;

  /* plot the data */
  for(t=0; t<num; ++t) {
    a = data[t];
    a = a-ymin;
    a*=norm; /* normalize */
    y = a; /* type conversion */
    point(189-y, ((t*incr)+20), color);
  }

}
```

In **scatterplot( )** the minimum and maximum data values are passed into the function, instead of being computed by the function as they are in **barplot( )**. This allows you to plot multiple data sets on the same screen without changing the scale. Figure 6-4 shows a sample scatter graph of 30 data elements produced by this function.

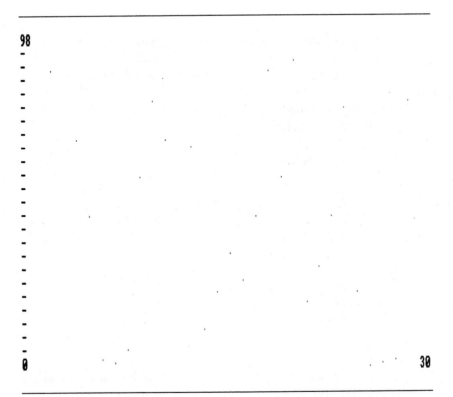

Figure 6-4. Sample scatter graph produced by **scatterplot( )**

PROJECTIONS AND THE
REGRESSION EQUATION

Statistical information is often used to make "informed guesses" about the future. Even though everyone knows that the past does not necessarily predict the future and that there are exceptions to every rule, historical data is still used in this way, because very often, past and present trends do continue into the future. When they do, you can try to determine specific values at future points in time. This process is called making a *projection* or *trend analysis*.

For example, consider a fictitious ten-year study of life spans, which collected the following data:

Year	Life Span
1970	69
1971	70
1972	72
1973	68
1974	73
1975	71
1976	75
1977	74
1978	78
1979	77

You might first ask yourself whether there is a trend here at all. If there is, you may want to know which way it is going. Finally, if there is indeed a trend, you might wonder what life expectancy will be in, say, 1985.

First, look at the bar graph of this data, as shown in Figure 6-5. By examining the graph you can conclude that life spans are getting longer in general. Also, if you placed a ruler on the graph to try to fit the data and drew a line that extended into 1985, you could project that that life span would be about 82 in 1985. However, while you may feel confident about your intuitive analysis, you would probably rather use a more formal and exact method of projecting life span.

Given a set of historical data, the best way to make projections is to find the *line of best fit* in relation to the data. This is what you did with the ruler. A line of best fit most closely represents each point of the data and its trend. Although some or even all of the actual data points may not be on the line, the line best represents

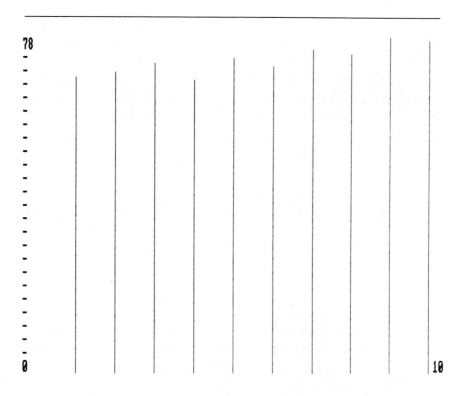

Figure 6-5.   Bar graph of life expectancy

them. The validity of the line is based on how close to the line the sample data points are.

A line in two-dimensional space has the basic equation

$$Y = a + bX$$

where X is the dependent variable, Y is the independent variable, a is Y-intercept, and b is the slope of the line. Therefore, to find a line that best fits a sample, you must determine a and b.

Any number of methods can be used to determine the values of a and b, but the most common and generally best is called the *method of least squares*. It attempts to minimize the distance between the actual data points and the line. The method involves two steps: the first computes b, the slope of the line, and the second finds a, the Y-intercept. To find b, use the formula

$$b = \frac{\sum\limits_{i=1}^{N} (X_i - M_x)(Y_i - M_y)}{\sum\limits_{i=1}^{N} (X_i - M_x)^2}$$

where M_x is the mean of the X coordinate and M_y is the mean of the y coordinate. The derivation of this formula is beyond the scope of this book, but having found b, you can use it to compute a as shown here:

$$a = M_y - bM_x$$

After you have calculated a and b, you can plug in any number for X and find the value of Y. For example, if you use the life-expectancy data, you find that the regression equation looks like

$$Y = 67.46 + 0.95 * X$$

Therefore, to find the life expectancy in 1985, which is 15 years from 1970, you have

$$\textit{Life expectancy} = 67.46 + 0.95 * 15$$

$$\cong 82$$

However, even with the line of best fit for the data, you may still want to know how well that line actually correlates with the data. If the line and data have only a slight correlation, then the regression line is of little use. However, if the line fits the data well, then it is a much more valid indicator. The most common way to determine and represent the correlation of the data to the regression line is to compute the *correlation coefficient*, which is a number between 0 and 1. The correlation coefficient is a percentage that is related to the distance of each data point in the sample from the line. If the correlation coefficient is 1, then the data corresponds perfectly to the line. A coefficient of 0 means that there is no correlation between the line and the points—in fact, any line would be as good (or bad) as the one used. The formula to find the correlation coefficient is

$$Cor = \frac{\dfrac{1}{N} \displaystyle\sum_{i=1}^{N} (X_i - M_x)(Y_i - M_y)}{\sqrt{\dfrac{1}{N} \displaystyle\sum_{i=1}^{N} (X_i - M_x)^2} \ \sqrt{\dfrac{1}{N} \displaystyle\sum_{i=1}^{N} (Y_i - M_y)^2}}$$

where M_x is the mean of X and M_y is the mean of Y. Generally, a value of 0.81 is considered a strong correlation. It indicates that about 66% of the data fits the regression line. To convert any correlation coefficient into a percentage, you simply square it.

Here is the function **regress( )**. It uses the methods just described to find the regression equation and the coefficient of correlation, as well as to make a scatter plot of both the sample data and the line:

```
/* Compute the regression equation. */
void regress(data, num)
float *data;
int num;
{
  float a, b, x_avg, y_avg, temp, temp2;
  float data2[280], cor;
```

```
float std_dev();
int t, min, max;
char s[80];

/* find mean of y */
y_avg = 0;
for(t=0; t<num; ++t)
  y_avg+=data[t];
y_avg/=num;

/* find mean of x */
x_avg = 0;
for(t=1; t<=num; ++t)
  x_avg+=t;
x_avg/=num;


/* now find b */
temp = 0; temp2 = 0;
for(t=1; t<=num; ++t) {
  temp+=(data[t-1]-y_avg)*(t-x_avg);
  temp2+=(t-x_avg) * (t-x_avg);
}

b = temp/temp2;

/* now find a */
a = y_avg-(b*x_avg);

/* now compute coefficient of correlation */
for(t=0; t<num; ++t) data2[t] = t+1; /* load x axis */
cor = temp/(num);
cor = cor/(std_dev(data, num) * std_dev(data2, num));

printf("regression equation is: Y = %f + %f * X\n", a, b);
printf("Correlation Coefficient: %f\n", cor);
printf("plot data points and regression line? (y/n) ");
gets(s);
if(toupper(*s)=='N') return;

mode(4); /* 320x200  graphics mode */
palette(0);
/* now do scatter graph and regression line */
for(t=0; t<num*2; ++t)    /* create plot regression line */
  data2[t] = a+(b*(t+1));
min = getmin(data, num)*2;
max = getmax(data, num)*2;
scatterplot(data, num, min, max, num*2, 1);  /* plot the points */
scatterplot(data2, num*2, min, max, num*2, 2);
gets(s);
mode(3);
}


/* Returns the maximum value of the data. */
getmax(data, num)
float *data;
int num;
{
  int t, max;

  for(max=data[0],t=1; t<num; ++t)
    if(data[t]>max) max=data[t];
  return max;
}
```

```
/* Returns the minimum value of the data. */
getmin(data, num)
float *data;
int num;
{
  int t, min;

  for(min=data[0],t=1; t<num; ++t)
    if(data[t]<min) min=data[t];
  return min;
}
```

A scatter plot of both the sample life-expectancy data and the regression line is shown in Figure 6-6. The important point to remember while using projections like this is that the past does not necessarily predict the future—if it did, it wouldn't be fun!

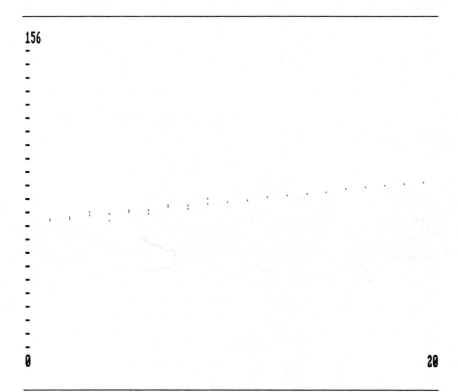

Figure 6-6.   Regression line for life expectancy

MAKING A COMPLETE STATISTICS PROGRAM

So far, this chapter has developed several functions that perform statistical calculations on single-variable populations. In this section you will put the functions together to form a complete program for analyzing data, printing bar charts or scatter plots, and making projections. Before you can design a complete program, you must define a data structure to hold the variable data information, as well as a few support functions.

First you need an array to hold the sample information. You can use a single-dimension floating-point array called **data** of size **MAX**. **MAX** is defined so that it fits the largest sample you will need, which in this case will be 100. The **main( )** function, along with the menu selection function **menu( )**, is shown here:

```c
#include "stdio.h"
#include "dos.h"
#include "ctype.h"

#define MAX 100

float mean(), std_dev(), median(), find_mode();
void goto_xy(), point(), palette(), mode(), line();
void save(), display(), regress(), barplot();
void scatterplot(), quick(), qs();

main()
{
  char ch;
  float data[MAX];  /* this array will hold data */
  float a, m, md, std; /* these hold the result of
                          the various analyses */
  int num=0; /* number of data items */

  for(;;) {
    ch = menu(); /* get user's selection */
    switch(ch) {
        case 'E':  /* enter date */
          num = enter_data(data);
          break;
        case 'B': /* compute basic stats */
          a = mean(data, num);
          std = std_dev(data, num);
          m = median(data, num);
          md = find_mode(data, num);
          printf("Average: %f\n", a);
          printf("Standard Deviation: %f\n", std);
          printf("Median: %f\n", m);
          printf("Mode: %f\n", md);
          break;
```

```
        case 'R': /* regression analysis and line */
          regress(data, num);
          break;
        case 'D': /* show the data */
          display(data, num);
          break;
        case 'L': /* load data from a file */
          num = load(data);
          break;
        case 'S': /* save data to a file */
          save(data, num);
          break;
        case 'P': /* bar plot */
          barplot(data, num);
          break;
        case 'Q': exit(0);
      }
    }
}

/* Return the user's selection. */
menu()
{
  char ch;
  do {
    printf("\nEnter data\n");
    printf("Basic statistics \n");
    printf("Regression line and scatter plot\n");
    printf("Plot a bar graph\n");
    printf("Save\n");
    printf("Load\n");
    printf("Display data\n");
    printf("Quit\n\n");
    printf("choose one (E, B, R, P, S, L, D, Q): ");
    ch = getche();
    ch = toupper(ch);
  } while(!strchr("BESLQDPR", ch));
  printf("\n");
  return ch;
}
```

Besides the statistical functions developed already, you also will need routines to save and load data. The **save()** routine must also store the number of data elements, and **load()** must read back that number.

```
/* Save the data file. */
void save(data, num)
float *data;
int num;
{
  FILE *fp;
  int t;
  char s[80];

  printf("enter filename: ");
  gets(s);
```

```
  if((fp=fopen(s, "w"))==0) {
    printf("cannot open file\n");
    exit(1);
  }
  putw(num, fp);  /* write out count */

  for(t=0; t<num; ++t) fprintf(fp, "%f ", data[t]);

  fclose(fp);
}

/* Load the data file. */
load(data)
float *data;
{
  FILE *fp;
  int t, num;
  char s[80];

  printf("enter filename: ");
  gets(s);
  if((fp=fopen(s, "r"))==0) {
    printf("cannot open file\n");
    exit(1);
  }

  num = getw(fp);
  for(t=0; t<num; ++t) fscanf(fp, "%f", &data[t]);

  fclose(fp);
  return num;
}
```

For your convenience, here is the entire program. Users of Microsoft C will need to specify the −STACK:4096 option when linking.

```
/* A statistics analysis and graphing program. */

#include "stdio.h"
#include "dos.h"
#include "ctype.h"

#define MAX 100

float mean(), std_dev(), median(), find_mode();
void goto_xy(), point(), palette(), mode(), line();
void save(), display(), regress(), barplot();
void scatterplot(), quick(), qs();

main()
{
  char ch;
  float data[MAX];  /* this array will hold data */
  float a, m, md, std; /* these hold the result of
                          the various analyses */
int num=0; /* number of data items */
```

```
    for(;;) {
      ch = menu(); /* get user's selection */
      switch(ch) {
          case 'E':  /* enter date */
            num = enter_data(data);
            break;
          case 'B': /* compute basic stats */
            a = mean(data, num);
            std = std_dev(data, num);
            m = median(data, num);
            md = find_mode(data, num);
            printf("Average: %f\n", a);
            printf("Standard Deviation: %f\n", std);
            printf("Median: %f\n", m);
            printf("Mode: %f\n", md);
            break;
          case 'R': /* regression analysis and line */
            regress(data, num);
            break;
          case 'D': /* show the data */
            display(data, num);
            break;
          case 'L': /* load data from a file */
            num = load(data);
            break;
          case 'S': /* save data to a file */
            save(data, num);
            break;
          case 'P': /* bar plot */
            barplot(data, num);
            break;
          case 'Q': exit(0);
      }
    }
}

/* Return the user's selection. */
menu()
{
  char ch;
  do {
    printf("\nEnter data\n");
    printf("Basic statistics \n");
    printf("Regression line and scatter plot\n");
    printf("Plot a bar graph\n");
    printf("Save\n");
    printf("Load\n");
    printf("Display data\n");
    printf("Quit\n\n");
    printf("choose one (E, B, R, P, S, L, D, Q): ");
    ch = getche();
    ch = toupper(ch);
  } while(!strchr("BESLQDPR", ch));
  printf("\n");
  return ch;
}

/* Display the data. */
void display(data, num)
float *data;
int num;
{
  int t;
```

```
   for(t=0; t<num; ++t)
     printf("item %d; %f\n", t+1, data[t]);

   printf("\n");
}

/* Read user's data and return number of items. */
enter_data(data)
float *data;
{

  int t, num;

  printf("number of items?: ");
  scanf("%d", &num);

  for(t=0; t<num; ++t) {
    printf("enter item %d: ", t+1);
    scanf("%f", &data[t]);
  }
  return num;
}

/* Compute the average. */
float mean(data, num)
float *data;
int num;
{
  int t;
  float avg;

  avg = 0;
  for(t=0; t<num; ++t)
    avg += data[t];

  avg /= num;

  return avg;
}

/* Compute the standard deviation. */
float std_dev(data, num)
float *data;
int num;
{
  register int t;
  float std, avg;
  double temp, sqrt();

  avg = mean(data, num);   /* get average */
  std = 0;
  for(t=0; t<num; ++t)
  {
    std += ((data[t]-avg) * (data[t]-avg));
  }
```

```
    std /= num;
    temp = std;
    temp = sqrt(temp);
    std = temp;
    return std;
}

/* Find the median. */
float median(data, num)
float *data;
int num;
{
  register int t;
  float dtemp[MAX];

  /* copy data for sorting */
  for(t=0; t<num; ++t) dtemp[t] = data[t];

  quick(dtemp, num);  /* sort data into ascending order */
  return dtemp[num/2]; /* return the middle value */
}

/* Find the mode. */
float find_mode(data, num)
float *data;
int num;
{
  register int t, w;
  float md, oldmode;
  int count, oldcount;

  oldmode = 0; oldcount = 0;
  for(t=0; t<num; ++t) {
    md = data[t];
    count = 1;
    for(w=t+1; w<num; ++w)
      if(md==data[w]) count++;
    if(count>oldcount) {
      oldmode = md;
      oldcount = count;
    }
  }
  return oldmode;
}

/* Compute the regression equation. */
void regress(data, num)
float *data;
int num;
{
  float a, b, x_avg, y_avg, temp, temp2;
  float data2[280], cor;
  float std_dev();
  int t, min, max;
  char s[80];
```

```
/* find mean of y */
y_avg = 0;
for(t=0; t<num; ++t)
  y_avg+=data[t];
y_avg/=num;

/* find mean of x */
x_avg = 0;
for(t=1; t<=num; ++t)
  x_avg+=t;
x_avg/=num;


/* now find b */
temp = 0; temp2 = 0;
for(t=1; t<=num; ++t) {
  temp+=(data[t-1]-y_avg)*(t-x_avg);
  temp2+=(t-x_avg) * (t-x_avg);
}

b = temp/temp2;

/* now find a */
a = y_avg-(b*x_avg);

/* now compute coefficient of correlation */
for(t=0; t<num; ++t) data2[t] = t+1; /* load x axis */
cor = temp/(num);
cor = cor/(std_dev(data, num) * std_dev(data2, num));

printf("regression equation is: Y = %f + %f * X\n", a, b);
printf("Correlation Coefficient: %f\n", cor);
printf("plot data points and regression line? (y/n) ");
gets(s);
if(toupper(*s)=='N') return;

mode(4); /* 320x200  graphics mode */
palette(0);
/* now do scatter graph and regression line */
for(t=0; t<num*2; ++t)    /* create plot regression line */
  data2[t] = a+(b*(t+1));
min = getmin(data, num)*2;
max = getmax(data, num)*2;
scatterplot(data, num, min, max, num*2, 1);  /* plot the points */
scatterplot(data2, num*2, min, max, num*2, 2);
gets(s);
mode(3);
}

/* Plot a bar chart of num items of data. */
void barplot(data, num)
float *data;
int num;
{
```

```
    int y, t, max, min, incr;
    float a, norm, spread;
    char s[80];

    mode(4); /* 320x200  graphics mode */
    palette(0);

    /* first find max value to enable normalization */
    max = getmax(data, num);
    min = getmin(data, num);
    if(min>0) min = 0;
    spread = max-min;
    norm = 200/spread;  /* absolute increment/spread */

    /* display the grid and range values */
    goto_xy(23, 0); printf("%d", min);
    goto_xy(0, 0); printf("%d", max);
    goto_xy(23, 38); printf("%d", num);

    /* print hash marks */
    for(t=1; t<23; ++t) {
      goto_xy(t, 0);
      printf("-");
    }

    /* plot the data */
    for(t=0; t<num; ++t) {
      a = data[t];
      a = a-min;
      a*=norm; /* normalize */
      y=a; /* type conversion */
      incr = 280/num;
      line(189, ((t*incr)+20), 189-y, ((t*incr)+20), 1);
    }
    gets(s);
    mode(3);
}

/* Display scatter chart of num items of data.
   Call with minimum value for Y and max values
   for Y and X.  Also specify color.
*/
void scatterplot(data, num, ymin, ymax, xmax, color)
float *data;
int num, ymin, ymax, xmax, color;
{
    int y, t, incr;
    float norm, a, spread;

    if(ymin>0) ymin = 0;
    spread = ymax-ymin;
    norm = 200/spread;  /* absolute increment/spread */

    /* display the grid and range */
    goto_xy(23, 0); printf("%d", ymin);
```

```
  goto_xy(0, 0); printf("%d", ymax);
  goto_xy(23, 38); printf("%d", xmax);

  o* hash marks */
  for(t=1; t<23; ++t) {
    goto_xy(t, 0);
    printf("-");
  }

  incr = 280/xmax;

  /* plot the data */
  for(t=0; t<num; ++t) {
    a = data[t];
    a = a-ymin;
    a*=norm; /* normalize */
    y = a; /* type conversion */
    point(189-y, ((t*incr)+20), color);
  }

}

/* Returns the maximum value of the data. */
getmax(data, num)
float *data;
int num;
{
  int t, max;

  for(max=data[0],t=1; t<num; ++t)
    if(data[t]>max) max=data[t];
  return max;
}

/* Returns the minimum value of the data. */
getmin(data, num)
float *data;
int num;
{
  int t, min;

  for(min=data[0],t=1; t<num; ++t)
    if(data[t]<min) min=data[t];
  return min;
}

/* Save the data file. */
void save(data, num)
float *data;
int num;
{
  FILE *fp;
  int t;
  char s[80];
```

```
  printf("enter filename: ");
  gets(s);

  if((fp=fopen(s, "w"))==0) {
    printf("cannot open file\n");
    exit(1);
  }
  putw(num, fp);  /* write out count */

  for(t=0; t<num; ++t) fprintf(fp, "%f ", data[t]);

  fclose(fp);
}

/* Load the data file. */
load(data)
float *data;
{
  FILE *fp;
  int t, num;
  char s[80];

  printf("enter filename: ");
  gets(s);
  if((fp=fopen(s, "r"))==0) {
    printf("cannot open file\n");
    exit(1);
  }

  num = getw(fp);
  for(t=0; t<num; ++t) fscanf(fp, "%f", &data[t]);

  fclose(fp);
  return num;
}

/* Quicksort setup routine */
void quick(item, count)
float *item;
int count;
{
  qs(item, 0, count-1);
}

void qs(item, left, right)  /* quick sort */
float *item;
int left, right;
{

  register int i, j;
  float x, y;

  i = left; j = right;
  x = item[(left+right)/2];
```

```
  do {
    while(item[i]<x && i<right) i++;
    while(x<item[j] && j>left) j--;

    if(i<=j) {
      y=item[i];
      item[i]=item[j];
      item[j]=y;
      i++; j--;
    }
  } while(i<=j);

  if(left<j)  qs(item, left, j);
  if(i<right) qs(item, i, right);
}

/* Set the palette. */
void palette(pnum)
int pnum;
{
  union REGS r;

  r.h.bh = 1;    /* code for mode 4 graphics */
  r.h.bl = pnum;
  r.h.ah = 11;   /* set palette function */
  int86(0x10, &r, &r);
}

/* Set the video mode. */
void mode(mode_code)
int mode_code;
{
  union REGS r;

  r.h.al = mode_code;
  r.h.ah = 0;
  int86(0x10, &r, &r);
}

/* Draw a line in specified color
   using Bresenham's integer-based algorithm.
*/
void line(startx, starty, endx, endy, color)
int startx, starty, endx, endy, color;
{
  register int t, distance;
  int x=0, y=0, delta_x, delta_y;
  int incx, incy;

  /* compute the distances in both directions */
  delta_x=endx-startx;
  delta_y = endy-starty;

  /* Compute the direction of the increment,
     an increment of 0 means either a vertical or horizontal
     line.
  */
  if(delta_x>0) incx = 1;
```

```
    else if(delta_x==0) incx = 0;
    else incx=-1;

    if(delta_y>0) incy = 1;
    else if(delta_y==0) incy = 0;
    else incy=-1;

    /* determine which distance is greater */
    delta_x = abs(delta_x);
    delta_y = abs(delta_y);
    if(delta_x>delta_y) distance = delta_x;
    else distance = delta_y;

    /* draw the line */
    for(t=0; t<=distance+1; t++) {
      point(startx, starty, color);
      x+=delta_x;
      y+=delta_y;
      if(x>distance) {
        x-=distance;
        startx+=incx;
      }
      if(y>distance) {
        y-=distance;
        starty+=incy;
      }
    }
}

/* Write a point to the CGA. */
void point(x, y, color_code)
int x, y, color_code;
{
  union REGS r;

  /* check range for mode 4 */
  if(x<0 || x>199 || y<0 || y>319) return;

  r.h.ah = 12; /* write a pixel */
  r.h.al = color_code; /* color to write */
  r.x.dx = x; /* row */
  r.x.cx = y; /* column */
  int86(0x10, &r, &r);  /* call BIOS */

}

/* Send the cursor to x,y. */
void goto_xy(x, y)
int x, y;
{
  union REGS r;

  r.h.ah = 2; /* cursor addressing function */
  r.h.dl = y; /* column coordinate */
  r.h.dh = x; /* row coordinate */
  r.h.bh = 0; /* video page */
  int86(0x10, &r, &r);
}
```

USING THE STATISTICS
PROGRAM

To give you an idea of how you can use the statistics program
developed in this chapter, here is an example of a simple stock-
market analysis for Widget, Incorporated. As an investor, you will
be trying to decide if it is a good time to buy stock in Widget; if
you should sell "short" (the process of selling shares you do not
have and hoping for a rapid price drop so that you can buy them
later at a cheaper price); or if you should invest elsewhere.

For the past 24 months, Widget's stock price has been as
follows:

Month	Stock Price ($)
1	10
2	10
3	11
4	9
5	8
6	8
7	9
8	10
9	10
10	13
11	11
12	11
13	11
14	11
15	12
16	13
17	14
18	16
19	17
20	15
21	15
22	16
23	14
24	16

You should first find out if Widget's stock price has established a trend. After entering the figures, you find the following basic statistics (rounded):

Mean: 12.08
Standard deviation: 2.68
Median: 11
Mode: 11

Next, you should plot a bar graph of the stock price, as shown in Figure 6-7. (Press the ENTER key to return to the main menu.)

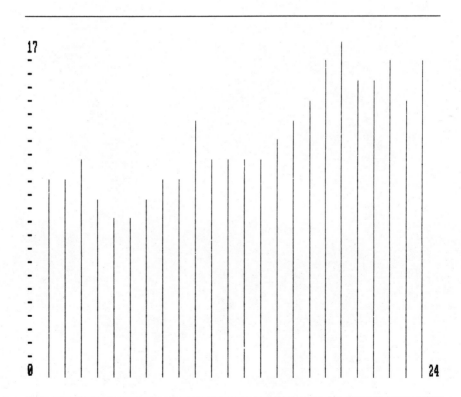

Figure 6-7.   Bar chart of Widget's stock price

The bar graph looks as if there might be a trend, but it is best to perform a formal regression analysis. The regression equation is

$$Y = 7.90 + 0.33 * X$$

with a correlation coefficient of about 0.87, or about 74%. This is quite good—in fact, a definite trend is clear. Printing a scatter graph, as shown in Figure 6-8, makes this strong growth readily apparent. Such results could cause an investor to throw caution to the wind and buy 1000 shares as quickly as possible!

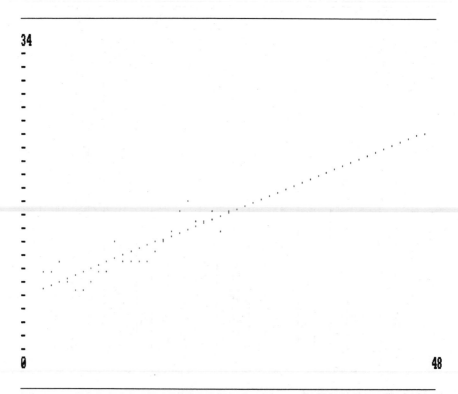

Figure 6-8.   Scatter graph of Widget's stock with regression line

FINAL THOUGHTS

The correct use of statistical analysis requires a general understanding of how the results are derived and what they really
mean. As with the Widget example, it is easy to forget that past
events cannot account for circumstances that can radically affect
the final outcome of a situation. Blind reliance on statistical evi-
dence can cause some very disturbing results.

7

ENCRYPTION AND DATA COMPRESSION

People who like computers and programming often like to play with codes and ciphers. Perhaps the reason for this is that all codes involve algorithms, just as programs do. Or perhaps these people simply have an affinity for cryptic things that most people cannot understand. All programmers seem to receive a great deal of satisfaction when a nonprogrammer looks at a program listing and says something like, "Wow, that sure looks complicated!" After all, the act of writing a program is called "coding."

Closely associated with the topic of cryptography is *data compression*. Data compression is the compacting of information into a smaller space than is usually used. Because data compression can play a role in encryption and uses many of the same principles, it is included in this chapter.

Computer-based cryptography is important for two primary reasons. The most obvious is the need to keep sensitive data on shared systems secure. Although password protection is adequate for many situations, important, confidential files are routinely coded to provide a higher level of protection. The second reason is that computer-based codes are used in data transmission. Not only are codes used for such things as secret government information, but they are starting to be used by broadcasters to protect their sky-to-earth station transmissions. Because these types of coding procedures are so complex, they are usually done by computer.

Data compression is commonly used to increase the storage capacity of various storage devices. Although the cost of storage devices has fallen sharply in the past few years, there can still be a need to fit more information into smaller areas.

A SHORT HISTORY OF CRYPTOGRAPHY

Although no one knows when secret writing began, one of the earliest examples is a cuneiform tablet made around 1500 B.C. It contains a coded formula for making pottery glaze. The Greeks and Spartans used codes as early as 475 B.C., and the upper class in Rome frequently used simple ciphers during the reign of Julius Caesar. During the Dark Ages, interest in cryptography (as well as many other intellectual pursuits) decreased except among monks, who used it occasionally. With the birth of the Italian Renaissance, the art of cryptography again flourished. By the time of Louis XIV of France, a code based on 587 randomly selected keys was used for government messages.

In the 1800s, two factors helped move cryptography forward. The first was Edgar Allan Poe's stories, such as "The Gold Bug," which featured coded messages and excited the imagination of many readers. The second was the invention of the telegraph and Morse code. Morse code was the first binary representation (dots and dashes) of the alphabet that received wide use.

By World War I, several nations had constructed mechanical "code machines" that permitted easy encoding and decoding of text by using sophisticated, complex ciphers. The story of cryptography changes slightly at this point, to the story of code-breaking. Before the use of mechanical devices to encode and decode messages, complex ciphers were used infrequently because of the time and effort required both for encoding and decoding. Hence, most codes could be broken within a relatively short period of time. However, the art of code-breaking became much more difficult when the code machines were used. Although modern computers would have made even those codes fairly easy to break, even computers cannot dwarf the incredible talent of Herbert Yardley, still considered the master code-breaker of all time. He not only broke the U.S. diplomatic code in 1915 in his spare time, but he also broke the Japanese diplomatic code in 1922—even though he did not know Japanese! He accomplished this by using frequency tables of the Japanese language.

By World War II, the major method used to break codes was to steal the enemy's code machine, thereby foregoing the tedious (if intellectually satisfying) process of code-breaking. In fact, the Allies' possession of a German code machine (unknown to the Germans) contributed greatly to the outcome of the war.

With the advent of computers—especially multiuser computers—secure and unbreakable codes have become even more important. Not only do computer files occasionally need to be kept secret, but access to the computer itself must also be managed and regulated. Numerous methods of encrypting data files have been developed, and the DES (Data Encryption Standard) algorithm, accepted by the National Bureau of Standards, is generally considered to be secure from code-breaking efforts. However, DES is very difficult to implement and may not be suitable for all situations.

Types of Ciphers

Of the more traditional coding methods, there are two basic types: *substitution* and *transposition*. A substitution cipher replaces one character with another, but leaves the message in the proper order. A transposition cipher essentially scrambles the characters of a message according to some rule. These types of codes can be used at whatever level of complexity is desired and can even be intermixed. The digital computer adds a third basic encryption technique, called *bit manipulation*, which alters the computerized representation of data by some algorithm.

All three methods may make use of a *key*. A key is a string of characters that is needed to decode a message. Do not confuse the key with the method, however, because the key itself is never sufficient to decode—the encryption algorithm must also be known. The key "personalizes" a coded message so that only those people that know the key can decode it, even though the method used to encode the message may be accessible.

Two terms that you should become familiar with are *plaintext* and *ciphertext*. The plaintext of a message is text you can read; the ciphertext is the encoded version.

This chapter presents computerized methods that use each of the three basic methods to code text files. You will see several short programs that encode and decode text files. With one exception, all of these programs have both a **code( )** and a **decode( )** function: the **decode( )** function always reverses the **code( )** process used to create the ciphertext.

SUBSTITUTION CIPHERS

One of the simplest substitution ciphers involves offsetting the alphabet by a specified amount. For example, if each letter were offset by three, then

abcdefghijklmnopqrstuvwxyz

would become

defghijklmnopqrstuvwxyzabc

Notice that the letters *abc* shifted off the front were added to the end. To encode a message using this method, you simply substitute the shifted alphabet for the real one. For example, the message

meet me at sunset

becomes

phhw ph dw vxqvhw

The program shown here enables you to code any text message using any offset after you specify which letter of the alphabet to begin with.

```
/* A simple substitution cipher. */

#include "ctype.h"
#include "stdio.h"

void code(), decode();

main(argc, argv)
int argc;
char *argv[];
{
  if(argc!=5) {
    printf("usage: input output encode/decode offset\n");
    exit(1);
  }
  if(!isalpha(*argv[4])){
    printf("start letter must be alphabetical character\n");
    exit(1);
  }

  if(toupper(*argv[3])=='E') code(argv[1], argv[2], *argv[4]);
  else decode(argv[1], argv[2], *argv[4]);
}

void code(input, output, offset)
char *input, *output;
char offset;
{
  int ch;
  FILE *fp1, *fp2;

  if((fp1=fopen(input, "r"))==NULL) {
    printf("cannot open input file\n");
    exit(1);
  }

  if((fp2=fopen(output, "w"))==NULL) {
    printf("cannot open output file\n");
    exit(1);
  }

  offset = tolower(offset);
  offset = offset-'a';
  do {
    ch = getc(fp1);
    ch = tolower(ch);
    if(isalpha(ch)) {
      ch+=offset; /* shift the letter */
      if(ch>'z') ch-=26; /* wrap around */
    }
    putc(ch, fp2);
    if(feof(fp1)) break;
  } while(!ferror(fp1) && !ferror(fp2));
  fclose(fp1); fclose(fp2);
}
```

```
void decode(input, output, offset)
char *input, *output;
char offset;
{
  int ch;
  FILE *fp1, *fp2;

  if((fp1=fopen(input, "r"))==NULL) {
    printf("cannot open input file\n");
    exit(1);
  }

  if((fp2=fopen(output, "w"))==NULL) {
    printf("cannot open output file\n");
    exit(1);
  }

  offset = tolower(offset);
  offset = offset-'a';
  do {
    ch = getc(fp1);
    ch = tolower(ch);
    if(isalpha(ch)) {
      ch-=offset; /* shift letter back to original */
      if(ch<'a') ch+=26;  /* wrap around */
    }
    putc(ch, fp2);
    if(feof(fp1)) break;
  } while(!ferror(fp1) && !ferror(fp2));
  fclose(fp1); fclose(fp2);
}
```

As an example, you could use this program to encode a file called "message," to put the coded version into a file called "cmess," and to offset the alphabet by two places. Assuming your program was named "code," you would first type at the command line

```
>code message cmess encode c
```

To decode, you would then type

```
>code cmess message decode c
```

Although a substitution cipher based on a constant offset will generally fool grade-schoolers, it is not suitable for most purposes because it is too easy to crack. After all, there are only 26 possible offsets, and it is easy to try all of them within a short period of time. An improvement on the substitution cipher is to use a scrambled alphabet instead of a simple offset.

A second failing of the simple substitution cipher is that it pre-serves the spaces between words, which makes it doubly easy for a code-breaker to crack. Another improvement would be to encode spaces. (Actually, all punctuation should be encoded, but for sim-plicity, the examples will not do this.) For example, you could map this random string containing every letter of the alphabet and a space.

    abcdefghijklmnopqrstuvwxyz<space>

into this string:

    qazwsxedcrfvtgbyhnujm ikolp

You may wonder if there is a significant improvement in the security of a message encoded by using a randomized version of the alphabet compared to using a simple offset version. The answer is *yes* —there are 26 factorial (26!) ways to arrange the alphabet; with the space, that number becomes 27 factorial (27!) ways. The factorial of a number is that number times every whole number smaller than it, down to 1. For example, 6! is 6*5*4*3*2*1 = 720. Therefore, 26! is a very large number.

The program shown here is an improved substitution cipher that uses the randomized alphabet shown earlier. If you encoded the message

    meet me at sunset

by using the improved substitution cipher program, it would look like

    tssjptspqjpumgusj

which is definitely a harder code to break.

```
/* Substitution Cipher that uses a randomized alphabet; */
#include "ctype.h"
```

```
#include "stdio.h"

void code(), decode();

char sub[28]=     "qazwsxedcrfvtgbyhnujm ikolp";
char alphabet[28]="abcdefghijklmnopqrstuvwxyz ";

main(argc, argv)
int argc;
char *argv[];
{
  if(argc!=4) {
    printf("usage: input output encode/decode\n");
    exit();
  }
  if(toupper(*argv[3])=='E') code(argv[1], argv[2]);
  else decode(argv[1], argv[2]);
}

void code(input, output)
char *input, *output;
{
  int ch;
  FILE *fp1, *fp2;

  if((fp1=fopen(input, "r"))==NULL) {
    printf("cannot open input file\n");
    exit();
  }

  if((fp2=fopen(output, "w"))==NULL) {
    printf("cannot open output file\n");
    exit();
  }

  do {
    ch = getc(fp1);
    ch = tolower(ch);
    if(isalpha(ch) || ch==' ')
      ch = sub[find(alphabet, ch)];
    putc(ch, fp2);
    if(feof(fp1)) break;
  } while(!ferror(fp1) && !ferror(fp2));
  fclose(fp1); fclose(fp2);
}

void decode(input, output)
char *input, *output;
{
  int ch;
  FILE *fp1, *fp2;

  if((fp1=fopen(input, "r"))==NULL) {
    printf("cannot open input file\n");
    exit();
  }

  if((fp2=fopen(output, "w"))==NULL) {
    printf("cannot open output file\n");
    exit();
  }

  do {
    ch = getc(fp1);
    ch = tolower(ch);
```

```
    if(isalpha(ch) || ch==' ')
      ch = alphabet[find(sub, ch)];
    putc(ch, fp2);
    if(feof(fp1)) break;
  } while(!ferror(fp1) && !ferror(fp2));

  fclose(fp1); fclose(fp2);
}

/* Find the correct index. */
find(s, ch)
char *s;
char ch;
{
  register int t;
  for(t=0;t<28;t++) if(ch==s[t]) return t;
  return -1;
}
```

Although code-breaking is examined later in this chapter, you should know that even this improved substitution code can still be broken easily by using a frequency table of the English language, in which the statistical information of the use of each letter of the alphabet is recorded. By looking at the coded message of the example, you can probably deduce that "s" represents "e," the most common letter in the English language, and that "p" represents the space. You can probably decode the rest. (You use the same process to solve the "cryptogram," which is next to the crossword puzzle in your newspaper.) Furthermore, the larger the coded message is, the easier it is to crack with a frequency table.

To impede the progress of a code-breaker who applies frequency tables to a coded message, you can use a *multiple substitution cipher* in which the same letter in the plaintext message would not necessarily be mapped to the same letter in the coded form. You can do this by adding a second randomized alphabet, and switching between it and the first alphabet each time a space is encountered. For example, the program can be rewritten to use this second string:

poi uytrewqasdfghjklmnbvcxz

The multiple substitution cipher shown here will work only with letters of the alphabet, switching randomized alphabets each time a space is encountered. It requires that all messages be only one line long. Note that the spaces beteen words are preserved, which is a definite drawback.

```
/* A multiple substitution cipher. */
#include "ctype.h"
#include "stdio.h"

void code(), decode();

char sub[28]=     "qazwsxedcrfvtgbyhnujm ikolp";
char sub2[28]=    "poi uytrewqasdfghjklmnbvcxz";
char alphabet[28]="abcdefghijklmnopqrstuvwxyz ";

main(argc,argv)
int argc;
char *argv[];
{
  register int t;

  if(argc!=4) {
    printf("usage: input output encode/decode\n");
    exit();
  }
  if(toupper(*argv[3])=='E') code(argv[1],argv[2]);
  else decode(argv[1],argv[2]);
}

void code(input, output)
char *input, *output;
{
  int ch, change, t;
  FILE *fp1, *fp2;

  if((fp1=fopen(input,"r"))==NULL) {
    printf("cannot open input file\n");
    exit();
  }

  if((fp2=fopen(output,"w"))==NULL) {
    printf("cannot open output file\n");
    exit();
  }

  change = 1;
  do {
    ch = getc(fp1);
    ch = tolower(ch);
    if(isalpha(ch) && ch!=' ')
      if(change)
        ch = sub[find(alphabet,ch)];
      else
        ch = sub2[find(alphabet,ch)];
    putc(ch, fp2);
    if(feof(fp1)) break;

    /* change alphabets each time a space is encountered */
    if(ch==' ') change=!change;
  } while(!ferror(fp1) && !ferror(fp2));
  fclose(fp1); fclose(fp2);
}

void decode(input,output)
char *input,*output;
{
  int ch, change;
  FILE *fp1, *fp2;
```

```
if((fp1=fopen(input,"r"))==NULL) {
  printf("cannot open input file\n");
  exit();
}

if((fp2=fopen(output,"w"))==NULL) {
  printf("cannot open output file\n");
  exit();
}
change = 1;
do {
  ch = getc(fp1);
  ch = tolower(ch);
  if(isalpha(ch))
    if(change)
      ch = alphabet[find(sub,ch)];
    else
      ch = alphabet[find(sub2,ch)];
  putc(ch, fp2);
  if(feof(fp1)) break;
  if(ch==' ')  change=!change;
} while(!ferror(fp1) && !ferror(fp2));
fclose(fp1); fclose(fp2);
}

/* Find an element */
find(s, ch)
char *s;
char ch;
{
  register int t;

  for(t=0; t<28; t++) if(ch==s[t]) return t;
  return -1;
}
```

For example, after you use the program on the message

meet me at sunset

it appears as

tssj fu qj kmdkul

To see how this works, examine the ordered alphabet and the two randomized alphabets (called R1 and R2) set up over one another:

alphabet	abcdefghijklmnopqrstuvwxyz<space>
R1	qazwsxedcrfvtgbyhnujm ikolp
R2	poi uytrewqasdfghjklmnbvcxz

When the program begins execution, R1 is used to code the word "meet." When the first space is encountered, the second randomized alphabet, R2, is used to code "me." The program continues to switch between the two alphabets after each space until the end of the message is reached.

Using a multiple substitution cipher makes it much harder to break a code by using frequency tables. It would be possible to use several different randomized alphabets and a more complex switching routine to have all letters in the coded text occur equally. In this case, a frequency table would be useless in breaking the code.

TRANSPOSITION CIPHERS

One of the earliest known transposition codes was designed by the Spartans around 475 B.C. It used a device called a *skytale*. A skytale is basically a strap that is wrapped around a cylinder upon which a message is written crossways. The strap is then unwound and delivered to the recipient of the message, who also has a cylinder of equal size. Theoretically, it is impossible to read the strap without the cylinder, because the letters are out of order. In actual practice, however, this method leaves something to be desired because many different cylinder sizes can be tried until the message begins to make sense.

You can create a computerized version of a skytale by placing your message into an array a certain way and writing it out a different way. For example, if the following **union**

```
union message {
  char s[100];
  char s2[20][5];
} skytale;
```

is initialized to nulls, and if you then placed the message

    meet me at sunset

into array **skytale.s** but viewed it as the two-dimensional array **skytale.s2**, it would look like this.

m	e	e	t	
m	e		a	t
	s	u	n	s
e	t	0	0	0
0	0	0	0	0

⋮

If you then wrote the array out by column, the message would look like this:

    mm e...eest...e u...tan... ts...

where the periods indicate the null padding. To decode the message, columns are fed into **skytale.s2**. Then the array **skytale.s** can be displayed in normal order. The **skytale.s** array can be printed as a string because the message will be null-terminated. The Skytale Cipher program uses this method to code and decode messages.

```
/* One approach to a skytale cipher. */
#include "ctype.h"
#include "stdio.h"
union message {
  char s[100];
  char s2[20][5];
} skytale;

void code(), decode();

main(argc, argv)
int argc;
```

```
char *argv[];
{
  int t;

  for(t=0;  t<100;  ++t) skytale.s[t]='\0';   /* load array */

  if(argc!=4) {
    printf("usage: input output encode/decode\n");
    exit();
  }

  if(toupper(*argv[3])=='E') code(argv[1], argv[2]);
  else decode(argv[1], argv[2]);
}

void code(input, output)
char *input, *output;
{
  int t, t2;
  FILE *fp1, *fp2;

  if((fp1=fopen(input, "r"))==NULL) {
    printf("cannot open input file\n");
    exit();
  }

  if((fp2=fopen(output, "w"))==NULL) {
    printf("cannot open output file\n");
    exit();
  }

  /* read in message as a one-dimensional string */
  for(t=0;  t<100;  ++t) {
    skytale.s[t] = getc(fp1);
    if(feof(fp1))  break;
  }

  /* write it out as a two-dimensional array of chars */
  for(t=0;  t<5;  ++t)
    for(t2=0;  t2<20;  ++t2)
      putc(skytale.s2[t2][t], fp2);

  fclose(fp1);  fclose(fp2);
}

void decode(input, output)
char *input, *output;
{
  int t, t2;
  FILE *fp1, *fp2;

  if((fp1=fopen(input, "r"))==NULL) {
    printf("cannot open input file\n");
    exit();
  }

  if((fp2=fopen(output, "w"))==NULL) {
    printf("cannot open output file\n");
    exit();
  }

  /* read in cipher-text as a two-dimensional arrray
     of chars
```

```
*/
for(t=0;  t<5 && !feof(fp1);  ++t)
  for(t2=0;  t2<20 && !feof(fp1);  ++t2)
    skytale.s2[t2][t] = getc(fp1);

/* write it out as a string */
for(t=0;  t<100;  ++t)
  putc(skytale.s[t], fp2);

fclose(fp1);  fclose(fp2);
}
```

Naturally, there are other methods of obtaining transposed messages. One method particularly suited for computers swaps letters within the message as defined by some algorithm. For example, here is a program that transposes letters by an even distance that is specified by the user, starting from the front of the array and alternating its exchange with the end of the array:

```
/* A transposition cipher. */
#include "ctype.h"
#include "stdio.h"

void code(), decode();

main(argc, argv)
int argc;
char *argv[];
{
  int dist;

  if(argc!=5) {
      printf("usage: input output encode/decode distance\n");
      exit();
  }

  dist=atoi(argv[4]);
  if(dist % 2) dist++; /* swap distance must be even */
  if(toupper(*argv[3])=='E') code(argv[1], argv[2], dist);
  else decode(argv[1], argv[2], dist);
}

void code(input, output, dist)
char *input, *output;
int dist;  /* max distance between swaps */
{
  char done, temp;
  int t;
  char s[256];
  FILE *fp1, *fp2;

  if((fp1=fopen(input, "r"))==0) {
    printf("cannot open input file\n");
    exit();
  }
```

```
  if((fp2=fopen(output, "w"))==0) {
    printf("cannot open output file\n");
    exit();
  }

  done = 0;
  do {
    for(t=0; t<(dist*2); ++t) {
      s[t] = getc(fp1);
      if(feof(fp1)) {
        s[t]='\0';  /* if eof then null */
        done = 1;
      }
    }

    /* exchange elements up to specified swap distance */
    for(t=0; t<dist; t++) {
      temp = s[t];
      s[t] = s[t+dist];
      s[t+dist] = temp;
      t++;
      temp = s[t];
      s[t] = s[dist*2-t];
      s[dist*2-t] = temp;
    }
    for(t=0; t<dist*2; t++) putc(s[t], fp2);
  } while(!done);
  fclose(fp1);  fclose(fp2);
}

void decode(input, output, dist)
char *input, *output;
int dist;
{
  char done, temp;
  int t;
  char s[256];
  FILE *fp1, *fp2;

  if((fp1=fopen(input, "r"))==0) {
    printf("cannot open input file\n");
    exit();
  }

  if((fp2=fopen(output, "w"))==0) {
    printf("cannot open output file\n");
    exit();
  }

  done = 0;
  do {
    for(t=0; t<(dist*2); ++t) {
      s[t] = getc(fp1);
      if(feof(fp1)) {
        s[t] = 0;  /* if eof then null */
        done = 1;
      }
    }

    /* re-exchanged items previously swapped */
    for(t=0; t<dist; t++) {
      t++;
      temp = s[t];
      s[t] = s[dist*2-t];
      s[dist*2-t] = temp;
```

```
      t--;
      temp = s[t];
      s[t] = s[t+dist];
      s[t+dist] = temp;
      t++;
    }
    for(t=0; t<dist*2; t++) putc(s[t], fp2);
  } while(!done);
  fclose(fp1);   fclose(fp2);
}
```

If you use this method with a distance of 10, the message

    meet me at sunset

will look something like this:

    <space>usetn smte metae

Used by themselves, transposition ciphers can accidentally create "clues" in the transposition process. In the sample text just given, the partial words "set" and "me" are suspiciously suggestive.

BIT-MANIPULATION CIPHERS

The digital computer has given rise to a new method of encoding: manipulating the bits that compose the actual characters of the plaintext. Although the real purist would claim that *bit manipulation* (or *alteration*, as it is sometimes called) is really just a variation on the substitution cipher, the concepts, methods, and options differ so significantly that it must be considered a cipher method in its own right.

Bit-manipulation ciphers are well-suited for computer use because they employ operations easily performed by the system. Also, the ciphertext tends to look completely unintelligible, which adds to security by making the data look like unused or crashed files and thereby confusing anyone who tries to gain access to the file.

Generally, bit-manipulation ciphers are applicable only to computer-based files and cannot be used to create hardcopy messages because the bit manipulations tend to produce nonprinting characters. For this reason, you should assume that any file coded by bit-manipulation methods will remain in a computer file.

Bit-manipulation ciphers convert plaintext into ciphertext by altering the actual bit pattern of each character through the use of one or more of the following logical operators:

AND
OR
NOT
XOR
1's complement

C is perhaps the best language for creating bit-manipulation ciphers because it supports the following bitwise operators:

Operator	Meaning
|	OR
&	AND
^	XOR
~	1's complement

The simplest and least secure bit-manipulation cipher uses only ~, the 1's complement operator. (Remember that the ~ operator causes each bit within a byte to be inverted: 1 becomes 0, and 0 becomes 1.) Therefore, a byte complemented twice is the same as the original. The 1's Complement Cipher program presented here encodes any text file.

```
/* 1's complement cipher */
#include "stdio.h"

void code(), decode();

main(argc, argv)
int argc;
char *argv[];
{
  if(argc!=4) {
```

```
      printf("usage: input output encode/decode\n");
      exit();
   }
   if(toupper(*argv[3])=='E') code(argv[1], argv[2]);
   else decode(argv[1], argv[2]);
}

void code(input, output)
char *input, *output;
{
   int ch;
   FILE *fp1, *fp2;

   if((fp1=fopen(input, "r"))==NULL) {
     printf("cannot open input file\n");
     exit();
   }

   if((fp2=fopen(output, "w"))==NULL) {
     printf("cannot open output file\n");
     exit();
   }

   do {
     ch = getc(fp1);
     ch = ~ch;
     putc(ch, fp2);
     if(feof(fp1)) break;
   } while(!ferror(fp1) && !ferror(fp2));
   fclose(fp1); fclose(fp2);
}

void decode(input, output)
char *input, *output;
{
   int ch;
   FILE *fp1, *fp2;

   if((fp1=fopen(input, "r"))==NULL) {
     printf("cannot open input file\n");
     exit();
   }

   if((fp2=fopen(output, "w"))==NULL) {
     printf("cannot open output file\n");
     exit();
   }

   do {
     ch = getc(fp1);
     ch = ~ch;
     putc(ch, fp2);
     if(feof(fp1)) break;
   } while(!ferror(fp1) && !ferror(fp2));
   fclose(fp1); fclose(fp2);
}
```

It is not possible to show what the ciphertext of a message would look like, because the bit manipulation used here generally creates nonprinting characters. Try it on your computer and examine the file—it will look quite cryptic, indeed!

There are two problems with this simple coding scheme. First, the encryption program does not use a key to decode, so anyone with access to the program can decode an encoded file. Second, and perhaps more important, this method would be easily spotted by any experienced computer programmer.

An improved method of bit-manipulation coding uses the XOR operator. The XOR operator has the following truth table:

XOR	0	1
0	0	1
1	1	0

The outcome of the XOR operation is TRUE if and only if one operand is TRUE and the other is FALSE. This gives the XOR a unique property: if you XOR a byte with another byte called the *key*, and then take the outcome of that operation and XOR it again with the key, the result will be the original byte, as shown here:

```
        1 1 0 1     1 0 0 1  ┐
XOR     0 1 0 1     0 0 1 1  (key)
        ───────     ───────        │
        1 0 0 0     1 0 1 0         ├ same
        1 0 0 0     1 0 1 0         │
XOR     0 1 0 1     0 0 1 1  (key)
        ───────     ───────  │
        1 1 0 1     1 0 0 1  ┘
```

When used to code a file, this process solves the two inherent problems of the method that uses 1's complement. First of all, because it uses a key, the encryption program alone cannot decode a file; second, because using a key makes each file unique, what has been done to the file is not obvious to someone schooled only in computer science.

The key does not have to be just one byte long. For example, you could use a key of several characters and alternate the characters through the file. However, a single-character key is used here to keep the program uncluttered.

```
/* An XOR cipher that uses a single character key. */

#include "stdio.h"

void code(), decode();

main(argc, argv)
int argc;
char *argv[];
{
  if(argc!=5) {
    printf("usage: input output decode/encode key\n");
    exit();
  }
  if(toupper(*argv[3])=='E')
    code(argv[1], argv[2], *argv[4]);
  else
    decode(argv[1], argv[2], *argv[4]);

}

void code(input, output, key)
char *input, *output;
char key;
{
  int ch;
  FILE *fp1, *fp2;

  if((fp1=fopen(input, "r"))==NULL) {
    printf("cannot open input file\n");
    exit();
  }

  if((fp2=fopen(output, "w"))==NULL) {
    printf("cannot open output file\n");
    exit();
  }

  do {
    ch = getc(fp1);
    ch = ch^key;
    if(feof(fp1)) break;
    putc(ch, fp2);
  } while(!ferror(fp1) && !ferror(fp2));
  fclose(fp1);  fclose(fp2);
}

void decode(input, output, key)
char *input, *output;
char key;
{
  int ch;
  FILE *fp1, *fp2;

  if((fp1=fopen(input, "r"))==NULL) {
    printf("cannot open input file\n");
    exit();
```

```
    }
    if((fp2=fopen(output, "w"))==NULL) {
      printf("cannot open output file\n");
      exit();
    }
    do {
      ch = getc(fp1);
      ch = ch^key;
      if(feof(fp1)) break;
      putc(ch, fp2);
    } while(!ferror(fp1) && !ferror(fp2));
    fclose(fp1);   fclose(fp2);
}
```

DATA COMPRESSION

Data-compression techniques essentially squeeze a given amount of information into a smaller area. Data compression is often used in computer systems to increase the available storage (by reducing the storage needs of the computer user), to save transfer time (especially over phone lines), and to provide a level of security. Although there are many data-compression schemes available, this chapter will examine only two of them. The first is *bit compression*, where more than one character is stored in a single byte, and the second is *character deletion*, in which actual characters from the file are deleted.

Eight into Seven

Most modern computers use byte sizes that are even powers of two because of the binary representation of data in the machine. The uppercase and lowercase letters and the punctuation only require about 63 different codes needing only 6 bits to represent a byte. (A 6-bit byte could have values of 0 through 63.) However, most computers use an 8-bit byte; thus, 25% of the byte's storage is wasted in simple text files. You could, therefore, actually compact 4 characters into 3 bytes if you could use the last 2 bits in each byte. The

only problem is the way in which ASCII codes are organized—
there are more than 63 different ASCII character codes, and the
uppercase and lowercase alphabet falls more or less in the middle.
This means that some of the characters will require at least 7 bits.
It is possible to use a non-ASCII representation (which, on rare
occasions, is done), but it is not generally advisable. An easier
option is to compact 8 characters into 7 bytes, exploiting the fact
that no letter or common punctuation mark uses the eighth bit of
a byte. Therefore, you can use the eighth bit of each of the 7 bytes
to store the eighth character. However, you should realize that
many computers—including the IBM PC—do use 8-bit characters to represent special characters or graphics characters. Also,
some word processors use the eighth bit to indicate text-
processing instructions. Therefore, the use of this type of data
compaction will only work on "straight" ASCII files that do not
use the eighth bit for anything.

To visualize how this works, consider the following 8 characters represented as 8-bit bytes:

byte 1   0 1 1 1   0 1 0 1

byte 2   0 1 1 1   1 1 0 1

byte 3   0 0 1 0   0 0 1 1

byte 4   0 1 0 1   0 1 1 0

byte 5   0 0 0 1   0 0 0 0

byte 6   0 1 1 0   1 1 0 1

byte 7   0 0 1 0   1 0 1 0

byte 8   0 1 1 1   1 0 0 1

As you can see, the eighth bit is always 0. This is always the case
unless the eighth bit is used for parity checking. The easiest way
to compress 8 characters into 7 bytes is to distribute the 7 significant bits of byte 1 into the 7 unused eighth-bit positions of bytes 2
through 8. The 7 remaining bytes then appear as follows:

byte 1 — read down

byte 2	1	1	1	1	1	1	0	1
byte 3	1	0	1	0	0	0	1	1
byte 4	1	1	0	1	0	1	1	0
byte 5	0	0	0	1	0	0	0	0
byte 6	1	1	1	0	1	1	0	1
byte 7	0	0	1	0	1	0	1	0
byte 8	1	1	1	1	1	0	0	1

To reconstruct byte 1, you just put it back together again by taking the eighth bit off of each of the 7 bytes.

This compression technique compresses any text file by 1/8, or 12.5%. This is quite a substantial savings. For example, if you were transmitting the source code for your favorite program to a friend over long-distance phone lines, you would be saving 12.5% of the expense of transmission. (Remember, the object code, or executable version of the program, needs the full 8 bits.)

The following program compresses a text file using the method just described:

```
/* A Bit compression program that compresses
   8 bits into 7.  This program only works for
   text files.
*/
#include "stdio.h"

void compress(), decompress();

main(argc, argv)
int argc;
char *argv[];
{
  if(argc!=4) {
    printf("usage: input output compress/decompress\n");
    exit();
  }
  if(toupper(*argv[3])=='C')
    compress(argv[1], argv[2]);
  else
    decompress(argv[1], argv[2]);

}
```

```
void compress(input, output)
char *input, *output;
{
  char ch, ch2, done, t;
  FILE *fp1, *fp2;

  if((fp1=fopen(input, "r"))==NULL) {
    printf("cannot open input file\n");
    exit();
  }

  if((fp2=fopen(output, "w"))==NULL) {
    printf("cannot open output file\n");
    exit();
  }

  done = 0;
  do {
      ch = getc(fp1);  /* get a byte */
      ch = ch << 1;   /* shift off the top bit */
      for(t=0; t<7; ++t) {
        ch2 = getc(fp1);
        if(feof(fp1)) {
          ch2 = 0;
          done = 1;
        }
        ch2 = ch2 & 127;   /* turn off top bit */
        /* OR in the proper bit into the recieving byte's
           high-order bit
        */
        ch2 = ch2 | ((ch<<t) & 128);
        putc(ch2, fp2);
      }
      if(feof(fp1)) break;
  } while(!done && !ferror(fp1) && !ferror(fp2));
  fclose(fp1);  fclose(fp2);
}

void decompress(input, output)
char *input, *output;
{
  unsigned char ch, ch2, t;
  char s[7], temp;
  FILE *fp1, *fp2;

  if((fp1=fopen(input, "r"))==NULL) {
    printf("cannot open input file\n");
    exit();
  }

  if((fp2=fopen(output, "w"))==NULL) {
    printf("cannot open output file\n");
    exit();
  }

  do {
    ch = 0;
    for(t=0;  t<7;  ++t) {
      temp = getc(fp1);
      ch2 = temp; /* type conversion */
      s[t] = ch2 & 127;  /* turn off top bit */
      ch2 = ch2 & 128;   /* turn off all but top bit */
```

```
    ch2 = ch2 >> t+1; /* reconstruct the byte, bit at a time */
    ch = ch | ch2;
  }
  putc(ch, fp2);
  for(t=0; t<7; ++t) putc(s[t], fp2);
  if(feof(fp1)) break;
} while(!ferror(fp1) && !ferror(fp2));
fclose(fp1);   fclose(fp2);
}
```

This program is fairly complex because the bits that make up the first byte must be shifted into their proper positions in the next seven bytes. Be aware that in order for the algorithm to work correctly at the end of the file, as many as seven extra bytes may be appended to the output file. Thus, on extremely short files (less than 56 bytes), the compressed file can be longer than the uncompressed file. However, these extra bytes become insignificant in longer files. You may find it useful to alter the algorithm so that the extra bytes are avoided. (Be prepared however: this is not a trivial task.)

The 16-Character Language

Although unsuitable for most situations, an interesting method of data compression deletes unnecessary letters from words, in essence making most words into abbreviations. Data compression is accomplished because the unused characters are not stored. The use of abbreviations to save space is very common: for example, "Mr." is commonly used instead of "Mister." Instead of using actual abbreviations, the method presented in this section automatically removes certain letters from a message. To do this, a *minimal alphabet* will be needed. A minimal alphabet is one in which several seldom-used letters have been removed, leaving only those necessary to form most words or avoid ambiguity. Therefore, any character not in the minimal alphabet will be extracted from any word in which it appears. Exactly how many characters there are in a minimal alphabet is a matter of choice. However, this section uses the 14 most common letters, plus spaces and newlines.

Automating the abbreviation process requires that you know what letters in the alphabet are used most frequently so that you can create a minimal alphabet. In theory, you could count the letters in each word in a dictionary; however, different writers use a different frequency mix than others, so a frequency chart based just on the words that make up the English language may not reflect the actual usage frequency of letters. (It would also take a *long* time to count the letters!) As an alternative, you can count the frequency of the letters in this chapter and use them as a basis for our minimal alphabet. To do this, you could use this simple program. The program skips all punctuation except periods, commas, and spaces.

```
/* The program counts the number of times a character
   appears in a file.
*/

#include "stdio.h"
#include "ctype.h"

main(argc, argv)
int argc;
char *argv[];
{
  FILE *fp1;
  int alpha[26], t;
  int space=0, period=0, comma=0;
  char ch;

  if(argc!=2) {
    printf("Please specify text file.\n");
    exit(1);
  }

  if((fp1=fopen(argv[1], "r"))==NULL) {
    printf("cannot open input file\n");
    exit(1);
  }

  for(t=0; t<26; t++) alpha[t]=0;

  do {
    ch=getc(fp1);
    if(isalpha(ch))
      alpha[toupper(ch)-'A']++;
    else switch(ch) {
      case ' ': space++;
        break;
      case '.': period++;
        break;
      case ',': comma++;
        break;
    }
  } while(!feof(fp1));

  for(t=0; t<26; ++t)
    printf("%c: %d\n", 'A'+t, alpha[t]);

  printf("period: %d\n", period);
```

```
   printf("space: %d\n", space);
   printf("comma: %d\n", comma);
   fclose(fp1);
}
```

By running the program on the text of this chapter, you get the following frequency:

A	2525
B	532
C	838
D	1145
E	3326
F	828
G	529
H	1086
I	2242
J	39
K	94
L	1103
M	1140
N	2164
O	1767
P	697
Q	62
R	1656
S	1672
T	3082
U	869
V	376
W	370
X	178
Y	356
Z	20
Space	5710
Period	234
Comma	513

The frequency of letters in this chapter compares well with the standard English mix and is offset only by the repeated use of the C keywords in the programs.

To achieve significant data compression, you need to cut the alphabet substantially by removing the letters used least frequently. Although there are many different ideas about exactly what a workable minimum alphabet is, the 14 most common letters and the space account for about 85% of all the characters used in this chapter. Because the newline character is also necessary to preserve word breaks, it must also be included. Therefore, the minimal alphabet used in this section consists of 14 characters, a space, and a newline.

A C D E H I L M N O R S T U <space> <newline>

Here is a program that removes all characters except the 16 selected:

```
/*   This program compresses a file by removing
     seldom used characters.
*/

#include "stdio.h"

void comp2();

main(argc,argv)
int argc;
char *argv[];
{
   if(argc!=3) {
     printf("usage: input output\n");
     exit();
   }
   comp2(argv[1],argv[2]);
}
void comp2(input,output)
char *input,*output;
{
   char ch;
   FILE *fp1,*fp2;

   if((fp1=fopen(input,"r"))==NULL) {
     printf("cannot open input file\n");
     exit();
   }

   if((fp2=fopen(output,"w"))==NULL) {
```

```
    printf("cannot open output file\n");
    exit();
  }
do {
  ch=getc(fp1);
  if(feof(fp1)) break;
  /* if char is part of acceptable characters,
     then write it to disk - otherwise ignore
     it
  */
  if(strchr("ACDEJILMNORSTU '\n'", toupper(ch))) {
    if(ch=='\n') putc('\r',fp2);
    putc(ch,fp2);
  }
} while(!ferror(fp1) && !ferror(fp2));
fclose(fp1); fclose(fp2);
}
```

If you use this program on the message

Attention i Command

Attac successul lease send additional sulies and res
troos Tis is essential to maintain our ootold

eneral rasier

the compressed message would look like this:

Attention i Command

Attac successul lease send additional sulies and
res troos Tis is essential to maintain our

ootold eneral rasier

As you can see, the message is largely readable, although some ambiguity is present. Ambiguity is the chief drawback of this method of data compression. However, if you are familiar with the vocabulary of the writer of the message, you could probably select a better minimal alphabet that would remove some of this ambiguity. In spite of the potential for ambiguity, quite a bit of space was saved. The original message was 168 bytes long and the compacted message was 142 bytes long—a savings of about 16%.

If both character deletion and bit compression were applied to the message, then about 28% less storage space would have been needed, which could be important. For example, if you were a submarine captain and wanted to send a message to headquarters but did not want to give away your position, you might want to compress the message by using both methods so that it would be as short as possible.

Both the bit-compression and character-deletion methods of data compression have uses in encryption. Bit compression further encrypts the information and makes decoding more difficult. If used before encryption, the character-deletion method has one wonderful advantage: it disguises the character frequency of the source language.

CODE-BREAKING

No chapter on encryption is complete without a brief look at code-breaking. The art of code-breaking is essentially one of trial and error. With the use of digital computers, relatively simple ciphers can easily be broken through exhaustive trial and error. However, the more complex codes either cannot be broken or require techniques and resources not commonly available. For simplicity, this section focuses on breaking the more straightforward codes.

If you wish to break a message that was ciphered using a simple substitution method and only an offset alphabet, then all you need to do is try all 26 possible offsets to see which one fits. A program to do this is shown here:

```
/* Code breaker for simple substitution cipher. */

#include "ctype.h"
#include "stdio.h"

main(argc, argv)
int argc;
char *argv[];
{
  if(argc!=2) {
    printf("usage: input\n");
    exit();
  }
  bc(argv[1]);
}

/* Try to break a simple substitution cipher. */
bc(input)
```

```
char *input;
{
  register int t, t2;
  unsigned char ch, s[1000], q[10];
  FILE *fp1;

  if((fp1=fopen(input, "r"))==NULL) {
    printf("cannot open input file\n");
    exit();
  }

  for(t=0; t<1000; ++t) {
    if(feof(fp1)) break;
    s[t] = getc(fp1);
  }
  s[t] = '\0';
  fclose(fp1);

  /* try each offset in turn */
  for(t=0; t<26; ++t) {
    for(t2=0; s[t2]; t2++) {
      ch = s[t2];
      if(isalpha(ch) && ch!=' ') {
        ch = tolower(ch)-t;
        if(ch<'a') ch += 26;
      }
      printf("%c", ch);
    }
    printf("\n");
    printf("decoded? (y/n): ");
    gets(q);
    if(*q=='y') break;
  }
  printf("\noffset is: %d", t);

}
```

With only a slight variation, you could use the same program to break ciphers that use a random alphabet. In this case, substitute manually entered alphabets, as shown in this program:

```
/* Code breaker for random substitution cipher .*/

#include "ctype.h"
#include "stdio.h"
char sub[28];
char alphabet[28]="abcdefghijklmnopqrstuvwxyz ";

void bc2();

main(argc, argv)
int argc;
char *argv[];
{
  char s[80];

  if(argc!=2) {
    printf("usage: input");
    exit();
  }
```

```
  do {
    printf("enter test alphabet:\n");
    gets(sub);
    bc2(argv[1]);
    printf("\nIs this right?: (y/n) ");
    gets(s);
  } while(tolower(*s)!='y');
}

/* Try to break a random substitution cipher. */
void bc2(input)
char *input;
{
  char ch;
  FILE *fp1;

  if((fp1=fopen(input, "r"))==NULL) {
    printf("cannot open input file\n");
    exit();
  }

  do {
    ch = getc(fp1);
    if(feof(fp1)) break;
    if(isalpha(ch) || ch==' ') {
      printf("%c", alphabet[find(sub, ch)]);
    }
  } while(!ferror(fp1));
  fclose(fp1);
}

/* find the corresponding character */
find(s, ch)
char *s;
char ch;
{
  register int t;

  for(t=0; t<28; t++) if(ch==s[t]) return t;
}
```

Unlike substitution ciphers, transposition and bit-manipulation ciphers are harder to break using the trial-and-error methods. If you have to break such complex codes, good luck!

Oh, and by the way—hsaovbno wlymljapvu pz haahpuhisl, pa vjjbyz vusf hz hu hjjpklua.

8

RANDOM NUMBER GENERATORS AND SIMULATIONS

Random number sequences are used in a variety of programming situations, ranging from simulations, which are the most common, to games and other recreational software. The study of random number generators is important for several reasons. First, although the ANSI standard defines the random number generator function **rand()**, many nonstandard compilers do not supply a random number generator. Second, and probably most important, one random number generator may not be sufficient for complex simulations in which many random events must operate independently. Third, it is sometimes desirable to have a random number generator that produces numbers skewed in some fashion. Finally, the quality of many random number generators is not sufficient for some demanding situations, and at times it is important to have control over the way random numbers are produced.

In this chapter you will study the way various random number generating functions are written and learn how to evaluate them. You will also look at two interesting simulations that use the random number generators developed in the chapter. The first is a grocery store check-out simulation and the second is a random-walk stock portfolio manager.

RANDOM NUMBER GENERATORS

Technically, the term *random number generator* is absurd; numbers, in and of themselves, are not random. For example, is 100 a random number? Is 25? Of course not. What is really meant by "random number generator" is something that creates a *sequence* of numbers that appear to be in random order. This raises a more complex question: What is a random sequence of numbers? The only correct answer is that a random sequence of numbers is one in which all elements are completely unrelated. This definition leads to the paradox that any sequence can be both random and nonrandom, depending on the way the sequence was obtained. For example, the following list of numbers:

1 2 3 4 5 6 7 8 9 0

was created by typing the top row of keys on the keyboard in order, so the sequence certainly cannot be construed as random. But what if you happened to pull out exactly that sequence from a barrel full of ping-pong balls that had numbers written on them? Then it *would* be a random sequence. This discussion shows that the randomness of a sequence depends on *how it was generated*, not on what the actual sequence is.

Keep in mind that sequences of numbers generated by a computer are *deterministic:* each number other than the first depends on the number that precedes it. Technically, this means that only a *quasi-random* sequence of numbers can be created by a computer. However, this is sufficient for most problems, and for the purposes of this book, the sequences will simply be called random.

Generally, it is best if the numbers in a random sequence are *uniformly distributed.* (Do not confuse this with the normal distribution, or bell-shaped curve.) In a uniform distribution, all events are equally probable, so that a graph of a uniform distribution is a flat line rather than a curve.

Before the widespread use of computers, whenever random numbers were needed they were produced by either throwing dice or pulling numbered balls from a jar. In 1955, the RAND Corporation published a table of 1 million random digits obtained with the help of a computer-like machine. In the early days of computer science, although many methods were devised to generate random numbers, most were discarded.

One particularly interesting method that almost worked was developed by John von Neumann—the father of the modern computer. Often referred to as the *middle-square method*, it squares the previous random number, and then extracts its middle digits. For example, if you were creating three-digit numbers and the previous value was 121, then you would square 121 to make 14641. Extracting the middle three digits would give you 464 as the next number. The problem with this method is that it tends to lead to a very short repeating pattern called a *cycle*, especially after a zero has entered the pattern. For this reason the method is not presently used.

Today, the most common way to generate random numbers is by using the following equation:

$$R_{n+1} = (aR_n + c) \bmod m$$

where

$R >= 0$
$a >= 0$
$c >= 0$
$m > R$, a, and c

This method is sometimes referred to as the *linear congruential method*. Looking at the equation, you probably think that random number generation seems simple. There is a catch, though—how well this equation performs depends heavily on the values of a, c, and m. Choosing these values is sometimes more of an art than a science. There are complex rules that can help you choose those values; however, this discussion will cover only a few simple rules and experiments.

The modulus (m) should be fairly large because it determines the range of the random numbers. The modulus operation yields the remainder of a division that uses the same operands. Hence,

10 % 4 = 2

because 4 goes into 10 twice with a remainder of 2. Therefore, if the modulus is 12, then only the numbers 0 through 11 can be produced by the randomizing equation, whereas if the modulus is 21,425, the numbers 0 through 21,424 can be produced. Remember, a small modulus does not actually affect randomness, only range. The choice of the multiplier, a, and the increment, c, is much harder. Usually, the multiplier can be fairly large and the increment fairly small. A lot of testing is needed to confirm that a good generator has been created.

As a first example, here is a common random number generator. The equation shown in **ran1()** has been used as the basis for the random number generator in a number of popular languages.

```
float ran1()
{
   static long int a=100001;

   a = (a*125) % 2796203;
   return (float) a / 2796203;
}
```

This function has three important features. First, the random number is actually an integer—**long int** in this case—even though the function returns a **float**. The integers are necessary for the linear congruential method, but random number generators, by convention, are expected to return a number between 0 and 1, which means it is a floating point. In contrast, as defined by the ANSI standard, the function **rand( )** returns an integer.

Second, the *seed*, or starting value, is hard-coded into the function by using the **static long int a**. This method provides a seed value to the next call. Although this feature is fine for most situations, it is possible to let the user specify the initial value. If a user-specified seed value is used, the function is as follows:

```
float ran1(seed)
float seed;
{
  static long int a;
  static char once=1;

  if(once){
    a = seed*1000;   /* get a first value */
    once = 0;
}

      a = (a*125) % 2796203;
      return (float) a / 2796203;
}
```

However, for the rest of this chapter, the seed will be hard-coded into the functions for the sake of simplicity.

Third, the random number is divided by the modulus prior to the return. This obtains a number between 0 and 1. If you study this, you will see that the value of **a** prior to the return line must be between 0 and 2,796,202. Therefore, when **a** is divided by 2,796,203, a number equal to or greater than 0 but less than 1 is obtained.

Many random number generators are not useful because they produce nonuniform distributions or have short, repeating sequences. Even when they are very slight, these problems can produce biased results if the same random number generator is used over and over again. The solution is to create several different generators and use them either individually or jointly to obtain more random numbers. Therefore, the code for two other random number generators is presented here. The following generator, called **ran2( )**, produces a good distribution:

```
float ran2()
{
   static long int a=1;

   a = (a * 32719+3) % 32749;
   return (float) a / 32749;
}
```

The generator called **ran3( )** uses fairly small numbers:

```
float ran3()
{
   static long int a=203;

   a = (a *10001 + 3) % 1717;
   return (float) a / 1717;
}
```

Each of these random number generators produces a good sequence of random numbers. Yet the questions remain: How "random" are the numbers? How good are these generators?

Determining the Quality of a Generator

You can use several tests to determine the randomness of a number sequence. None of these tests will tell you if a sequence is random, but they will tell you if it is not. The tests can identify a nonrandom sequence, but just because a test does not find a problem does not mean that a given sequence is indeed random. The test does, however, raise your confidence in the random number generator that produced the sequence. For the purposes of this chapter most of these tests are either too complicated or time-consuming in their most rigorous forms. Therefore, you will look briefly at some of the ways a sequence can be tested and how it can fail.

To begin, here is the way to find out how closely the distribution of the numbers in a sequence conforms to what you would expect a random distribution to be. For example, say that you are attempting to generate random sequences of the digits 0 through 9. Therefore, the probability of each digit occurring is 1/10, because there are ten possibilities for each number in the sequence, all of which are equally possible. Assume that the sequence

9 1 8 2 4 6 3 7 5 8 2 9 0 4 2 4 7 8 6 2

was actually generated. If you count the number of times each digit occurs, the result is

Digit	Occurrences
0	1
1	1
2	4
3	1
4	3
5	1
6	2
7	2
8	3
9	2

The question you should ask next is if this distribution is sufficiently similar to the expected distribution.

Remember that if a random number generator is good, it generates sequences randomly; in a truly random state, all sequences are possible. This seems to imply that any sequence generated should qualify as a valid random sequence. So how can you tell if this sequence is random? In fact, how could any sequence of the ten digits be nonrandom, since any sequence is possible? The answer is that some sequences are *less likely* to be random than others. You can determine the *probability* of a given sequence's randomness by using the *chi-square test*. The chi-square test basically subtracts the expected number of occurrences from the observed number of occurrences for all possible outcomes to produce a

	p=99%	p=95%	p=75%	p=50%	p=25%	p=5%
n=5	0.5543	1.1455	2.675	4.351	6.626	11.07
n=10	2.558	3.940	6.737	9.342	12.55	18.31
n=15	5.229	7.261	11.04	14.34	18.25	25.00
n=20	8.260	10.85	15.45	19.34	23.83	31.41
n=30	14.95	18.49	24.48	29.34	34.80	43.77

Figure 8-1.   Selected chi-square values

number, generally called V. You can then look up this number in a table of chi-square values to find the likelihood that the sequence is random in distribution. A small chi-square table is given in Figure 8-1; you can find complete tables in most books on statistics.

The formula to obtain V is

$$V = \sum_{1 \le i \le N} \frac{(O_i - E_i)^2}{E_i}$$

where O_i is the number of observed occurrences, E_i is the expected occurrences, and N is the number of discrete elements. The value for E_i is determined by multiplying the probability of that element occurring by the number of observations. In this case, because each digit is expected to occur one-tenth of the time, if 20 samples are taken, the value for E will be 2 for all digits. N is 10 because there are 10 possible elements, the digits 0 through 9. Therefore,

$$V= \frac{(1-2)^2}{2} + \frac{(1-2)^2}{2} + \frac{(4-2)^2}{2} + \frac{(1-2)^2}{2} + \frac{(3-2)^2}{2} +$$

$$\frac{(1-2)^2}{2} + \frac{(2-2)^2}{2} + \frac{(2-2)^2}{2} + \frac{(3-2)^2}{2} + \frac{(2-2)^2}{2} = 5$$

To determine the likelihood that the sequence is not random, find the row in the table in Figure 8-1 that equals the number of observations; in this case, it is 20. Then read across until you find a number that is greater than V. In this case, it is column 1. This means that that there is a 99% likelihood that a sample of 20 elements will have a V greater than 8.260. Therefore, there is only a 1% probability that the sequence is random. To "pass" the chi-square test, the probability of V must fall between 25% and 75%. (This range is derived from mathematics beyond the scope of this book.)

You might, however, counter this conclusion with the following question: Since all sequences are possible, how can this sequence have only a 1% chance of being legitimate? The answer is that it is just a probability—the chi-square test is actually not a test at all, only a confidence builder. In fact, if you use the chi-square test, you should obtain several different sequences and average the results to avoid rejecting a good random number generator. Any single sequence might be rejected, but averaging several sequences together should provide a good test.

On the other hand, a sequence can pass the chi-square test and still not be random. For example,

1 3 5 7 9 7 5 3 1

would pass the chi-square test but does not appear very random. In this case, a *run* has been generated. A run is simply a sequence of strictly ascending or descending numbers that are at evenly spaced intervals. Each group of four digits is in strictly ascending order and as such (assuming it continued) would not be a random sequence. Runs can be separated by "noise" digits as well: the digits that comprise the run can be interspersed throughout an otherwise random sequence. It is possible to design tests to detect these situations, but they are beyond the scope of this book.

Another feature to test for is the length of the *period;* that is, how many numbers can be generated before the sequence begins to repeat—or worse, degenerate into a short cycle. All computer-based random number generators eventually repeat a sequence. The longer the period, the better the generator. Even though the frequency of the numbers within the period is uniformly distributed, the numbers do not constitute a random series, because a truly random series will not repeat itself consistently. Generally, a period of several thousand numbers is sufficient for most applications. (Again, a test for this can be performed, but it is beyond the scope of this book.)

Several other tests can be applied to determine the quality of a random number generator. In fact, there probably has been more code written to test random number generators than has been written to construct them. Here is yet another test that allows you to test random number generators "visually" by using a graph to show how the sequence is generated.

Ideally, the graph should be based on the frequency of each number. However, since a random number generator can produce thousands of different numbers, this is impractical. Instead, you will create a graph grouped by the tenths digit of each number; for example, since all random numbers produced are between 0 and 1, the number 0.9365783 is grouped under 9 and 0.34523445 is grouped under 3. This means that the graph of the output of the Random Number Generator Display program has 10 lines, with each line representing the number of times a particular number in the group occurs. The program also prints the mean of each sequence, which can be used to detect a bias in the numbers. Like the other graphics programs in this chapter, this program runs only on an IBM PC that is equipped with a color-graphics display adapter.

```
/* Random number generator display program. */

#include "dos.h"

int freq1[10]={0, 0, 0, 0, 0, 0, 0, 0, 0, 0};
int freq2[10]={0, 0, 0, 0, 0, 0, 0, 0, 0, 0};
int freq3[10]={0, 0, 0, 0, 0, 0, 0, 0, 0, 0};

float ran1(), ran2(), ran3();
void point(), mode(), goto_xy();
void line(), display();

main()
{

  int x, y;
  float f, f2, f3, r, r2, r3;
  char s[80];

  mode(4); /* 320 x 200 graphics */

  f=0; f2=0; f3=0;

  goto_xy(0, 6);
  printf("Comparison of Random Number");
  goto_xy(2, 15);
  printf("Generators");
  line(180, 0, 180, 90, 1);
  line(180, 110, 180, 200, 1);
  line(180, 220, 180, 310, 1);
  goto_xy(23, 3);
  printf("ran1()       ran2()        ran3()");

  for(x=0; x<1000; ++x) {
    r = ran1();
    f+=r;
    y = r*10;
    freq1[y]++;

    r2 = ran2();
    f2+=r2;
    y = r2*10;
    freq2[y]++;

    r3 = ran3();
    f3 += r3;
    y = r3*10;
    freq3[y]++;

    display();
  }
  gets(s);
  mode(3);
  printf("mean of ran1() function 1: %f\n", f/1000);
  printf("mean of ran2() function 2: %f\n", f2/1000);
  printf("mean of ran3() function 3: %f\n", f3/1000);
}

/* Display the graph of the random numbers. */
void display()
{
  register int t;
  for(t=0; t<10; ++t) {
    line(180, t*10, 180-freq1[t], t*10, 2);
```

```
      line(180, t*10+110, 180-freq2[t], t*10+110, 2);
      line(180, t*10+220, 180-freq3[t], t*10+220, 2);
  }
}

float ran1()
{
   static long int a=100001;

   a = (a*125) % 2796203;
   return (float) a/2796203;
}

float ran2()
{
   static long int a=1;

   a = (a * 32719+3) % 32749;
   return (float) a/32749;
}

float ran3()
{
   static long int a=203;

   a = (a *10001 + 3) % 1717;
   return (float) a/1717;
}

/* set the video mode */
void mode(mode_code)
int mode_code;
{
   union REGS r;

   r.h.al = mode_code;
   r.h.ah = 0;
   int86(0x10, &r, &r);
}

/* Draw a line in specified color
     using Bresenham's integer based algorithm.
*/
void line(startx, starty, endx, endy, color)
int startx, starty, endx, endy, color;
{
   register int t, distance;
   int x=0, y=0, delta_x, delta_y;
   int incx, incy;

   /* compute the distances in both directions */
   delta_x = endx-startx;
   delta_y = endy-starty;

   /* Compute the direction of the increment,
      an increment of 0 means either a vertical or horizontal
      line.
   */
   if(delta_x>0) incx = 1;
   else if(delta_x==0) incx = 0;
   else incx = -1;

   if(delta_y > 0) incy = 1;
   else if(delta_y==0) incy = 0;
   else incy = -1;
```

```
/* determine which distance is greater */
delta_x = abs(delta_x);
delta_y = abs(delta_y);
if(delta_x > delta_y) distance = delta_x;
else distance = delta_y;

/* draw the line */
for(t=0; t<=distance+1; t++) {
  point(startx, starty, color);
  x += delta_x;
  y += delta_y;
  if(x > distance) {
    x -= distance;
    startx+=incx;
  }
  if(y > distance) {
    y -= distance;
    starty += incy;
  }
}
}

/* Write a point to the CGA. */
void point(x, y, color_code)
int x, y, color_code;
{
  union REGS r;

  /* check range for mode 4 */
  if(x<0 || x>199 || y<0 || y>319) return;

  r.h.ah = 12; /* write a pixel */
  r.h.al = color_code; /* color to write */
  r.x.dx = x; /* row */
  r.x.cx = y; /* column */
  int86(0x10, &r, &r);  /* call BIOS */

}

/* send the cursor to x,y */
void goto_xy(x, y)
int x, y;
{
  union REGS r;

  r.h.ah = 2; /* cursor addressing function */
  r.h.dl = y; /* column coordinate */
  r.h.dh = x; /* row coordinate */
  r.h.bh = 0; /* video page */
  int86(0x10, &r, &r);
}
```

In this program, the functions **ran1()**, **ran2()**, and **ran3()** have been included to do a side-by-side comparison. Each function generates 1000 numbers, and based on the digit in the tenths position, the appropriate frequency array is updated. The function **display()** plots all three frequency arrays on the screen after each random number is generated, so you can watch the display grow. Figure 8-2 shows the output from each random number genera-

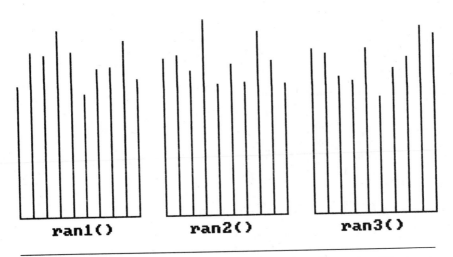

Figure 8-2.   Output from the Random Number Generator Display
program

tor at the end of the thousand numbers. The mean is 0.496960 for
ran1( ), 0.490550 for **ran2( )**, and 0.512488 for **ran3( )**. These are
acceptable results.

To use the display program effectively, you should watch both
the shape of the graph and the way that it grows to check for any
short, repeating cycles. This "test" is, of course, not conclusive, but
it does give you insight into the way a generator produces its
numbers, and it can speed up the testing process by allowing
obviously poor generating functions to be rejected quickly. (It also
makes a great program to run when someone asks you to show
them your computer!)

Using Multiple Generators

One simple technique that improves the randomness of sequences produced by the three generators is to combine them under the control of one master function. This function selects between two of them, based on the result of the third. With this method you can obtain very long periods and diminish the effects of any cycle. The function called **random()** shown here combines **ran1()**, **ran2()**, and **ran3()**:

```
float random()
{
   float f;

   f = ran3();

   if(f>.5) return ran1();
   else return ran2();
}
```

The result of **ran3()** is used to decide whether **ran1()** or **ran2()** becomes the value of the master function **random()**. Feel free to alter the mix between them by changing the constant in the **if** to obtain the exact distribution you require. Here is a program that displays the graph of **random()** and its mean:

```
/* This program uses random numbers to further randomize
      the output from the random number generators.
*/

#include "dos.h"

int freq1[10]={0,0,0,0,0,0,0,0,0,0};

float ran1(), ran2(), ran3(), random();
void point(), mode(), goto_xy();
void line(), display();

main()
{
   int x, y;
   float    f=0.0, r;
   char s[80];

   mode(4); /* 320 x 200 graphics */

   goto_xy(0, 6);
   printf("Output Obtained by Combining");
   goto_xy(2, 5);
   printf("Three Random Number Generators");
   line(180, 110, 180, 200, 1);
```

```
    for(x=0; x<1000; ++x) {
      r=random();
      f+=r;
      y=r*10;
      freq1[y]++;
      display();
    }
    gets(s);
    mode(3);
    printf("mean of random number function 1: %f\n", f/1000);
}

/* Display the frequency of the random numbers. */
void display()
{
  register int t;
  for(t=0; t<10; ++t)
    line(180, t*10+110, 180-freq1[t], t*10+110, 2);
}

float random()   /* random selection of generators */
{
  float f;
  f = ran3();

  if(f>.5) return ran1();
  else return ran2();
}


float ran1()
{
  static long int a=100001;

  a = (a*125) % 2796203;
  return (float) a / 2796203;
}

float ran2()
{
  static long int a=1;

  a = (a * 32719+3) % 32749;
  return (float) a / 32749;
}

float ran3()
{
  static long int a=203;

  a = (a *10001 + 3) % 1717;
  return (float) a / 1717;
}

/* Set the video mode. */
void mode(mode_code)
int mode_code;
{
  union REGS r;
```

```c
      r.h.al = mode_code;
      r.h.ah = 0;
      int86(0x10, &r, &r);
}

/* Draw a line in specified color
     using Bresenham's integer based algorithm.
*/
void line(startx, starty, endx, endy, color)
int startx, starty, endx, endy, color;
{
   register int t, distance;
   int x=0, y=0, delta_x, delta_y;
   int incx, incy;

   /* compute the distances in both directions */
   delta_x = endx-startx;
   delta_y = endy-starty;

   /* Compute the direction of the increment,
       an increment of 0 means either a vertical or horizontal
       line.
   */
   if(delta_x>0) incx = 1;
   else if(delta_x==0) incx = 0;
   else incx = -1;

   if(delta_y>0) incy = 1;
   else if(delta_y==0) incy = 0;
   else incy = -1;

   /* determine which distance is greater */
   delta_x = abs(delta_x);
   delta_y = abs(delta_y);
   if(delta_x>delta_y) distance = delta_x;
   else distance = delta_y;

   /* draw the line */
   for(t=0; t<=distance+1; t++) {
     point(startx, starty, color);
     x+=delta_x;
     y+=delta_y;
     if(x>distance) {
       x-=distance;
       startx+=incx;
     }
     if(y>distance) {
       y-=distance;
       starty+=incy;
     }
   }
}

/* Write a point to the CGA. */
void point(x, y, color_code)
int x, y, color_code;
{
   union REGS r;

   /* check range for mode 4 */
```

```
if(x<0 || x>199 || y<0 || y>319) return;

r.h.ah = 12; /* write a pixel */
r.h.al = color_code; /* color to write */
r.x.dx = x; /* row */
r.x.cx = y; /* column */
int86(0x10, &r, &r);  /* call BIOS */

}

/* send the cursor to x,y */
void goto_xy(x, y)
int x, y;
{
  union REGS r;

  r.h.ah = 2; /* cursor addressing function */
  r.h.dl = y; /* column coordinate */
  r.h.dh = x; /* row coordinate */
  r.h.bh = 0; /* video page */
  int86(0x10, &r, &r);
}
```

The mean of **random( )** is 0.494316.

Figure 8-3 shows the final graph after 1000 random numbers have been computed.

SIMULATIONS

For the remainder of this chapter, the application of random number generators will be examined for computer *simulations*. A simulation is a computerized model of a real-world situation. Anything can be simulated, and the success of the simulation is based primarily upon how well the programmer understands the event being simulated. Because real-world situations often have thousands of variables, many things are difficult to simulate effectively. However, there are several events that lend themselves very well to simulation.

Simulations are important for two reasons. First, they let you alter the parameters of a situation to test and observe the possible results, even though in real life such experimentation might be either too costly or dangerous. For example, a simulation of a nuclear power plant can be used to test the effects of certain types of failures without danger. Second, simulation allows you to create

Output Obtained by Combining
Three Random Number Generators

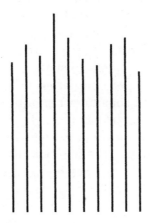

Figure 8-3.   The final graph of **random( )**

situations that cannot occur in the real world. For example, a psychologist might want to study the effects of gradually increasing the intelligence of a mouse to that of a human to see at what point the mouse runs a maze the fastest. Although this cannot be done in real life, a simulation may provide insight into the nature of intelligence versus instinct. Here is the first of two examples of simulations that use random number generators.

Simulating a Check-out Line

The first example simulates a check-out line in a grocery store. Assume that the store is open for ten hours a day, with peak hours from 12 to 1 P.M. and from 5 to 6 P.M. The 12 to 1 P.M. slot is twice as busy as normal, and the 5 to 6 P.M. slot is three times as busy. As the simulation runs, one random number generator "creates" customers, another generator determines how long it will take one customer to check out, and a third generator decides which of the open lines the customers will go to. The goal of the simulation is to help management find the optimal number of check-out lines that need to be available on a typical shopping day, while limiting the number of people in line at any time to ten or less and not having cashiers waiting for customers to serve.

The key to this type of simulation is to create multiple processes. Although C does not support simultaneity directly, you can simulate multiprocessing by having each function inside of a main program loop do some work and return — in essence, time-slicing the functions. For example, the function that simulated the check-out only checks out a part of each order each time it is called. In this way, each function inside the main loop continues to execute.

The **main( )** function for the Check-out program is shown here with its global data. The **mode( )** and **goto—xy( )** functions were developed in Chapter 6. The **circle( )** function included in the program listing uses Bresenham's circle-drawing algorithm to simulate a check-out station. While it is beyond the scope of this chapter to describe the operation of **circle( )**, you can refer to the book *C: Power User's Guide* by Herbert Schildt (Berkeley, Calif.: Osborne/McGraw-Hill, 1987) for a complete discussion of this and other graphics-related functions.

```
#include "dos.h"

float ran1(), ran2(), ran3();

void point(), mode(), goto_xy();
void line(), display(), add_cust();
void check_out(), add_queue(), circle(), plot_circle();

char queues[10];
char qopen[10];
int   cust;    /* total number of customers */
int   time=0;

double asp_ratio=1.0; /* used by circle drawing function */
```

```
main()
{

  int x, y;
  char s[80];

  mode(4);  /* 320 x 200 graphics */

  for(x=0; x<10; ++x) {
    queues[x]=0;
    qopen[x]=0;   /* all closed at start of day */
  }
  goto_xy(24, 20);  printf("1             10");
  goto_xy(24, 0);   printf("Check-out lines:");
  qopen[0]=1;  /* open up number 1 */
  do {
    add_cust();   /* add customers */
    add_queue();  /* add another check out line */
    display();    /* show state of system */
    check_out();  /* check the customer out */
    display();

    /* create high-traffic hours */
    if(time>30 && time<50) add_cust();
    if(time>70 && time < 80) {
       add_cust();
       add_cust();
    }
    time++;
  } while (!kbhit() && time<100);
  gets(s);
  mode(3);
}
```

The body of the main loop used to drive the simulation is shown here:

```
do {
  add_cust();   /* add customers */
  add_queue();  /* add another check out line */
  display();    /* show state of system */
  check_out();  /* check the customer out */
  display();

  /* create high-traffic hours */
  if(time>30 && time<50) add_cust();
  if(time>70 && time < 80) {
     add_cust();
     add_cust();
  }
  time++;
} while (!kbhit() && time<100);
```

The **add—cust()** function uses either **ran1()** or **ran3()** to generate the number of customers arriving at the check-out lines at each request. The **add—queue()** function is used to place the customers into an open check-out line according to the results of **ran2( )**, and it also opens a new line if all of the currently open lines are full. The **display( )** function shows a graphics representation of the simulation. The **check-out( )** function uses **ran2( )** to assign each customer a check-out count, and each call decrements that count by 1. When a customer's count is 0, the customer leaves the check-out line.

The variable **time** alters the rate at which customers are generated in order to match the peak hours of the store. In essence, each pass through the loop is one-tenth of an hour.

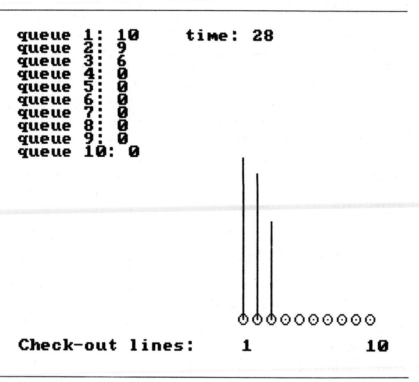

Figure 8-4.   The status of the check-out line when **time** = 28

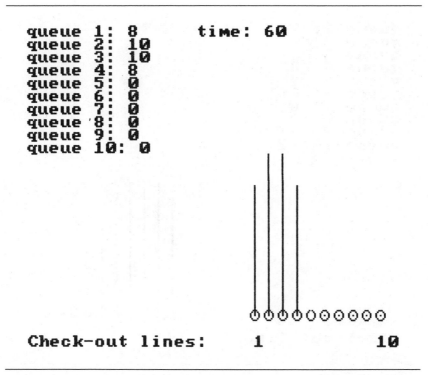

```
queue  1:  8        time:  60
queue  2:  10
queue  3:  10
queue  4:  8
queue  5:  0
queue  6:  0
queue  7:  0
queue '8:  0
queue  9:  0
queue 10:  0
```

Check-out lines: 1   10

Figure 8-5.   The status of the check-out line when **time** = 60

Figures 8-4, 8-5, and 8-6 show the state of the check-out lines when **time** = 28, **time** = 60, and **time** = 88, corresponding to normal time, the end of the first peak, and the end of the second peak, respectively. Notice that at the end of the second peak, a maximum of six check-out lines is needed. This means that if the simulation was completed properly, the grocery store does not need to operate the remaining four lines.

You can directly control several variables in the program. First, you can alter the way customers arrive and the number of customers that arrive. You can also change **add—cust( )** to return gradually more or fewer customers as the peak hours approach

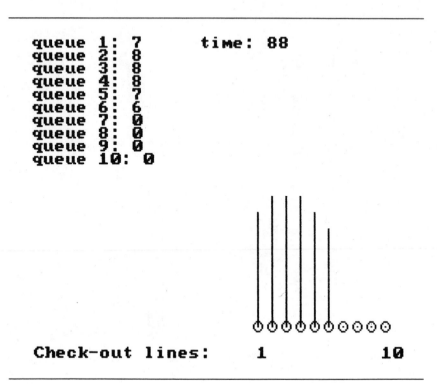

Figure 8-6.   The status of the check-out line when **time** = 88

or wane. The program assumes that customers will randomly choose which line to stand in. Although this may be true of some customers, others will obviously choose the shortest line. You can account for this by altering the **add—queue( )** function to put customers into the shortest line at some times and to place customers randomly at other times. The simulation does not account for the occasional accident—such as a dropped catsup bottle—or for an unruly customer at the check-out counter, both of which would cause a line to stall temporarily.

The entire program is shown here:

```
/* Check-out line simulation. */

#include "dos.h"

float ran1(), ran2(), ran3();

void point(), mode(), goto_xy();
void line(), display(), add_cust();
void check_out(), add_queue(), circle(), plot_circle();

char queues[10];
char qopen[10];
int  cust;    /* total number of customers */
int time=0;

double asp_ratio=1.0; /* used by circle drawing function */

main()
{

  int x, y;
  char s[80];

  mode(4);  /* 320 x 200 graphics */

  for(x=0; x<10; ++x) {
    queues[x]=0;
    qopen[x]=0;    /* all closed at start of day */
  }
  goto_xy(24, 20);  printf("1              10");
  goto_xy(24, 0);  printf("Check-out lines:");
  qopen[0]=1;  /* open up number 1 */
  do {
    add_cust();  /* add customers */
    add_queue(); /* add another check out line */
    display();   /* show state of system */
    check_out(); /* check the customer out */
    display();

    /* create high-traffic hours */
    if(time>30 && time<50) add_cust();
    if(time>70 && time < 80) {
        add_cust();
        add_cust();
    }
    time++;
  } while (!kbhit() && time<100);
  gets(s);
  mode(3);
}

/* Add a customer to a line. */
void add_cust()
{

  float f, r;
  static char swap=0;
```

```
   /* use two different number generators */
   if(swap) f=ran1();    /* to get a random number */
   else f = ran3();
   swap = !swap;

   if(f<.5) return;    /* no customers */
   else if(f<.6) {
     cust++;    /* add one customer */
     return;
   }
   else if(f<.7) {
     cust+=2;    /* add two customers */
     return;
   }
   else if(f<.8) {
     cust+=3;
     return;
   }
   else cust+=4;
}

/* Check out the customer. */
void check_out()
{
   static char count[10]={0, 0, 0, 0, 0, 0, 0, 0, 0, 0};
   register int t;

   for(t=0; t<10; ++t) {
     if(queues[t]) {
       /* get check out time */
       while(count[t]==0) count[t]=ran2()*5;
       count[t]--;
       if(count[t]==0) queues[t]--;
     }
     if(!queues[t]) qopen[t]=0;    /* close the line */
   }
}

/* Add another check out line. */
void add_queue()
{
   register int t;
   int line;

   while(cust) {
     if(allfull())
       for(t=0; t<10; t++) if(!qopen[t]) {
         qopen[t]=1;
         break;
       }
     line = ran3() * 10;
     if(qopen[line] && queues[line]<10) {
       queues[line]++;
       cust--;
     }
     if(t==10) return;    /* all queues full */
   }
}
```

```
/* Return 1 if all lines are full; 0 otherwise. */
allfull()
{
  register int t;

  for(t=0; t<10; t++) if(queues[t]<10 && qopen[t]) return 0;
  return 1;
}

/* Show the current state of the system. */
void display()
{
  register int t;

  goto_xy(0, 15);
  printf("time: %d", time);
  for(t=0; t<10; ++t) {
    /* first, erase the old line by printing in 0 color */
    line(180, (t*10)+160, 80, (t*10)+160, 0);
    /* now, draw the circle */
    circle(180, (t*10)+160, 3, 1);
    /* now draw current state of the queue */
    line(180, (t*10)+160, 180-queues[t]*10, (t*10)+160, 2);
    goto_xy(0+t, 0);  printf("queue %d: %d  ", t+1, queues[t]);
  }
}

float ran1()
{
  static long int a=100001;

  a = (a*125) % 2796203;
  return (float) a/2796203;
}

float ran2()
{
  static long int a=1;

  a = (a * 32719+3) % 32749;
  return (float) a/32749;
}

float ran3()
{
  static long int a=203;

  a = (a *10001 + 3) % 1717;
  return (float) a/1717;
}

/* Set the video mode. */
void mode(mode_code)
int mode_code;
{
  union REGS r;

  r.h.al = mode_code;
```

```
     r.h.ah = 0;
     int86(0x10, &r, &r);
}

/* Draw a line in specified color
   using Bresenham's integer based algorithm.
*/
void line(startx, starty, endx, endy, color)
int startx, starty, endx, endy, color;
{
   register int t, distance;
   int x=0, y=0, delta_x, delta_y;
   int incx, incy;

   /* compute the distances in both directions */
   delta_x = endx-startx;
   delta_y = endy-starty;

   /* Compute the direction of the increment,
      an increment of 0 means either a vertical or horizontal
      line.
   */
   if(delta_x>0) incx = 1;
   else if(delta_x==0) incx = 0;
   else incx=-1;

   if(delta_y>0) incy = 1;
   else if(delta_y==0) incy = 0;
   else incy = -1;

   /* determine which distance is greater */
   delta_x=abs(delta_x);
   delta_y=abs(delta_y);
   if(delta_x>delta_y) distance=delta_x;
   else distance=delta_y;

   /* draw the line */
   for(t=0; t<=distance+1; t++) {
     point(startx, starty, color);
     x+=delta_x;
     y+=delta_y;
     if(x>distance) {
       x-=distance;
       startx+=incx;
     }
     if(y>distance) {
       y-=distance;
       starty+=incy;
     }
   }
}

/* Write a point to the CGA. */
void point(x, y, color_code)
int x, y, color_code;
{
   union REGS r;

   /* check range for mode 4 */
```

```
   if(x<0 || x>199 || y<0 || y>319) return;

   r.h.ah = 12; /* write a pixel */
   r.h.al = color_code; /* color to write */
   r.x.dx = x; /* row */
   r.x.cx = y; /* column */
   int86(0x10, &r, &r);   /* call BIOS */

}

/* send the cursor to x,y */
void goto_xy(x, y)
int x, y;
{
  union REGS r;

  r.h.ah = 2; /* cursor addressing function */
  r.h.dl = y; /* column coordinate */
  r.h.dh = x; /* row coordinate */
  r.h.bh = 0; /* video page */
  int86(0x10, &r, &r);
}

/* Draw a circle using Bresenham's integer based Algorithm. */
void circle(x_center, y_center, radius,  color_code)
int x_center, y_center, radius, color_code;
{
  register int x, y, delta;

  asp_ratio = 1.0;  /* for different aspect ratios, alter
                       this number */

  y = radius;
  delta = 3 - 2 * radius;

  for(x=0; x<y; ) {
    plot_circle(x, y, x_center, y_center, color_code);

    if (delta < 0)
      delta += 4*x+6;
    else {
      delta += 4*(x-y)+10;
      y--;
    }
    x++;
  }
  x=y;
  if(y) plot_circle(x, y, x_center, y_center, color_code);
}

/* plot_circle actually prints the points that
   define the circle */
void plot_circle(x, y, x_center, y_center, color_code)
int x, y, x_center, y_center, color_code;
{
  int startx, endx, x1, starty, endy, y1;

  starty = y*asp_ratio;
  endy = (y+1)*asp_ratio;
```

```
startx = x*asp_ratio;
endx = (x+1)*asp_ratio;

for (x1=startx; x1<endx; ++x1)  {
  point(x1+x_center, y+y_center, color_code);
  point(x1+x_center, y_center-y, color_code);
  point(x_center-x1, y_center-y, color_code);
  point(x_center-x1, y+y_center, color_code);
}

for (y1=starty; y1<endy; ++y1) {
  point(y1+x_center, x+y_center, color_code);
  point(y1+x_center, y_center-x, color_code);
  point(x_center-y1, y_center-x, color_code);
  point(x_center-y1, x+y_center, color_code);
}
}
```

Random-Walk
Portfolio Management

The art of stock portfolio management is generally based on various theories and assumptions about many factors, some of which cannot be easily known unless you are an insider. There are buy/sell strategies based on statistical analyses of stock prices and PE ratios; there are correlations with the price of gold, the GNP, and even the cycles of the moon. The programmer's revenge is to use the computer to simulate the free marketplace—the stock exchange—without all the theoretical worry.

You may think that the stock exchange is simply too hard to simulate; that it has too many variables and too many unknowns; and that it swings wildly at times and coasts smoothly at others. However, the problem itself is the solution: because the marketplace is so complex, it can be thought of as being composed of *randomly occurring* events. This means that you can simulate the stock exchange as a series of disconnected, random occurrences. This simulation is affectionately referred to as the *random-walk method* of portfolio management. The term is derived from the classic experiment to determine the direction of the next step of a drunk wandering a street, randomly weaving from lamppost to lamppost. With the random-walk theory, you let chance be your guide because it is as good as any other method.

Before you continue, be warned: the random-walk method is

generally discredited by professional money managers; it is presented here for your enjoyment, not for actual investing.

To implement the random-walk method, first select ten companies from the *Wall Street Journal* by some chance method, such as throwing darts at it and using the companies whose names you hit. After you have selected ten companies, feed their names into the Random-Walk Simulation program so that it can tell you what to do with them.

Basically, the program can tell you five things to do with the stock of each company:

- Sell

- Buy

- Sell short

- Buy on margin

- Hold (do nothing)

The operations of selling, buying, and holding stock are obvious. When you *sell short*, you sell stock that you do not own in the hopes that soon you can buy it cheaper and deliver it to the person you sold it to. Selling short is a way to make money when the market is going down. When you *buy on margin*, you use, for a small fee, the money of the brokerage house to finance part of the cost of the stock that you purchased. The idea behind buying on margin is that if the stock increases enough, then you make more money than you could if you only bought a smaller amount of stock with cash. This makes money only in a bull (rising) market.

The Random-Walk Simulation program is shown here. The **kbhit()** function checks for keyboard status and waits for a keypress. This allows you to use the sequence produced by the random number generator at a random point—in essence, creating a random seed value. This prevents the program from always producing the same advice.

```
/* Random Walk stock portfolio simulation. */

char stock[10][30];  /* company names */
```

```c
float ran3();
char *action();
void enter();

main()
{
  register int t;
  char ch, s[80];

  printf("Wait awhile, then strike a key.\n");
  do {   /* start at random place in number generator */
    ran3();
  } while(!kbhit());
  getch();

  enter(); /* get company names */

  do {
        for(t=0;t<10;++t)
        printf("%30s: %s\n",stock[t],action());
    printf("\nagain? (y/n)");
    gets(s);
  } while(toupper(*s)=='Y' || *s==0);
}

/* Enter company names. */
void enter()
{
  register int t;

  for(t=0; t<10; t++) {
    printf("enter company name: ");
    gets(stock[t]);
  }
}

/* Determine action to take with stock. */
char *action()
{
  register int x;
  float f;

  f = ran3();
  x = f*10;

  switch(x) {
    case 0: return "sell";
    case 1: return "buy";
    case 3: return "sell short";
    case 4: return "buy on margin";
    default: return "hold";
  }
}

float ran3()
{

  static long int a=203;

  a = (a *10001 + 3) % 1717;
  return (float) a / 1717;
}
```

The program requires that you interpret the instructions in the following way:

Instruction	Interpretation
Buy	Buy as much of the specified stock as you can afford with borrowing
Sell	Sell all of the stock if any is owned. Then randomly select a new company for reinvesting your money
Sell short	Sell 100 shares of the specified company, even though you don't own it, in the hopes that you can buy it cheaper in the future
Buy on margin	Borrow money to buy shares of the specified stock
Hold	Do nothing

For example, if you were to run this program using the fictitious company names of Com1 through Com10, the first day's advice would look like this:

```
Com1:    sell
Com2:    buy
Com3:    buy on margin
Com4:    sell short
Com5:    hold
Com6:    hold
Com7:    hold
Com8:    buy
Com9:    hold
Com10:   sell short
```

The second day's advice might be

```
Com1:    hold
```

Com2:   hold
Com3:   sell
Com4:   sell short
Com5:   hold
Com6:   hold
Com7:   buy
Com8:   buy on margin
Com9:   hold
Com10:   sell

If you prefer, you can run the program weekly instead of daily.

Feel free to alter the program in any way. For example, you could change the program to give you amounts of stock to buy and sell, depending on your available investment dollars. Again, remember that this program is only for fun and is not recommended as a way to make actual investments in the market. However, it is interesting to create a portfolio on paper and to track its performance.

9

EXPRESSION PARSING AND EVALUATION

How do you write a program that will take as input a string containing a numeric expression, for example 10−5*3, and return the answer, in this case −5? If a "high priesthood" still exists among programmers, then it must be made up of those few who know how to do this. Almost everyone who uses a computer is mystified by the way high-level language compilers, spreadsheet programs, and database managers convert complex expressions, such as 10*3−(4+c)/12, into instructions that a computer can execute. This conversion process is called *expression parsing*. It forms the backbone of all language compilers and interpreters, spreadsheet programs, and anything else that converts those numeric expressions understood by humans into forms that a computer can use. Few programmers know how to write an expression parser; this realm of programming is generally thought of as "off limits," except by those enlightened few.

However, this is not the case. Expression parsing is actually very straightforward and is similar to other programming tasks. In some ways it is easier, because it works within the strict rules of algebra. This chapter develops what is commonly referred to as a *recursive descent parser*, as well as all of the necessary support routines to enable you to evaluate complex numeric expressions. After you have mastered the parser, you can enhance and modify it to suit your needs—and join the "high priesthood" yourself.

EXPRESSIONS

Although expressions can be made up of all types of information, you will be studying only one type: *numeric expressions*. For the purposes of this chapter, assume that numeric expressions can be made up of the following:

- Numbers
- The operators +, −, /, *, ^, %, and =
- Parentheses
- Variables

The ^ symbol indicates exponentiation, as in BASIC, and the = symbol represents the assignment operator. All of these items follow the rules of algebra with which you are familiar. Some examples of expressions are

    10−8
    (100−5) * 14/6
    a+b−c
    10^5
    a=10−b

Assume the following precedence for each operator:

    highest: ^
             * / %
             + −
    lowest: =

Operators of equal precedence evaluate from left to right.

For the examples in this chapter, the following assumptions will be made. All variables are single letters, which means that 26 variables—the letters A through Z—are available for use. All numbers are floating point, although you could easily write the routines to handle other types of numbers. Finally, only a minimal amount of error checking is included in the routines to keep the logic uncluttered.

Take a look at the sample expression

10−2*3

This expression has the value 4. Although you could easily create a program that would compute that specific expression, you may wonder how to create a computer program that will give you the correct answer for any arbitrary expression of this type. At first you might think that you could use a routine like this:

> **a** = *get first operand*
> **while**(*operands present*) {
>   **op** = *get operator*
>   **b** = *get second operand*
>   **a** = *a op b*
> }

According to this routine, you could get the first operand, the operator, and the second operand; perform the operation; then get the next operator and operand, if any; perform that operation; and so on. If you use this basic method, the expression 10−2*3 evaluates to 24 (that is, 8*3) instead of the correct answer, 4, because the procedure neglects the precedence of the operators. You cannot take the operands and operators in order from left to right, because the multiplication must be done before the subtraction. A beginner may think that this problem could be easily overcome — and sometimes, in very restrictive cases, it can — but the problem only gets worse when parentheses, exponentiation, variables, function calls, and the like are added in.

Although there are a few ways to write functions that evaluate expressions of this sort, you will study the one that is most easily written and is also the most common. The method that you will examine is called a recursive descent parser, and you will see how it got its name in the course of this chapter. (Some other methods used to write parsers employ complex tables that almost require another computer program to generate them. These are sometimes called *table-driven parsers*.)

Dissecting an Expression

Before you can develop a parser to evaluate expressions, you must get pieces of the expression easily. For example, given the expression

$$A * B - (W + 10)$$

has the components A, B, W, and 10, the parentheses, and the operators $*$, $+$, and $-$. In general, you need a routine that returns each item in the expression individually. The routine also needs to be able to skip over spaces and tabs, and it must know when the end of the expression has been reached.

Formally, each piece of an expression is called a *token*. Therefore, the function that returns the next token in the expression is called **get_token()**. A global character pointer is needed to point to the expression string. This pointer is called **prog**. The variable **prog** is global because it must maintain its value between calls to **get_token()** and it must allow other functions to use it. You also need to know what *type* of token you are getting. For the parser developed in this chapter, you only need three types: VARIABLE, NUMBER, and DELIMITER, where DELIMITER is used for both operators and parentheses. Here is **get_token()** with its necessary globals, **#define** statements, and support functions:

```
#define DELIMITER      1
#define VARIABLE       2
#define NUMBER         3

extern char *prog;   /* points to the expression */
char token[80];
char tok_type;


/* Get a token from the input stream. */
void get_token()
{

  register char *temp;

  tok_type = 0;
  temp = token;
```

```
      while(isspace(*prog)) ++prog;    /* skip over white space */

      if(strchr("+-*/%^=()", *prog)){ /* is delimiter */
         tok_type = DELIMITER;
         *temp++ = *prog++;
         /* advance to next position */
      }
      else if(isalpha(*prog)) { /* is variable */
         while(!isdelim(*prog)) *temp++ = *prog++;
         tok_type = VARIABLE;
      }
      else if(isdigit(*prog)) { /* is number */
         while(!isdelim(*prog)) *temp++ = *prog++;
         tok_type = NUMBER;
      }

      *temp = '\0';

}

/* Return true if c is a delimiter. */
isdelim(c)
char c;
{
   if(strchr(" +-/*%^=()", c) || c==9 || c=='\r' || c==0)
      return 1;
   return 0;
}
```

This function's first step is to check for the null terminator, which indicates the end of the expression string. Because C uses null-terminated strings, if a null is reached, you know that the expression has ended and a null token is returned. Although spaces are added into expressions to add clarity, these spaces only confuse the parser and you must skip over them.

After the spaces have been skipped, **prog** will be pointing to either a number, a variable, an operator, or a null, if trailing spaces end the expression. If the next character is an operator, that character is returned as a string in the global variable **token**, and the type of DELIMITER is placed in **tok—type**. If the next character is a letter instead, it will be assumed to be one of the variables and will be returned as a string in **token**; **tok—type** will be assigned the value VARIABLE. If the next character is a number, then the integer is returned as a string **token** with a type of NUMBER. Finally, if the next character is none of these, you can then assume that the end of the expression has been reached and that **token** is null.

As stated earlier, to keep the code clean in this function, a certain amount of error checking has been omitted and some assumptions have been made. For example, any unrecognized character may end an expression. Also, in this version, variables may be any length, but only the first letter is significant. However, you can fill in these and other details according to your specific application. You can modify or enhance **get_token( )** easily to enable character strings, function calls, or whatever you want to be returned from an input-string token.

To understand how **get_token( )** works, study what it returns for each token from the expression A+100−(B*C)/2:

Token	Token Type
A	VARIABLE
+	DELIMITER
100	NUMBER
−	DELIMITER
(	DELIMITER
B	VARIABLE
*	DELIMITER
C	VARIABLE
)	DELIMITER
/	DELIMITER
2	NUMBER
null	null

Don't forget that **token( )** always holds a null-terminated string, even if that string is just a single character.

PARSING AND EVALUATION

Remember that there are several possible ways to parse and evaluate an expression. For the purposes of this chapter, think of expressions as *recursive data structures* that are defined in terms of themselves. If, for the moment, you restrict expressions to using only +, −, *, /, and parentheses, you could say that all expressions can be defined by using these rules:

Expression => Term [+ *Term*] [− *Term*]
Term => Factor [* *Factor*] [/ *Factor*]
Factor => Variable, Number or (*Expression*)

where any part can be null. The square brackets mean optional, and the => means "produces." In fact, the rules are called the *production rules* of the expression. Therefore, you would read the second rule as "Term produces factor times factor, or factor divided by factor." The precedence of the operators is implicit in the way an expression is defined.

The expression

10+5*B

has two terms: 10 and 5*B. However, it has three factors: 10, 5, and B. These factors consist of two numbers and one variable.

On the other hand, the expression

14*(7−C)

has two factors, 14 and (7−C), which is one number and one parenthesized expression. The parenthesized expression evaluates to one number and one variable.

These production rules form the basis for a recursive descent parser, which is basically a set of mutually recursive routines that work in a chainlike fashion. At each appropriate step, the parser can perform the specified operations in the algebraically correct sequence. To see how this process works, follow the parsing of the input expression

10/3−(100+56)

and perform the arithmetic operations at the right time:

Step 1. Get first term: 10/3.

Step 2. Get each factor and divide integers. That value is 3.

Step 3. Get second term: (100+56). At this point, you must analyze the second expression recursively.

Step 4. Get each factor and add. The result is 156.

Step 5. Return from the recursive call and subtract 156 from 3, which yields an answer of −153.

If you are a little confused at this point, don't worry. This is a complex concept that takes getting used to. There are two things to remember about this recursive view of expressions: first, the precedence of the operators is *implicit* in the way the production rules are defined; second, this method of parsing and evaluating expressions is similar to the way you would parse and evaluate without a computer.

A SIMPLE EXPRESSION PARSER

In the remainder of this chapter, two parsers are developed. The first one parses and evaluates only constant expressions—that is, expressions with no variables. This is the parser in its simplest form. The second parser includes the 26 user variables A through Z.

Here is the entire simple version of the recursive descent parser for integer expressions:

```
/* Recursive descent parser */

#include "stdlib.h"
#include "ctype.h"

#define DELIMITER  1
#define VARIABLE   2
#define NUMBER     3

extern char *prog;  /* points to the expression */
char token[80];
char tok_type;

void get_exp(), level2(), level3(), level4(), level5();
void level6(), primitive(), get_token(), arith(), unary();
void serror(), putback();
```

```
/* Entry point into the parser. */
void get_exp(result)
float *result;
{
  get_token();
  if(!*token) {
    serror(2);
    return;
  }
  level2(result);

}

/* Add or subtract two terms. */
void level2(result)
float *result;
{
  register char  op;
  float hold;

  level3(result);
  while((op = *token) == '+' || op == '-') {
    get_token();
    level3(&hold);
    arith(op, result, &hold);
  }
}

/* Multiply or divide two factors. */
void level3(result)
float *result;
{
  register char  op;
  float hold;

  level4(result);
  while((op = *token) == '*' || op == '/' || op == '%') {
    get_token();
    level4(&hold);
    arith(op, result, &hold);
  }
}

/* Process an exponent. */
void level4(result)
float *result;
{
  float hold;

  level5(result);
  if(*token== '^') {
    get_token();
    level4(&hold);
    arith('^', result, &hold);
  }
}

/* Processs a unary + or -. */
void level5(result)
float *result;
{
  register char  op;

  op = 0;
  if((tok_type == DELIMITER) && *token=='+' || *token == '-') {
    op = *token;
```

```
     get_token();
   }
   level6(result);
   if(op)
     unary(op, result);
}

/* Process a parenthesized expression. */
void level6(result)
float *result;
{
   if((*token == '(') && (tok_type == DELIMITER)) {
     get_token();
     level2(result);
     if(*token != ')')
       serror(1);
     get_token();
   }
   else
     primitive(result);
}

/* Get actual value of a number. */
void primitive(result)
float *result;
{

   if(tok_type==NUMBER) {
     *result=atof(token);
     get_token();
     return;
   }
   serror(0);  /* otherwise syntax error in expression */
}

/* Perform the indicated arithmetic operations. */
void arith(o, r, h)
char o;
float *r, *h;
{
   register float t, ex;

   switch(o) {
     case '-':
       *r = *r-*h;
       break;
     case '+':
       *r = *r+*h;
       break;
     case '*':
       *r = *r * *h;
       break;
     case '/':
       *r = (*r)/(*h);
       break;
     case '%':
       t = (*r)/(*h);
       *r = *r-(t*(*h));
       break;
     case '^':
       ex = *r;
       if(*h==0) {
         *r = 1;
         break;
```

```
    }
    for(t=*h-1; t>0; --t) *r=(*r) * ex;
    break;
  }
}

/* Process a unary - */
void unary(o, r)
char o;
float *r;
{
  if(o=='-') *r = -(*r);
}

/* Return a token to the input stream. */
void putback()
{
  char *t;

  t = token;
  for(; *t; t++) prog--;
}

/* Display a syntax error. */
void serror(error)
int error;
{
  static char *e[]= {
      "syntax error",
      "unbalanced parentheses",
      "no expression present"
          };
  printf("%s\n", e[error]);
}

/* Read a token from the input stream. */
void get_token()
{

  register char *temp;

  tok_type = 0;
  temp = token;

  while(isspace(*prog)) ++prog;  /* skip over white space */

  if(strchr("+-*/%^=()", *prog)){ /* is a delimiter */
    tok_type = DELIMITER;
    *temp++ = *prog++;
    /* advance to next position */
  }
  else if(isalpha(*prog)) { /* is a variable */
    while(!isdelim(*prog)) *temp++ = *prog++;
    tok_type = VARIABLE;
  }
  else if(isdigit(*prog)) { /* is a number */
    while(!isdelim(*prog)) *temp++ = *prog++;
    tok_type = NUMBER;
  }

  *temp = '\0';

}
```

```
/* Return true if c is a delimiter. */
isdelim(c)
char c;
{
  if(strchr(" +-/*%^=()", c) || c==9 || c=='\r' || c==0)
    return 1;
  return 0;
}
```

The parser as shown can accept the operators $+$, $-$, $*$, $/$, and %, as well as exponentiation ($^$), the unary minus, and parentheses. It has six levels and the **primitive()** function, which returns the value of a number. Also included are the routines **arith()** and **unary()** for performing the various arithmetic operations, as well as **get_token()**. As discussed previously, the two globals **token** and **tok_type** return the next token and its type from the expression string. The **extern prog** is a pointer to the expression string, which is assumed to be loaded by another part of the program.

A simple **main()** function that demonstrates the use of the parser is shown here:

```
#include "stdlib.h"

char *prog;

main()   /* Parser driver program */
{
  float answer;
  char *p;

  p = (char *) malloc(100);
  if(!p) {
    printf("allocation failure\n");
    exit(1);
  }

  /* Process expressions until a blank line
     is entered.
  */
  do {
    prog = p;
    printf("enter expression: ");
    gets(prog);
    if(!*prog) break;
    get_exp(&answer);
    printf("answer is: %.2f\n", answer);
  } while(*p);
}
```

To understand exactly how the parser evaluates an expression, work through the following expression, which you can assume is contained in **prog**:

10−3*2

When **get—exp( )** (the entry routine into the parser) is called, it gets the first token, and if that token is null, it prints the message **no expression present** and returns. If a token is present, then **level2( )** is called. (A **level1( )** will be added to the parser momentarily when the assignment operator is added, but it is not needed here.)

Now the token contains the number 10. The **level2( )** function calls **level3( )**, and **level3( )** calls **level4( )**, which in turn calls **level5( )**. The **level5( )** function checks to see if the token is a unary + or −; in this case it is not, so **level6( )** is called. The **level6( )** function either recursively calls **level2( )** in the case of a parenthesized expression, or in this case calls **primitive( )** to find the value of the integer.

Finally, when **primitive( )** is executed and **result** contains the number 10, **get—token** obtains another token, and the functions begin to return up the chain. The token is now the operator − and the functions return up to **level2( )**.

The next step is very important. Because the token is −, it is saved, **get—token** obtains new token 3, and the descent down the chain begins again. Again, **primitive( )** is entered, the number 3 is returned in **result**, and the token * is read. This causes a return back up the chain to **level3( )**, where the final token 2 is read. At this point, the first arithmetic operation occurs with the multiplication of 2 and 3. This result is then returned to **level2( )** and the subtraction is performed to yield an answer of 4. Although the process may seem complicated at first, you should work through some other examples to verify for yourself that it functions correctly every time.

You could use this parser as a desktop calculator, as illustrated by the sample driver program. You could also use it in a database or a simple spreadsheet application. Before it could be used in a language or a sophisticated calculator, the parser would have to be able to handle variables, which is the subject of the next section.

Adding Variables to the Parser

All programming languages and many calculators and spreadsheets use variables to store values for later use. The simple parser in the preceding section must be expanded to include variables before you can use it for this purpose. First you need the variables themselves. Since the parser uses floating-point numbers only, you can use floating-point variables. The parser will only recognize the variables A through Z, although you could expand it if you wanted. Each variable uses one array location in a 26-element array. Therefore, you should add the following:

```
float vars[26]= {      /* 26 user variables,  A-Z */
  0.0, 0.0, 0.0, 0.0, 0.0, 0.0, 0.0, 0.0, 0.0, 0.0,
  0.0, 0.0, 0.0, 0.0, 0.0, 0.0, 0.0, 0.0, 0.0, 0.0,
  0.0, 0.0, 0.0, 0.0, 0.0, 0.0
};
```

As you can see, the variables are initialized to zero as a courtesy to the user.

You also need a routine to look up the value of a given variable. Because you are using the letters A through Z as variable names, you can easily index the array **vars** based on its name. Here is the function **find_var ()**:

```
/* Find the value of a variable. */
float find_var(s)
char *s;
{
  if(!isalpha(*s)){
    serror(1);
    return 0.0;
  }
  return vars[toupper(*token)-'A'];
}
```

As written, this function actually accepts long variable names, but only the first letter is significant. You can modify this feature to fit your needs.

You must also modify the **primitive( )** function to treat both numbers and variables as primitives, as shown here:

```
/* Find value of number or variable. */
void primitive(result)
float *result;
{
  switch(tok_type) {
  case VARIABLE:
    *result = find_var(token);
    get_token();
    return;
  case NUMBER:
    *result = atof(token);
    get_token();
    return;
  default:
    serror(0);
  }
}
```

Technically, this is all you need for the parser to use variables correctly; however, there is no way for these variables to be assigned values. Often you can assign variables outside the parser, but since it is possible to treat the = as an assignment operator, there are many ways to make it part of the parser. One method is to add a **level1( )** to the parser, as shown here:

```
/* Process an assignment statement. */
void level1(result)
float *result;
{
  float hold;
  int slot, ttok_type;
  char temp_token[80];

  if(tok_type==VARIABLE) {
    /* save old token */
    strcpy(temp_token, token);
    ttok_type=tok_type;

    slot = toupper(*token)-'A';
    get_token();
    if(*token != '=') {
      putback();  /* return current token */
      /* restore old token - not assignment */
      strcpy(token, temp_token);
      tok_type = ttok_type;
    }
    else {
      get_token();  /* get next part of exp */
      level2(result);
      vars[slot] = *result;
      return;
    }
  }

  level2(result);
}
```

As you can see, you must look ahead to determine whether an assignment is actually being made; in this situation you need to save the state of the parser so that it can be restored if it is not an assignment.

Here is the entire enhanced parser:

```
/* recursive descent parser for floating point expressions
     which may include variables  */
#include "math.h"
#include "ctype.h"

#define DELIMITER  1
#define VARIABLE   2
#define NUMBER     3

extern char *prog;  /* holds expression to be analyzed */
char token[80];
char tok_type;

float vars[26]= {    /* 26 user variables,  A-Z */
  0.0, 0.0, 0.0, 0.0, 0.0, 0.0, 0.0, 0.0, 0.0, 0.0,
  0.0, 0.0, 0.0, 0.0, 0.0, 0.0, 0.0, 0.0, 0.0, 0.0,
  0.0, 0.0, 0.0, 0.0, 0.0, 0.0
};

void get_exp(),level2(), level3(), level4(), level5();
void level6(), primitive(), get_token(), arith(), unary();
void serror(), putback(), level1();

float find_var();
char *prog;

main()  /* Parser driver program */
{
  float answer;
  char *p;

  p = (char *) malloc(100);
  if(!p) {
    printf("allocation failure\n");
    exit(1);
  }

   /* Process expressions until a blank line
      is entered.
    */
  do {
    prog = p;
    printf("enter expression: ");
    gets(prog);
    if(!*prog) break;
    get_exp(&answer);
    printf("answer is: %.2f\n", answer);
  } while(*p);
}

/* Entry point into parser. */
void get_exp(result)
```

```
float *result;
{
  get_token();
  if(!*token) {
    serror(2);
    return;
  }
  level1(result);

}

/* Process an assignment statement. */
void level1(result)
float *result;
{
  float hold;
  int slot, ttok_type;
  char temp_token[80];

  if(tok_type==VARIABLE) {
    /* save old token */
    strcpy(temp_token, token);
    ttok_type=tok_type;

    slot = toupper(*token)-'A';
    get_token();
    if(*token != '=') {
      putback();  /* return current token */
      /* restore old token - not assignment */
      strcpy(token, temp_token);
      tok_type = ttok_type;
    }
    else {
      get_token();  /* get next part of exp */
      level2(result);
      vars[slot] = *result;
      return;
    }
  }

  level2(result);

}

/*  Add or subtract two terms. */
void level2(result)
float *result;
{
  register char  op;
  float hold;

  level3(result);
  while((op = *token) == '+' || op == '-') {
    get_token();
    level3(&hold);
    arith(op, result, &hold);
  }
}

/* Multiply or divide two factors. */
void level3(result)
```

```
float *result;
{
  register char  op;
  float hold;

  level4(result);
  while((op = *token) == '*' || op == '/' || op == '%') {
    get_token();
    level4(&hold);
    arith(op, result, &hold);
  }
}

/* Process an integer exponent. */
void level4(result)
float *result;
{
  float hold;

  level5(result);
  if(*token== '^') {
    get_token();
    level4(&hold);
    arith('^', result, &hold);
  }
}

/* Process a unary + or -. */
void level5(result)
float *result;
{
  register char  op;

  op = 0;
  if((tok_type==DELIMITER) && *token=='+' || *token=='-') {
    op = *token;
    get_token();
  }
  level6(result);
  if(op)
    unary(op, result);
}

/* process parenthesized expression */
void level6(result)
float *result;
{
  if((*token == '(') && (tok_type == DELIMITER)) {
    get_token();
    level1(result);
    if(*token != ')')
      serror(1);
    get_token();
  }
  else
    primitive(result);
}

/* Find value of number or variable. */
void primitive(result)
float *result;
{
```

```
  switch(tok_type) {
  case VARIABLE:
    *result = find_var(token);
    get_token();
    return;
  case NUMBER:
    *result = atof(token);
    get_token();
    return;
  default:
    serror(0);
  }
}

/* Perform the specified arithmetic operation. */
void arith(o, r, h)
char o;
float *r, *h;
{
  register int t, ex;

  switch(o) {
    case '-':
      *r = *r-*h;
      break;
    case '+':
      *r = *r+*h;
      break;
    case '*':
      *r = *r * *h;
      break;
    case '/':
      *r = (*r)/(*h);
      break;
    case '%':
      t = (*r)/(*h);
      *r = *r-(t*(*h));
      break;
    case '^':
      ex = *r;
      if(*h==0) {
        *r = 1;
        break;
      }
      for(t=*h-1; t>0; --t) *r = (*r) * ex;
      break;
  }
}

/* Process a unary -. */
void unary(o, r)
char o;
float *r;
{
  if(o=='-') *r = -(*r);
}

/* Return a token to the input stream. */
void putback()
{

  char *t;
```

```
  t = token;
  for(; *t; t++) prog--;
}

/* Find the value of a variable. */
float find_var(s)
char *s;
{
  if(!isalpha(*s)){
    serror(1);
    return 0;
  }
  return vars[toupper(*token)-'A'];
}

/* Display an error message. */
void serror(error)
int error;
{
  static char *e[]= {
      "syntax error",
      "unbalanced parentheses",
      "no expression present"
        };
  printf("%s\n", e[error]);
}

/* Get a token from the input stream. */
void get_token()
{

  register char *temp;

  tok_type = 0;
  temp = token;

  while(isspace(*prog)) ++prog;    /* skip over white space */

  if(strchr("+-*/%^=()", *prog)){ /* is delimiter */
    tok_type = DELIMITER;
    *temp++ = *prog++;
    /* advance to next position */
  }
  else if(isalpha(*prog)) { /* is variable */
    while(!isdelim(*prog)) *temp++ = *prog++;
    tok_type = VARIABLE;
  }
  else if(isdigit(*prog)) { /* is number */
    while(!isdelim(*prog)) *temp++ = *prog++;
    tok_type = NUMBER;
  }

  *temp = '\0';

}

/* Return true if c is a delimiter. */
isdelim(c)
char c;
{
  if(strchr(" +-/*%^=()", c) || c==9 || c=='\r' || c==0)
    return 1;
  return 0;
}
```

To see how this version of the parser functions, you can use the same **main( )** function you used for the simple parser. With the enhanced parser you can now enter expressions such as

$A = 10/4$
$A - B$
$C = A * (F - 21)$

SYNTAX CHECKING IN A RECURSIVE DESCENT PARSER

In expression parsing, a *syntax error* is a situation in which the input expression does not conform to the strict rules required by the parser. Usually this is caused by human error — most commonly by typing mistakes. For example, the following expressions will not be parsed correctly by the parsers in this chapter:

10**8
(10−5)*9)
/8

The first expression has two operators in a row; the second has unbalanced parentheses; and the last has a division sign starting an expression. None of these conditions are allowed by the parsers. Because syntax errors can cause the parser to give erroneous results, it is necessary to guard against them.

As you have studied the code to the parsers, you have probably noticed the function **serror( )**, which is called in certain situations. Unlike many other parsers, the recursive descent method makes syntax checking easy because, for the most part, syntax errors occur in either **primitive( )**, **find—var( )**, or **level6( )**, where parentheses are checked. The syntax checking as it now stands has only one problem: the entire parser is not aborted on syntax error. This can cause multiple error messages to be generated.

The best way to implement **serror( )** is to have it execute a **longjmp( )** routine. Many compilers come with a pair of companion functions called, for example, **setjmp( )** and **longjmp( )**. Together these two functions allow a program branch to a *different* function. Therefore, in **serror( )**, you would execute a **longjmp( )** to some safe point in your program outside the parser.

If your compiler does not have this type of routine pair or if you are trying to write portable code, your only other option is to add a global variable that is checked each level. The variable would initially be FALSE, and any call to **serror( )** would make it TRUE, causing the parser to abort one function at a time.

If you leave the code the way it is, all that will happen is that multiple syntax error messages may be issued. This could be an annoyance in some situations but a blessing in others because multiple errors will be caught. Generally, however, you will want to enhance the syntax checking before using it in commercial programs.

10

CONVERTING PASCAL AND BASIC TO C

Some programmers spend much of their time converting programs from one language into another. This is called *translating.* You may find the process either easy or difficult, depending on the methods you use to translate and how well you know the source and destination languages. This chapter presents some topics and techniques to help you convert Pascal and BASIC programs into C.

Why would anyone want to translate a program written in one language into another? One reason is *maintainability:* a program written in an unstructured language like BASIC is difficult to maintain or enhance. Another reason is *speed and efficiency:* C as a language is very efficient, and some demanding tasks have been translated into C for better performance. A third reason is *practicality:* you may see a useful program listed in one language but own or use a compiler for a different language. You will probably find that you want to translate a program into C for one or more of these reasons.

Pascal and BASIC were chosen from the field of nearly a hundred computer languages because they are popular languages among microcomputer users and because they represent opposite ends of the programming-language spectrum. Pascal is a structured language that has many similarities to C, whereas BASIC is a nonstructured language and has virtually no similarities to C. Although this chapter cannot cover each language in every detail, it will examine several of the most important problems that you will confront. It is assumed that you are familiar with either Pascal or BASIC; no attempt will be made to teach either language.

CONVERTING PASCAL TO C

Pascal and C have many similarities, especially in their control structures and their use of stand-alone subroutines with local variables. This makes it possible to do lots of *one-to-one translations:* you can often simply substitute the C equivalent keyword or function. With one-to-one translating you can use the computer to assist you with the translation process. A simple translation program will be developed later in the chapter.

Although Pascal and C are similar, there are four primary differences between them. The first is that Pascal is more restrictive and in some ways more limited than C. For example, standard Pascal not only makes it difficult to write system code (since memory addresses cannot be directly loaded into pointers, as in C), it also will not perform type conversions for you. A second and more important difference is that Pascal is formally block structured, whereas C is not. The term *block structured* refers to a language's ability to create logically connected units of code that can be referenced together. The term also means that procedures can have other procedures nested inside them, known only to the outer procedure. Although C is commonly called a block-structured language because it allows the easy creation of blocks of code, it does not allow functions to be defined inside other functions. For example, the following Pascal code is valid:

```
procedure A;
  var x:integer;

  procedure B;
  begin
    writeln('inside proc b');
  end;
```

```
begin
  writeln('starting A');
  B;
end;
```

Here, **procedure B** is defined inside of **procedure A**. This means that **procedure B** is known only to **procedure A** and may only be used by **procedure A**. Outside of **procedure A**, another **procedure B** could be defined without conflict. The same code translated into C, however, would need to have two functions:

```
A()
{
  printf("starting A\n");
  B();
}

B()
{
  printf("inside function B\n");
}
```

In addition, you would have to make sure that there were no other functions called B anywhere else in the program.

The third difference between Pascal and C is that all Pascal variables, functions, and procedures must be declared before they are used. In standard Pascal, this means that forward references are not allowed without the **forward** statement. In C, all variables must be declared before they are used, but forward references to functions are not restricted—in fact, they are very common.

A fourth difference is that standard Pascal does not support separate compilation, whereas separate compilation is encouraged in C.

A Comparison of Pascal and C

Figure 10-1 compares Pascal keywords with C keywords and operators. As you can see, many Pascal keywords have no C equivalent because Pascal uses keywords in places where C uses operators to accomplish the same steps. At times, Pascal is simply "wordier" than C.

Pascal	C
and	&&
array	
begin	{
case	switch
const	#define
div	/ (using integers)
do	
downto	
else	else
end	}
file	
forward	extern (on occasion)
for	for
function	
goto	goto
if	if
in	
label	
mod	%
nil	(sometimes \0)
not	!
of	
or	||
packed	
procedure	
program	
record	struct
repeat	do
set	
then	
type	
to	
until	while (as in do/while)
var	
while	while
with	

Figure 10-1.   Pascal keywords compared with C keywords and operators

Pascal	C
Boolean	char or integer
byte	char
char	char
EOF	EOF (in stdio library)
false	0
flush	flush( ) (in stdio library)
integer	integer
read	scanf( ) and others
real	float
true	any nonzero value
write	printf( )

Figure 10-2.   Some standard Pascal identifiers and their C equivalents

In addition to the keywords, Pascal has several built-in *standard identifiers* that can be used directly in a program. These identifiers may be functions (like **writeln**) or global variables (like **MaxInt**) that hold information about the state of the system. Also, Pascal uses standard identifiers to specify such data types as **real**, **integer**, **Boolean**, and **character**. Figure 10-2 shows several standard Pascal identifiers and their C equivalents. In addition to those in the figure, many of Pascal's built-in functions have equivalents in C that are found in the standard library; however, they may vary from compiler to compiler.

Pascal also differs from C in its operators. Figure 10-3 shows the Pascal operators and their C equivalents.

Converting Pascal Loops into C Loops

Because program control loops are fundamental to most programs, you should compare Pascal's loops with C's loops. Pascal

Pascal	C	Meaning
+	+	Addition
−	−	Subtraction
*	*	Multiplication
/	/	Division
div	/	Integer division
mod	%	Modulus
^		Exponentiation
:=	=	Assignment
=	==	Equals as a condition
<	<	Less than
>	>	Greater than
>=	>=	Greater than or equal to
<=	<=	Less than or equal to
<>	!=	Not equal

Figure 10-3.   Pascal operators and their C equivalents

has three built-in loops: **for, while,** and **repeat-until.** C has a corresponding loop for each.

The Pascal **for** has the general form

   for *initial value* **to** *target value* **do statement;**

The Pascal **for** is much more limited than the C **for** because it does not allow increments other than 1 (or −1 if the **downto** is used), and because the loop condition is rigidly tied to the counting mechanism, unlike C's more flexible design. However, these differences do not affect the process of translating from Pascal into C, because the Pascal **for** can be viewed simply as a C subset. For example, the Pascal statement

```
for x:=10 to 100 do writeln(x);
```

can be translated into C as

```
for(x=10; x<=100; ++x) printf("%d\n", x);
```

The Pascal **while** and the C **while** are virtually the same. However, Pascal's **repeat-until** and C's **do/while** require that you use different keywords and "reverse" the loop-test condition. The reason is that the Pascal **repeat-until** implies that a loop runs *until* something *becomes* true, whereas the C **do-while** loops *while* the loop condition *is* true. A sample translation of both these types of loops is shown here:

Pascal

```
while x<5 do
begin
   read(x);
   writeln(x);
end;

repeat
   read(x);
   writeln(x);
until x>5;
```

C

```
while(x<5)
{
   scanf("%d",&x);
   printf("%d\n", x);
}

do {
   scanf("%d", &x);
   printf("%d\n",x);
} while(x<=5);
```

Watch out for the translation of **repeat-until** into **do-while**: you must reverse the sense of the test condition.

A Sample Translation

For a taste of the translation process, follow the steps of converting a Pascal program into C. Here is a simple Pascal program:

```
program test (input,output);
var qwerty: real;

procedure func2 (x: integer);
begin
     writeln(x*2);
end;

function func1 (w: real): real;
begin
     func1:=w/3.1415;
     qwerty:=23.34
end;

begin
     qwerty:=0;
     writeln(qwerty);
     writeln('hello there');
     func2(25);
     writeln(func1(10));
     writeln(qwerty:2:4);
end.
```

This Pascal program has one function and one procedure
declared. Since functions and procedures are the same in C, you
do not need to worry about the difference, except to return the
value properly (although it is a good idea to declare functions as
void if they do not return values). Therefore, **procedure func2**
becomes

```
func2(x)
int x;
{
   printf("%d", x*2);
}
```

and **function func1** becomes

```
float func1(w)
float w;
{
   qwerty=23.34;
   return w/3.1415;
}
```

Because **func1( )** returns a **float**, you must explicitly declare it by
placing the type declaration **float** in front of the name **func1**.

Next, the **program** code (which starts with the first **begin**
that is not inside another function or procedure) must be converted into the **main( )** function. It becomes

```
main()
{
   qwerty=0;
   printf("%f",qwerty);
   printf("hello there\n");
   func2(25);
   printf("%f\n",func1(10));
   printf("%2.4f\n",qwerty);
}
```

Finally, you must declare the global variable **qwerty** as a
float. After you do this and put the pieces together, the C translation of the Pascal program looks like this:

```
float qwerty;

main()
```

```
{
  float func1();
  qwerty=0;
  printf("%f",qwerty);
  printf("hello there\n");
  func2(25);
  printf("%f\n",func1(10));
  printf("%2.4f\n",qwerty);
}

func2(x)
int x;
{
  printf("%d", x*2);
}

float func1(w)
float w;
{
  qwerty=23.34;
  return w/3.1415;
}
```

Using the Computer
to Help Convert
Pascal to C

It is possible to construct a computer program that accepts source code in one language and outputs it in another. The best way to do this is to implement an actual language parser for the source language.—but instead of generating executable code, it will output the destination language. You can occasionally find advertisements for such products in computer magazines, and their high prices reflect the complexity of the task.

A less ambitious approach is to construct a simple program to assist your program-conversion efforts by performing some of the simpler translation tasks. This "computer assist" can make conversion jobs much easier.

A computer-assist translator accepts as input a program in the source language and performs all one-to-one conversions into the destination language automatically, leaving the harder conversions up to you. For example, to assign **count** the value of 10 in Pascal you would write

```
count:=10;
```

In C, the statement is the same, except that there is no colon. Therefore, the computer-assist program can change the := assignment statement in Pascal to the = in C. However, the ways Pascal and C programs access disk files are different, and there is no straightforward way to perform such a conversion automatically. The translator leaves these types of translations for you to perform.

First, the translator needs a function that returns one token at a time from the Pascal program. The function **get—token( )**, developed in Chapter 9, can be modified for this use as shown here:

```
/* Read a token from the input stream. */
void get_token()
{

  register char *temp;

  tok_type = 0; tok = 0;
  temp = token;

  if(*prog=='\n') {
    *temp++ = '\r';
    *temp++ = '\n';
    *temp = '\0';
    prog++;
    tok_type = DELIM;
    return;
  }

  if(*prog=='\0') {
    *temp = '\0';
    tok_type = DELIM;
    return;
  }
  while(isspace(*prog)) ++prog;  /* skip over white space */

  /* relational equals */
  if(*prog=='=') {
    prog++;
    strcpy(token, "==");
    tok_type = OP;
    return;
  }

  /* assignment */
  if(*prog==':') {
    prog++;
    if(*prog=='=')
    {
      *temp++ = '=';
      prog++;
    }
```

```
    else *temp++ = ':';

    *temp = '\0';
    tok_type = OP;
    return;
}

/* strings */
if(is_in(*prog, "'")) {
    *temp++ = '"';  prog++;
    while(!is_in(*prog, "'")) *temp++ = *prog++;
    *temp = '"'; temp++; *temp = '\0'; prog++;
    tok_type = STRING;
    return;
}

/* other operators */
if(is_in(*prog, "+-*;.,/^%()")){
    *temp = *prog;
    prog++; /* advance to next position */
    if(*temp=='.') *temp = ' ';
    temp++;
    *temp = '\0';
    tok_type = OP;
    return;
}

/* variables */
if(isalpha(*prog)) {
    while(isalpha(*prog)) *temp++ = *prog++;
    *temp = '\0';
    tok_type = IDENTIFIER;
    return;
}

/* numbers */
if(isdigit(*prog)) {
    while(!isdelim(*prog)) *temp++ = *prog++;
    tok_type = NUMBER;
    *temp = '\0';
    return;
}
prog++;  /* unknown character */
}
```

In **get_token()**, the Pascal assignment := is converted into C as =, and = is converted into its C equivalent, ==. While this is sufficient for a simple translation program, a more complete translation program would have probably done this conversion in a larger operator-conversion routine.

The second important routine translates Pascal keywords and some functions into their C counterparts. The function **translate()** shown here uses the two-dimensional array **trans** to look up Pascal identifiers and return their C equivalents:

```
char * trans[][2] = {
  "and", "&&",
  "begin", "{",
  "case", "switch",
  "div", "/",
  "do", "do",
  "else", "else",
  "end", "}",
  "forward", "extern",
  "for", "for",
  "function", "\n",
  "goto", "goto",
  "if", "if",
  "then", " ",
  "mod", "%",
  "nil", "'\0'",
  "not", "!",
  "procedure", "\n",
  "record", "struct",
  "repeat", "do",
  "until", " while",
  "while", "while",
  "writeln", "printf",
  "read", "scanf",
  "readln", "scanf",
  "write", "printf",
  "real", "float",
  "integer", "int",
  "char", "char",
  "", ""
};


/* translate Pascal identifiers into C */
void translate(s)
char *s;
{
  register int i;

  for(i=0; *trans[i][0]; i++)
    if(!strcmp(s, trans[i][0])) {
      strcpy(s, trans[i][1]);
      return;
    }
}
```

Some words (such as **program**) have no equivalent in C, and in this case, a newline is substituted. A null string is not used, because it is reserved to indicate the end of the array.

Here is the entire translation program:

```
/* A computer assisted Pascal to C converter. */

#include "stdio.h"
#include "ctype.h"

#define OP        1
#define IDENTIFIER 2
```

```
#define VAR      3
#define NUMBER   4
#define DELIM    5
#define STRING   6

char token[80];
int tok_type;
int tok;

void get_token(), translate();

char s[10000];  /* holds source file */
char *prog;

char * trans[][2] = {
  "and", "&&",
  "begin", "{",
  "case", "switch",
  "div", "/",
  "do", "do",
  "else", "else",
  "end", "}",
  "forward", "extern",
  "for", "for",
  "function", "\n",
  "goto", "goto",
  "if", "if",
  "then", " ",
  "mod", "%",
  "nil", "'\0'",
  "not", "!",
  "procedure", "\n",
  "record", "struct",
  "repeat", "do",
  "until", " while",
  "while", "while",
  "writeln", "printf",
  "read", "scanf",
  "readln", "scanf",
  "write", "printf",
  "real", "float",
  "integer", "int",
  "char", "char",
  "",""
};

main(argc, argv)
int argc;
char *argv[];
{
  FILE *fp1, *fp2;
  char *p;
  int indent=0, i;

  prog = s;

  if(argc!=3) {
    printf("usage: input output");
    exit(1);
  }

  if((fp1=fopen(argv[1], "r"))==0) {
    printf("cannot open input file\n");
    exit(1);
```

```
  }

  if((fp2=fopen(argv[2], "w"))==0) {
    printf("cannot open output file\n");
    exit(1);
  }

  while((*prog=getc(fp1))!=EOF)
    prog++; /* read in source */

  *prog = '\0'; /* null terminate the source code */
  prog = s;

  for(;;) {
    get_token();
    if(!*token) break;  /* end of input file */
    p = token;
    /* if token is an indentifier then translate it */
    if(tok_type==IDENTIFIER) translate(token);

    while(*p) putc(*p++, fp2); /* write it */

    /* put a space between tokens */
    if(*token!='\r') putc(' ', fp2);

    /* indent code to proper level */
    if(*token=='\r') {
      for(i=0; i<indent; i++) {
        putc(' ', fp2);
        putc(' ', fp2);
      }
    }

    if(*token=='}') indent--;
    if(*token=='{') indent++;
  }
  fclose(fp1); fclose(fp2);
}

/* Read a token from the input stream. */
void get_token()
{
  register char *temp;

  tok_type = 0; tok = 0;
  temp = token;

  if(*prog=='\n') {
    *temp++ = '\r';
    *temp++ = '\n';
    *temp = '\0';
    prog++;
    tok_type = DELIM;
    return;
  }

  if(*prog=='\0') {
    *temp = '\0';
    tok_type = DELIM;
    return;
  }
  while(isspace(*prog)) ++prog;  /* skip over white space */
```

```
/* relational equals */
if(*prog=='=') {
  prog++;
  strcpy(token, "==");
  tok_type = OP;
  return;
}

/* assignment */
if(*prog==':') {
  prog++;
  if(*prog=='=')
  {
    *temp++ = '=';
    prog++;
  }
  else *temp++ = ':';

  *temp = '\0';
  tok_type = OP;
  return;
}

/* strings */
if(strchr("'", *prog)) {
  *temp++ = '"';  prog++;
  while(!strchr("'", *prog)) *temp++ = *prog++;
  *temp = '"'; temp++; *temp = '\0'; prog++;
  tok_type = STRING;
  return;
}

/* other operators  */
if(strchr("+-*;.,/^%()", *prog)){
  *temp = *prog;
  prog++; /* advance to next position */
  if(*temp=='.') *temp = ' ';
  temp++;
  *temp = '\0';
  tok_type = OP;
  return;
}

/* variables */
if(isalpha(*prog)) {
  while(isalpha(*prog)) *temp++ = *prog++;
  *temp = '\0';
  tok_type = IDENTIFIER;
  return;
}

/* numbers */
if(isdigit(*prog)) {
  while(!isdelim(*prog)) *temp++ = *prog++;
  tok_type = NUMBER;
  *temp = '\0';
  return;
}
prog++;  /* unknown character */
}

isdelim(c)
```

```
char c;
{
  if(strchr(" ;,+-/*^%()", c) || c==9 || c=='\r' || c==0)
    return 1;
  return 0;
}

/* translate Turbo Pascal identifiers into Turbo C */
void translate(s)
char *s;
{
  register int i;

  for(i=0; *trans[i][0]; i++)
    if(!strcmp(s, trans[i][0])) {
      strcpy(s, trans[i][1]);
      return;
    }
}
```

In essence, the Computer Assisted Pascal to C program reads in the entire source code of the Pascal program, takes a token at a time from it, performs any translations it can, and writes out a C version. Except for a few operator changes, the standard function **strcmp( )** detects a translatable token, and **strcpy( )** converts it to the proper C token. To see how this simple program can make translating from Pascal to C easier, run this Pascal program through the translator program:

```
program test (input,output);

procedure f1(x: integer);
begin
    writeln(x*2);
end;

function f2 (w: real): real;
begin
    if w=100 then writeln('w is 100 inside f2');
    f2:= w/3.1415;
end;

begin
    writeln('hello there');
    f1(25);
    writeln(f2(10));
end.
```

The pseudo-C output is

```
test ( input , output ) ;

f1 ( x : int ) ;
{
```

```
    printf ( x * 2 ) ;
    } ;

f2 ( w : float ) : float ;
{
    if w == 100 printf ( " w is 100 inside f2 " ) ;
    f2 = w / 3.1415;
    } ;

{
    printf ( " hello there " ) ;
    f1 ( 25 ) ;
    printf ( f2 ( 10 ) ) ;
    }
```

As you can see, this is not C code, but you have saved a lot of typing. All you need do is edit this a line at a time to correct the differences.

CONVERTING BASIC TO C

The task of converting BASIC to C is much more difficult than that of converting Pascal to C. BASIC is not a structured language, and it bears little similarity to C, which means not only that it does not have a complete set of control structures but, more important, it also does not have stand-alone subroutines with local variables. The translation task is very tricky. Generally, it requires extensive knowledge of both BASIC and C, and an understanding of the program, because in essence you will be rewriting the program in C and using the BASIC version as a guide. Because of the complexity of the task, this section will look at some of the more troublesome translations and offer suggestions.

Converting BASIC Loops into C Loops

The **FOR/NEXT** loop is the only form of loop control in many versions of BASIC. The overall form of the **FOR/NEXT** loop in BASIC and the **for** loop in C is generally the same; there is initialization, test condition, and increment. The C **for** loop is much more sophisticated and flexible than the BASIC **FOR/NEXT**, but when you translate from BASIC to C, this does not matter. For example, this BASIC **FOR/NEXT** loop:

```
10 FOR X=1 TO 100
20   PRINT X
30 NEXT
```

translates into C as

```
for(x=1; x<=100; ++x) printf("%d\n", x);
```

As you can see, the conversion is essentially a one-to-one substitution. The real trick in converting the **FOR/NEXT** loop is making sure that the loop control variable is not modified inside the loop. For example, in

```
10 FOR COUNT=10 TO 0 STEP -1
20   INPUT A
30   PRINT A*COUNT
40   IF A=100 THEN COUNT = 0
50 NEXT
```

the **IF/THEN** statement in line 40 could cause the loop to exit early. To translate this properly into C code, you must allow for this contingency as well:

```
for(count=10; count>=0; --count) {
  scanf("%d", &a);
  printf("%d\n", a*count);
  if(a==100) break;
}
```

Some forms of BASIC have a **WHILE/WEND** loop available. In such a case, you would use a C **while** loop and your translation would be straightforward. If the BASIC you are using does not have the **WHILE/WEND** loop or if the programmer chooses not to use it, your job will be harder because you must recognize a *constructed loop* using **GOTO** statements. This will also be the case if a **do/while** type of loop is needed in BASIC. These types of translations become nightmarish because you must actually understand how the code works in order to recognize the loop and translate it into one of C's built-in loop control structures.

After finding the loop, there is an easy way to tell whether a constructed loop in BASIC should be translated into a C **while** or **do/while**. Recall that a **do/while** loop *always executes at least once* because the loop condition is checked at the bottom of the loop, whereas a **while** loop may or may not execute because its condition is checked at the top. Therefore, you must look carefully at each constructed loop in BASIC and determine where the loop test is applied. For example, the BASIC code

```
100 S=S+1
200 Q=S/3.1415
300 PRINT Q;
400 IF S <100 THEN GOTO 100
```

is actually a **do/while** loop in disguise because it will always execute at least once. After line 100 has been executed, lines 200 through 400 will execute as well. If **S** is less than 100, the program will loop back to line 100. In C, this code would be

```
do {
  s++;
  q = s/3.1415;
  printf("%f ",q);
} while(s<100);
```

In the following BASIC example, the loop test is performed at the start of the loop, so it requires the use of the **while** loop:

```
10 A=1
20 IF A>100 THEN GOTO 80
30 PRINT A
40 INPUT B
50 A=A+B
60 GOTO 20
80 PRINT "DONE"
```

The C equivalent is

```
a = 1;
while(a<=100) {
  printf("%d\n", a);
  scanf("%d", &b);
  a = a+b;
}
printf("done");
```

Avoid placing any initialization inside the loop itself by accident. In this example, the statement **a=1** has to be outside the loop because it is a start-up condition and does not belong in the loop itself.

Converting the IF/THEN/ELSE Statement

Most forms of BASIC have only the single-line **IF/THEN/ELSE** statement. This means that when a block of statements must be executed based on the outcome of an **IF**, the **GOTO** or **GOSUB** must be used. You must recognize this situation, because you will want to structure the code into a proper C **if/else** statement when you translate it. As an example, consider the following BASIC code fragment:

```
120 IF T<100 THEN GOTO 500
130    Y=W
140    T=10
150    INPUT A$
.
.
.
500 REM RESUME DISK READS
```

To achieve an **IF** block in a BASIC program, the **IF** condition must be cast in the negative: it must not be the condition that you want to enter in the **IF** block, but rather the one that causes a jump around it. This is one of the worst problems in BASIC. Using **GOSUB** routines as the target of the **IF** or the **ELSE** does ease the problem slightly, but not entirely. If the BASIC code fragment were translated directly into C, it would look like this:

```
if(t<100);
else {
   y = w;
   t = 10;
   gets(a);
}
/* resume disk reads */
```

You can now see the problem: the target of the **if** is really an empty statement. The only way to resolve this is to recode the **if** condition so that if it is true, the block of code is entered. The code fragment then becomes

```
if(t>=100) {
  y = w;
  t = 10;
  gets(a);
}
/* resume disk reads */
```

Now the code, as written in C, makes sense.

The differences between the way the BASIC **IF/THEN** is used and the way the C **if** is used illustrate that the programming language often governs the approach to solving a problem. Most people find the positive form of the **if** more natural to use than the negative form.

Creating C Functions from BASIC Programs

One reason that translating BASIC into C is difficult is that it does not support stand-alone subroutines with local variables. This means that a literal translation of a BASIC program into C would produce a large **main( )** and only a few other functions. A better translation would create a C program with a fairly small **main( )** and many other functions, but to do this requires knowledge of the program and a keen eye for reading code. However, here are a few rules to guide you.

First, make all **GOSUB** routines into functions. Also look for similar functions in which only the variables have changed, and collapse them into one function with parameters. For example, this BASIC code has two subroutines—one at 100 and the second at 200:

```
10 A=10
20 B=20
30 GOSUB 100
```

```
40  PRINT A,B
50  C=20
60  D=30
70  GOSUB 200
80  PRINT C,D
90  END
100 A=A*B
110 B=A/B
120 RETURN
200 C=C*D
210 D=C/D
220 RETURN
```

Both subroutines do exactly the same thing, except they operate on separate sets of variables. A proper translation of this program into C has only one function that uses parameters to avoid having two dedicated functions:

```c
void f1();

main()
{
  int a,b,c,d;

  a = 10; b = 20;
  f1(&a, &b);
  printf("%d %d\n", a, b);
  c = 20; d = 30;
  f1(&c, &d);
  printf("%d %d\n",c, d);
}

void f1(x, y)
int *x, *y;
{
  *x = *x*(*y);
  *y = *x/ *y;
}
```

This C translation approximates the meaning of the code to the reader more closely than does the BASIC version, which implies that there are actually two separate functions involved.

The second rule is to make all repeated code into a function. In a BASIC program, the same few lines of code may be repeated. A programmer often does this to make the code slightly faster. Because C is generally a compiled language, using functions, as opposed to using in-line code, has minimal effect; the increased clarity outweighs any gain in speed.

Getting Rid of Global Variables

In BASIC, all variables are global: they are known throughout the program and may be modified anywhere in the program. In the translation process, try to convert as many of these global variables as possible into local ones, because it makes the program more resilient and bug-free. The more global variables there are, the more likely it is that side effects will occur.

It is sometimes difficult to know when to make a variable local to a function. The easiest choices are the ones that control counters in short sections of code. For example, in this code

```
10 FOR X=1 TO 10
20    PRINT X
30 NEXT
```

X is used only to control the **FOR/NEXT** loop and can therefore be made into a local variable within a function.

Another type of variable that is a candidate for becoming local is a temporary variable. A temporary variable holds an intermediate result in a calculation. Temporary variables are often spread out in a program and can be hard to recognize. For example, the variable C12 shown here holds a temporary result in the calculation.

```
10  INPUT A,B
20  GOSUB 100
30  PRINT C12
40  END
100 C12=A*B
110 C12=C12/0.142
120 RETURN
```

The same code in C, with C12 as a local variable, would be

```
main()
{
   float a,b;
```

```
   float f1();
   scanf("%f%f", &a, &b);
   printf("%f", f1(a, b));
}

float f1(a, b)
float a, b;
{
   float c12;

   c12 = a*b;
   c12 /= 0.142;
   return c12;
}
```

Remember that it is always best to have as few global variables as possible, so it is important to find good candidates for local variables.

FINAL THOUGHTS ON TRANSLATING

Although translating programs can be the most tedious of all programming tasks, it is also one of the most common. A good approach is to understand the way the program you are translating works, and to learn to use it. Once you know how it operates, the program is easier to recode; you know whether your new version is working correctly. Also, when you know the program you are translating, the job becomes more interesting because it is not just a simple symbol-substitution process.

The next chapter includes a specialized case of translating. In this situation, you will be translating a C program that you wrote with one compiler into a program that will compile and run with a different C compiler. Although this sounds easy, it is often the hardest translating task of all.

11

EFFICIENCY, PORTING, AND DEBUGGING

The ability to write programs that use system resources efficiently, are error-free, and are easily transported to other computers is the mark of a professional programmer. It is also this ability that transforms computer science into the "art of computer science," because so few formal techniques are available to ensure success. This chapter presents some of the methods by which efficiency, program debugging, and portability may be achieved.

EFFICIENCY

When it pertains to a computer program, the term *efficiency* refers to the program's speed of execution, its use of system resources, or both. System resources include RAM, disk space, printer paper, and basically anything that can be allocated and used up. Whether or not a program is efficient is sometimes a subjective judgment—it depends on the situation. Consider a program that uses 47K of RAM to execute, 2 megabytes of disk space, and that has an average run time of 7 minutes. If this is a sort program running on an Apple II, then the program is probably not very efficient. However, if it is a weather-forecasting program running on a Cray Supercomputer, then the program is probably very efficient.

Another consideration when you are concerned with efficiency is that optimizing one aspect of a program will often degrade another. For example, making a program execute faster often means making it bigger if you use in-line code instead of function calls to speed up the calling sequence. Also, making more efficient use of disk space by compacting the data invariably makes disk access slower. These and other types of efficiency trade-offs can be frustrating—especially to the nonprogramming end-user, who cannot see why one thing should affect the other.

In light of these problems, you may wonder how efficiency can be discussed at all. Actually, there are some programming practices that are always efficient—or at least are more efficient than others. There are also a few techniques that make programs *both* faster and smaller.

The Increment and Decrement Operators

Discussions on the efficient use of C almost always start by considering the increment and decrement operators. Remember that the increment operator ++ increases its argument by one, and the decrement operator −− decreases its argument by one. The increment operator essentially replaces this type of assignment statement:

```
x = x+1;
```

and the decrement operator replaces assignment statements of this type:

```
x = x-1;
```

Besides the obvious advantage of reducing the number of key-strokes it takes to enter the statement, the increment and decrement operators have another glorious advantage: they execute faster and need less RAM than their statement counterparts on most microcomputer C compilers. This is because of the way object code is generated by the compiler. For example, if you use a simple, imaginary assembly language that approximates the assembly language found on most microprocessors, the statement

```
x=x+1;
```

will generate this sequence of code:

```
move A,x   ; load value of x from memory into
           ;   accumulator
move B,1   ; put 1 into B register
add B      ; add B to the accumulator
store x    ; store new value back in x
```

However, if you use the increment operator, the following code will be produced:

```
incr x   ; increment x
```

Here, three entire instructions have been eliminated, which means the code will execute faster and will be smaller.

Some C compilers automatically recognize such expressions as **x=x+1** and to produce better object code will output the code as if it had been written as **x++**. This process is called *optimizing*. However, you should not count on it very often, and if you have to port your code to a new computer using a different compiler, you should use the increment and decrement operators explicitly.

Pointers Versus Array Indexing

Another technique that almost always produces both smaller and faster code is substituting pointer arithmetic for array indexing. To help you understand why this could make a difference, take a look at the following two code fragments, which both do the same thing.

```
move B, stack-1  ; get value in temporary t
return  ; return to the calling routine
; calling routine then does the following
pop A    ; clear parameter used in the call
```

Using the **compute()** function inside the loop causes the calling and returning sequences to be executed 100 times. If you really want to write fast code, then using **compute()** inside a loop is not the right idea.

By now you may think that you should write a program that has just a few large functions so that it will run quickly. In the majority of cases, however, the slight time differential will not be meaningful, and the loss of structure will be acute. But there is another problem. Replacing functions that are used by several routines with in-line code will make your program very large, because the same code will be duplicated several times. Keep in mind that subroutines were invented primarily as a way to make efficient use of memory. A rule of thumb is that making a program faster means making it bigger, while making it smaller means making it slower.

Finally, it only makes sense to use in-line code instead of a function call when speed is of absolute priority. Otherwise, the liberal use of functions is definitely recommended.

Overdoing It

In some circles, C has gained a reputation for being a cryptic, hard-to-read language. This reputation is due entirely to overzealous programmers who confuse efficiency with the terseness of the program. Because C allows very complex expressions to be written in one line, which can sometimes make the program run a little faster, some C programs are hard to decipher. An intensely optimized program is sometimes necessary, but in most cases it gains little and greatly reduces the program's maintainability. In all cases, you should have a very good reason when you reduce the readability of your code.

PORTING PROGRAMS

It is common for a program written on one machine to be transported to another computer with a different processor, operating system, or both. This process is called *porting* and can be either very easy or extremely difficult, depending on the way the program was originally written. A program is *portable* if it can be easily ported. A program is not easily portable if it contains numerous *machine dependencies* — code fragments that will work only with one specific operating system or processor. C has been designed to allow portable code, but it still requires care, attention to detail, and often the sacrifice of maximum efficiency to actually achieve portable code. In this section you will examine a few specific problem areas and learn about some solutions.

Using #define

Perhaps the simplest way to make programs portable is to make *every* system- or processor-dependent "magic number" into a #**define** macro-substitution directive. These "magic numbers" include buffer sizes for disk accesses, special screen and keyboard commands, memory allocation information, and anything else that has even the slightest chance of changing when the program is ported. If you make the magic numbers into #**define** directives, these "defines" not only make the magic numbers obvious to the person doing the porting, but they also simplify editing; their values have to be changed only once instead of throughout the program.

For example, here are two functions that use **fread( )** and **fwrite( )** to access information in a disk file:

```
f1()
{
  fwrite(buf,128,1,fp);
}

f2()
{
  fread(buf,128,1,fp);
}
```

Array Indexing

```
for(;;) {
    a = array[t++];
    .
    .
    .
}
```

Pointer Arithmetic

```
p = array;
for(;;) {
    a = *(p++);
    .
    .
    .
}
```

With the pointer method, after **p** has been loaded with the address of **array**, perhaps in an index register (such as SI on the 8086 processor), only an increment must be performed each time the loop repeats. However, the array-index version forces the program to compute the array index based on the value of **t** for every pass through the loop. The disparity between pointer arithmetic and array indexing grows as multiple indexes are used: pointer arithmetic can use simple addition, whereas each index requires its own sequence of instructions.

However, as a precaution, you may want to use array indexes when the index is derived through a complex formula and when the use of pointer arithmetic would obscure the meaning of the program. It is usually better to degrade performance slightly than to sacrifice clarity.

Use of Functions

Always remember that the use of stand-alone functions with local variables forms the basis of structured programming. Functions are the building blocks of C programs, and they are one of C's strongest assets. Do not let anything that is discussed in this section be construed otherwise. Now that you have been warned, you should know a few aspects of C functions and their effects on the size and speed of your code.

First and foremost, C is a *stack-oriented language:* all local variables and parameters passed to functions use the stack for temporary storage. When a function is called, the return address of the calling routine is placed on the stack as well. This allows the subroutine to return to the location from which it was called.

When a function returns, this address—as well as all local variables and parameters—must be removed from the stack. The process of pushing this information onto the stack is generally referred to as the *calling sequence*, and the process of popping the information off of the stack is called the *returning sequence*. These sequences take time—sometimes quite a bit of time.

To understand how a function call can slow down your program, look at the two code examples shown here.

Version 1   **Version 2**

```
for(x=1;x<100;++x) {
        t=compute(x);
}

float compute(q)
int q;
{
        float t;

        t=abs(sin(q)/100/3.1416);
        return t;
}
```

```
for(x=1;x<100;++x) {
        t=abs(sin(x)/100/3.1416);
}
```

Although each loop performs the same function, Version 2 is much faster because the overhead of the calling and returning sequences has been eliminated by using in-line code. To understand just how much time is taken up, study the following pseudo-assembly code, which shows the calling and returning sequences for the function **compute( )**. The actual code used depends on how the compiler is implemented and what processor is being used. Although most compilers will have more complex sequences than shown here, they generally follow the pattern in this pseudocode example.

```
; Calling sequence
move A, x  ; put value of x into accumulator
push A
call compute  ; the call instruction places
              ; the return address on the stack
.
.
.
; Returning sequence
; The return value of the function must be placed
; into a register - we will use B.
```

The problem is that the number **128** is hard-coded into both **fread( )** and **fwrite( )**. This might be acceptable for one operating system but less than optimal for another. A better way to code it is shown here:

```
#define buf_size 128

f1()
{
   fwrite(buf,buf_size,1,fp);
}

f2()
{
   read(buf,buf_size,1,fp);
}
```

In this case, only the #**define** would have to change and all references to **buf_size** would be automatically corrected. This version not only is easier to change, it also avoids many editing errors. Remember that there will probably be many references to **buf_size** in a real program, so the gain in portability is often substantial.

Operating-System Dependencies

Virtually all commercial programs have code in them that is specific to the operating system. For example, a spreadsheet program might make use of the IBM PC's video memory to allow fast switching between screens, or a graphics package may use special graphics commands that are only applicable to that operating system. Some operating-system dependencies are necessary for fast, commercially viable programs. However, there is no reason to hard-code any more dependencies than necessary.

As suggested earlier, disk-file functions can sometimes contain implicit machine dependencies. The **read( )** and **write( )** functions found in the standard library, for example, can work with various buffer sizes, but an operating system may require an even multiple of some number to operate most efficiently. Therefore, a buffer size of 128 might be fine for CP/M 2.2 but is not optimal for MS-DOS. In this case the buffer size should be defined, as discussed earlier.

When you must use system calls to access the operating system, it is best to do them all through one master function so that you only have to change it to accommodate a new operating system and can leave the rest of the code intact. For example, if system calls were needed to clear the screen and the end-of-line, and to locate the cursor at an X,Y coordinate, then you would create a master function like **op—sys—call( )**, shown here:

```
void op_sys_call(op,x,y)
char op;
int x,y;
{
  switch(op) {
    case 1: clear_screen();
    break;
    case 2: clear_eol();
    break;
    case 3: goto_xy(x,y);
    break;
  }
}
```

Only the code that forms the actual functions would have to change, leaving a common interface intact.

DEBUGGING

To paraphrase Thomas Edison, programming is 10% inspiration and 90% debugging. Good programmers are usually good debuggers. Although you probably have good debugging skills, you should watch for certain types of bugs that can occur easily while you are using C.

Order-of-Process Errors

When the increment and decrement operators are used in programs written in C, the order in which the operations take place is affected by whether these operators precede or follow the variable. For example, the two statements

Version 1   **Version 2**

```
y = 10;              y = 10;

x = y++;             x = ++y;
```

are not the same. The first one assigns the value of 10 to **x** and then increments **y**. The second increments **y** to 11 and then assigns the value 11 to **x**. Therefore, in Version 1, **x** contains 10; in Version 2, **x** contains 11. The rule is that increment and decrement operations occur before other operations if they precede the operand; otherwise, they occur afterwards.

An order-of-process error usually occurs when changes are made to an existing statement. For example, you may enter the statement

```
x = *p++;
```

which assigns the value pointed to by **p** to **x** and then increments the pointer **p**. However, say that you decide later that **x** really needs the value pointed to by **p** times the value pointed to by **p**. To do this, you might rewrite the statement to

```
x = *p++ * (*p); /* WRONG */
```

However, this version doesn't work, because **p** has already been incremented. The proper solution is to write

```
x = *p * (*p++);
```

Errors like this can be hard to find. There may be clues, such as loops that don't run correctly or routines that are off by one. If you have any doubt about a statement, recode it in a way that you have confidence in.

Pointer Problems

A common error in C programs is the misuse of pointers. Pointer problems fall into two general categories: misunderstanding of indirection and the pointer operators, and the accidental use of invalid pointers. To solve the first type of problem, you must understand the C language; to solve the second, you must always verify the validity of a pointer before you use it.

The following program illustrates a typical pointer error that C programmers make:

```
#include "stdlib.h"

main()   /* this program is WRONG */
{
  char *p;

  *p = (char *) malloc(100); /* this line is wrong */

  gets(p);
  printf(p);

}
```

This program will most likely crash, probably taking with it the operating system. It will crash because the address returned by **malloc()** was *not* assigned to **p**, but to the memory location pointed to by **p**, which is completely unknown in this case. To correct this program, you must substitute

```
p = (char *) malloc(100); /* this is correct */
```

for the incorrect line.

The program has a second and more insidious error: there is no run-time check on the address returned by **malloc()**. Remember, if memory is exhausted, **malloc()** will return 0, which is never a valid pointer in C. The malfunction caused by this type of bug is difficult to find because it occurs rarely, only when an allocation request fails. Prevention is the best way to deal with this. Here is a corrected version of the program, which now includes a check for pointer validity:

```
#include "stdlib.h"

main()   /* this program is now correct */
{
  char *p;

  p = (char *) malloc(100); /* this is correct */

  if(!p) {
    printf("out of memory\n");
    exit(1);
  }

  gets(p);
  printf(p);
}
```

"Wild" pointers are extremely difficult to track down. If you are making assignments to a pointer variable that does not contain a valid pointer address, your program may appear to function correctly sometimes but crash at other times. Statistically, the smaller your program, the more likely it will run correctly even with a stray pointer, because very little memory is in use. As your program grows, failures become more common, but as you try to debug you will be thinking about recent additions or changes to your program, not about pointer errors. Hence, you will probably look in the wrong spot for the bug.

One indication of a pointer problem is that errors tend to be erratic. Your program may work right one time and wrong another. Sometimes other variables will contain garbage for no explainable reason. If these problems occur, check your pointers. As a matter of procedure, you should check all pointers when bugs begin to occur.

Although pointers can be troublesome, they are also one of the most powerful and useful aspects of the C language, and they are worth whatever trouble they may cause. Make the effort early on to learn to use them correctly.

One final point to remember about pointers is that you must initialize them before they are used. This seems simple enough, but many excellent C programmers still fall into this trap occasionally. For example, the following code fragment will be a disaster because you don't know where x is pointing:

```
int *x;

*x = 100; /* WRONG */
```

Assigning a value to that unknown location will probably destroy something of value—perhaps other code or data for your program.

Redefining Functions

You can—but should not—call your functions by the same names as those in the C standard library. Most compilers will use your function over the one in the library, causing direct and indirect problems.

Here is an example of an indirect problem caused by redefining a library function:

```
char text[1000];

main()
{
  int x;

  scanf("%d",&x);
  .
  .
  .
}

getc(p)   /* return char from array */
{
  return text[p];
}
.
.
.
```

This program will not work correctly with many compilers because **scanf()**, a standard C function, will probably call **get()**, another standard C function, which has been redefined in the program. This problem can be difficult to find because you will have no clue that you have created a side effect. It will simply seem that **scanf()** is not working correctly.

The only way to avoid such problems is never to give a function you have written the same name as one in the standard library. If you are not sure, append your initials to the start of the name, as in **hsgetc()** instead of **getc()**.

Bizarre Syntax Errors

Occasionally you will see a syntax error that you cannot understand or even recognize as an error. The C compiler itself may
sometimes have a bug that causes it to report false errors. The
only solution is to redesign your code. Other unusual errors
simply require some backtracking to find.

One particularly unsettling error will occur when you try to
compile this code:

```
main()
{
   char *p, *myfunc();   /* myfunc() is supposed to return
                            char pointer */
                .
                .
                .
}

myfunc()                 /* by default, myfunc() returns an int */

{
                .
                .
                .
}
```

Most compilers will issue an error message such as **function
redefined** and point to **myfunc()**. How can this be? There are not
two **myfunc()**s. The answer is that you have declared **myfunc()**
to be returning a character pointer inside **main()**. This declaration causes a symbol-table entry to be made with that information.
When the compiler encounters **myfunc()** later in the program,
there is no indication that **myfunc()** will return anything other
than an integer, the default type. Hence, you have "redefined" the
function. The correct program would be as follows:

```
main()
{
   char *p, *myfunc();   /* myfunc() is supposed to return
                            char pointer */
                .
                .
                .
}
```

```
char *myfunc()          /* myfunc() now defined to return
                           char pointer */
{
            .
            .
            .
}
```

This code will generate another syntax error that is difficult to understand:

```
main() /* this program has a syntax error in it */
{
  func1();
}

func1();
{
  printf("this is func1 \n");
}
```

The error here is the semicolon after the declaration of **func1()**. The compiler will see it as a statement outside of any function, which is an error; however, compilers will report this error in different ways. Many compilers will issue an error message such as **bad declaration syntax** while pointing at the first open brace after **func1()**. Because you are used to seeing semicolons after statements, you may find it difficult to see where this error message is coming from.

"One Off" Errors

By now you know that all C indexes start at 0. A common error involves using a **for** loop to access the elements of an array. Consider the following program, which is supposed to initialize an array of 100 integers:

```
main()  /* this program will not work */
{

  int x, num[100];

  for(x=1; x<=100; ++x) num[x]=x; /* indexing off by one */
}
```

The **for** loop in this program is wrong for two reasons. First, it does not initialize **num[0]**, the first element of array **num**. Second, it goes one past the end of the array; **num[99]** is the last element in the array and the loop runs to 100. The correct way to write this program is

```
main()   /* this is right */
{
   int x, num[100];

   for(x=0; x<100; ++x) num[x]=x;
}
```

Remember, an array of 100 has elements 0 through 99.

Boundary Errors

The C language and many standard library functions have very little or no run-time boundary checking. For example, it is possible to overwrite arrays, disk files, and (through pointer assignments) variables. These things usually do not occur, but when they do, it can be very difficult to link the symptom to its cause.

For example, this program is supposed to read a string from the keyboard and display it on the screen:

```
#include "stdio.h"
main()
{
   int var1;
   char s[10];
   int var2;

   var1 = 10;  var2 = 10;
   get_string(s);
   printf("%s %d %s", s, var1, var2);
}

get_string(string)
char *string;
{
   register int t;

   printf("enter twenty characters\n");
   for(t=0; t<20; ++t) {
     *string++ = getchar();
   }
}
```

Here there are no direct coding errors. However, an indirect error arises when **get_string( )** is called with **s**. The **s** is declared to be 10 characters long, but **get_string( )** will read 20 characters, causing **s** to be overwritten.

The actual problem is that while **s** may display all 20 characters correctly, either **var1** or **var2** will not contain the correct value. All C compilers must allocate a region of memory—usually the stack region—for local variables. The variables **var1**, **var2**, and **s** will be located in memory as shown in Figure 11-1.

Your C compiler may exchange the order of **var1** and **var2**, but they will still bracket **s**. When **s** is overwritten, the additional information is placed into the area that is reserved for **var2**, destroying any previous contents. Therefore, instead of printing the number 10 for both integer variables, the program will display something else for the one destroyed by the overrun of **s**. This will cause you to look for the problem in the wrong place.

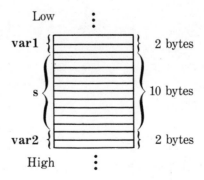

Figure 11-1.   The variables **var1**, **var2**, and **s** in memory

Function Declaration
Omissions

Any time a function returns a value type other than integer, the function must be declared to do this inside any other function that uses it. For example, this program multiplies two floating-point numbers together:

```
main() /* this is wrong */
{
   float x, y;

   scanf("%f%f", &x, &y);
   printf("%f", mul(x, y));

}

float mul(a, b)
float a, b;
{
   return a*b;
}
```

Although **main()** expects an integer value from **mul()**, **mul()** returns a floating-point number. You will get meaningless answers, because **main()** will only copy two bytes out of the eight needed for a **float**.

To correct this program, declare **mul()** in **main()** as shown:

```
main() /* this is right */
{
   float x, y, mul(); /* declare mul() */

   scanf("%f%f", &x, &y);
   printf("%f", mul(x, y));

}

float mul(a, b)
float a, b;
{
   return a*b;
}
```

Adding **mul()** to the **float** declaration list tells **main()** it should expect a floating-point value to be returned from **mul()**.

Function-argument type mismatches can be avoided by using function prototypes if you have an ANSI standard compiler. (Function prototypes are discussed in Appendix A.)

Calling-Argument Errors

You must be sure to match whatever type of argument a function expects with the type you give it. For example, remember that **scanf( )** expects to receive the *address* of its arguments, not the value. This means that you must call **scanf( )** with arguments by using the **&** operator. The following code is wrong:

```
int x;
char string[10];

scanf("%d%s", x, string); /* WRONG */
```

This code is correct:

```
int x;
char string[10];
scanf("%d%s", &x, string);
```

Remember, strings already pass their addresses to functions, so you should not use the **&** operator on them.

Another common error is to forget that C functions cannot modify their arguments. If it is necessary to modify an argument to a function, you must pass the address of the argument to the function and use pointer references to access the argument.

If a function's formal parameters are of type **float**, then you must pass floating-point variables to the function. For example, the following program will not function correctly:

```
main() /* this program is wrong */
{
  int x, y;
```

```
    scanf("%d%d", x, y);
    printf("%d", div(x, y));
}

float div(a, b)
float a, b;
{
    return a/b;
}
```

You cannot use a floating-point function such as **div( )** to return an integer value, and you cannot expect **div( )** to operate correctly — it expects floating-point numbers, not integers. You should remember that a cast can always be used to change one type to another if necessary. Again, using function prototypes will cause the compiler to check for this type of error.

General Debugging Theory

Everyone has a different approach to programming and debugging. However, some techniques have proved to be better than others. In the case of debugging, incremental testing is considered to be the least costly and most time-effective method, even though it can appear to slow the development process.

Incremental testing is simply the process of always having working code. As soon as it is possible to run a piece of your program, you should do so, testing that section completely. As you add to your program, continue to test the new sections as well as the way they connect to the established operational code. In this way you can be sure that any possible bugs are concentrated into a small area of code.

Incremental testing theory is generally based on probability and areas. As you know, *area* is a squared dimension. Each time you add length, you add area. Therefore, as your program grows, there is an n-squared area in which you must search for bugs. While debugging, you as a programmer want the smallest possible area to deal with. Through incremental testing you can subtract the area already tested from the total area, thereby reducing the region that may contain a bug.

FINAL THOUGHTS

Throughout this book, various algorithms and techniques have been discussed, some in considerable detail. Remember that computer science is both a theoretical and an empirical science. Although it is fairly easy to see why one algorithm is better than another, it is difficult to say what makes a successful program. When it comes to debugging, efficiency, and portability, experimenting will sometimes yield information more easily than would theoretical musing.

Programming is both a science and an art. It is a science because you must know logic and understand how and why algorithms work; it is an art because you create the total entity that is a program. As a programmer, you really have one of the best jobs on earth—you walk the line between art and science, and get the best of both.

A

A REVIEW OF C

This appendix serves as an aid to the inexperienced C programmer by clarifying aspects of the language. As such, it is a reference guide and not a tutorial.

THE ORIGINS OF C

The C language was invented and first implemented by Dennis Ritchie on a DEC PDP-11 using the UNIX operating system. The C language is the result of a development process that started with an older language called BCPL, which is still in use primarily in Europe. BCPL, developed by Martin Richards, influenced a language called B, which was invented by Ken Thompson and which led to the development of C.

For many years, the *de facto* standard for C was the one supplied with the UNIX Version 5 operating system and described in *The C Programming Language* written by Brian Kernighan and Dennis Ritchie (Englewood Cliffs: Prentice-Hall, Inc., 1978). As the popularity of microcomputers increased, a great number of C implementations were created. Most of these implementations were highly compatible with each other on the source-code level. However, because no standard existed, discrepancies did exist.

To correct this situation, a committee was established in the summer of 1983 to begin work on the creation of an ANSI standard that would finally define the C language. As of this writing, the proposed standard is almost complete and its adoption by ANSI is expected soon.

C AS A STRUCTURED LANGUAGE

C is commonly considered to be a structured language, with some similarities to ALGOL and Pascal. Although the term block-structured language does not strictly apply to C in an academic sense, C is informally part of that language group. The distinguishing feature of a block-structured language is *compartmentalization of code and data*. This means the language can section off and hide from the rest of the program all information and instructions necessary to perform a specific task. Generally, compartmentalization is achieved by subroutines with local variables, which are temporary. In this way, it is possible to write subroutines so that the events occurring within them cause no side effects in other parts of the program. Excessive use of global variables (variables known throughout the entire program) may allow bugs to creep into a program by allowing unwanted side effects. In C, all subroutines are discrete functions.

Functions are the building blocks of C in which all program activity occurs. They allow specific tasks in a program to be defined and coded separately. After debugging a function that uses only local variables, you can rely on the function to work properly in various situations without creating side effects in other parts of the program. All variables declared in that particular function will be known only to that function.

In C, using blocks of code also creates program structure. A *block of code* is a logically connected group of program statements that can be treated as a unit. It is created by placing lines of code between opening and closing curly braces, as shown here:

```
if(x<10) {
   printf("Invalid input - retry");
   done = 0;
}
```

In this example, the two statements after the **if** between curly braces are both executed if **x** is less than 10. These two statements together with the braces represent a block of code. They are linked together: one of the statements cannot execute without the other also executing. In C, every statement can be either a single statement or a block of statements. The use of code blocks creates readable programs with logic that is easy to follow.

C is a programmer's language. Unlike most high-level computer languages, C imposes few restrictions on what you can do with it. By using C a programmer can avoid assembly code in all but the most demanding situations. In fact, one motive for the invention of C was to provide an alternative to assembly language programming.

Assembly language uses a symbolic representation of the actual binary code that the computer directly executes. Each assembly language operation maps into a single operation for the computer to perform. Although assembly language gives programmers the potential for accomplishing tasks with maximum flexibility and efficiency, it is notoriously difficult to work with when developing and debugging a program. Furthermore, since assembly language is unstructured by nature, the final program tends to be "spaghetti code," a tangle of jumps, calls, and indexes. This makes assembly language programs difficult to read, enhance, and maintain.

Initially, C was used for systems programming. A *systems program* is part of a large class of programs that form a portion of the operating system of the computer or its support utilities. For example, the following are commonly called systems programs:

- Operating systems
- Interpreters
- Editors
- Assemblers
- Compilers
- Database managers

As C grew in popularity, many programmers began to use C to program all tasks because of its portability and efficiency. Since there are C compilers for virtually all computers, it is easy to take code written for one machine and then compile and run it on another machine with few or no changes. This portability saves both time and money. C compilers also tend to produce tight, fast object code—faster and smaller than most BASIC compilers, for example.

Perhaps the real reason that C is used in all types of programming tasks is because programmers like it. C has the speed of assembler and the extensibility of FORTH, while having few of the restrictions of Pascal. A C programmer can create and maintain a unique library of functions that have been tailored to his or her own personality. Because C allows—and indeed encourages—separate compilation, large projects are easily managed.

A REVIEW OF C

As defined by the proposed ANSI standard, the 32 keywords shown in Table A-1, combined with the formal C syntax, form the C programming language.

In addition to these keywords, several C compilers designed for use on the 8086 family of processors or multilanguage programming environments have added the following to allow greater control over the way memory and other system resources are used:

_cs	_ds	_es	_ss
cdecl	far	huge	interrupt
near	pascal		

All C keywords are in lowercase letters. In C, uppercase or lowercase makes a difference; that is, **else** is a keyword, ELSE is not.

VARIABLES—TYPES AND DECLARATION

C has five built-in data types, as shown in Table A-2. With the exception of **void**, all of these data types may be modified through the use of the C type modifiers:

signed
unsigned
short
long

Variable names are strings of letters from one to several characters in length. The ANSI standard states that at least six characters will be significant. For clarity, the underscore may also be used as part of the variable name (for example, **first_time**). Remember that in C, uppercase and lowercase are different—**test** and **TEST** will be two different variables.

All variables must be declared prior to use. The general form of the declaration is

type **variable_name;**

Table A-1.   List of Keywords

auto	double	int	struct
break	else	long	switch
case	enum	register	typedef
char	extern	return	union
const	float	short	unsigned
continue	for	signed	void
default	goto	sizeof	volatile
do	if	static	while

Table A-2.   Data Types and C Keyword Equivalents

Data Type	C Keyword Equivalent
character	**char**
integer	**int**
floating point	**float**
double floating point	**double**
value-less	**void**

For example, to declare **x** to be a float, **y** to be an integer, and **ch** to be a character, you would type

```
float x;
int y;
char ch;
```

In addition to the built-in types, you can create combinations of built-in types by using **struct** and **union**. You can also create new names for variable types by using **typedef**.

A *structure* is a collection of variables grouped and referenced under one name. The general form of a structure declaration is

> **struct struct—name** {
>   *element 1;*
>   *element 2;*
>   .
>   .
>   .
>   *element N;*
> } **struct—variable;**

As an example, the following structure has two elements: **name**, a character array, and **balance**, a floating-point number:

```
struct client {
  char name[80];
  float balance;
};
```

To reference individual structure elements, the dot operator is used if the structure is global or declared in the function referencing it. The arrow operator is used in all other cases.

When two or more variables share the same memory, a **union** is defined. The general form for a **union** is

union union—name {
   element 1;
   element 2;
   .
   .
   .
   element N;
 } **union—variable;**

The elements of a **union** overlay each other. For example, the following declares a **union t** that looks like Figure A-1 in memory:

```
union tom {
  char ch;
  int x;
} t;
```

The individual variables that comprise the **union** are referenced using the dot operator. The arrow operator is used with pointers to unions.

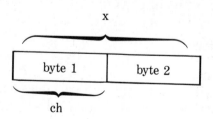

Figure A-1. The **union t** in memory

Another type of variable that can be created, called an *enumeration*, is a list of objects or values (depending upon how you interpret it). An *enumeration type* is a specification of the list of objects that belong to the enumeration. When a variable is declared to be of an enumeration type, then its only values may be those defined by the enumeration.

To create an enumeration, you must use the keyword **enum**. For example, the following short program defines an enumeration of cities called **cities**, and the variable **c** of type **cities**. Finally, the program assigns **c** the value "Houston."

```
enum cities {Houston, Austin, Amarillo };
enum cities c;

main()
{
   c=Houston;
}
```

The general form of an enumeration type is

enum *name* { *list of values* };

The Storage-Class Type Modifiers

The type modifiers **extern**, **auto**, **register**, **const**, **volatile**, and **static** are used to alter the way C creates storage for the variables that follow.

If the **extern** modifier is placed before a variable name, the compiler knows that the variable has been declared elsewhere. The **extern** modifier is most commonly used when two or more files share the same global variables.

An **auto** variable is created upon entry into a block and is destroyed upon exit. For example, all variables defined inside a function are **auto** by default. Although seldom used, **auto** variables can be valuable in specialized or dedicated systems where RAM is in short supply.

The **register** modifier can only be used on local integer or character variables. This modifier causes the compiler to attempt to keep that value in a register of the CPU instead of being placed in memory, which makes all references to that variable extremely fast. Throughout this book, **register** variables were used for loop control. For example, the following function uses a **register** loop control:

```
f1()
{

  register int t;
  for(t=0;t<10000;++t) {
     .
     .
     .
  }
}
```

Variables of type **const** may not be changed during your program's execution. The compiler is free to place variables of this type into ROM. For example, the following line

```
const int a;
```

creates an integer called **a** that cannot be modified by your program, but can be used in other types of expressions. A **const** variable recieves its value either from an explicit initialization or by some hardware-dependent means. The inclusion of *const* type variables aids in the development of applications for ROM.

The **volatile** modifier tells the compiler that a variable's value may be changed in ways not explicitly specified by the program. For example, a global variable's address may be passed to the clock routine of the operating system and used to hold the real time of the system. In this situation, the contents of the variable are altered without any explicit assignment statements in the program. In order to achieve higher performance, some C compilers automatically optimize certain expressions by assuming that the contents of a variable are unchanged inside that expression. The **volatile** modifier prevents this optimization in those rare instances where this is not true.

You can add the **static** modifier to any of the previously mentioned variables. The **static** modifier instructs the C compiler to keep a local variable in existence during the lifetime of the program, instead of creating and destroying it. Remember that the values of local variables are discarded when a function finishes and returns. Using **static** causes their values to be maintained between function calls.

Addressing Type Modifiers

Several C compilers designed for the 8086 processor family have added the following modifiers that may be applied to pointers so that you can explicitly control—and override—the default addressing mode used to compile your program:

    _cs _ds _es _ss
    far   near huge

These modifiers are discussed in Chapter 4.

Arrays

You can declare arrays on any of the previously mentioned data types. For example, to declare an integer array **x** of 100 elements, you write

```
int x[100];
```

This creates an array that is 100 elements long with the first element being 0 and the last being 99. For example, the following loop loads the numbers 0 through 99 into array **x**:

```
for(t=0;t<100; t++) x[t]=t;
```

Multidimensional arrays are declared by placing the additional dimensions inside additional brackets. For example, to declare a 10 × 20 integer array, you write

```
int x[10][20];
```

OPERATORS

C has a rich set of operators that can be divided into the following classes: *arithmetic, relational and logical, bitwise, pointer, assignment,* and *miscellaneous.*

Arithmetic Operators

C has the seven arithmetic operators shown in Table A-3.
  The precedence of these operators is

Highest	++ –– – (unary minus)
	* / %
Lowest	+ –

Operators on the same precedence level are evaluated left to right.

Table A-3. Arithmetic Operators

Operator	Action
–	Subtraction, unary minus
+	Addition
*	Multiplication
/	Division
%	Modulo division
––	Decrement
++	Increment

Table A-4.   Relational and Logical Operators

Relational Operators

Operator	Meaning
>	Greater than
>=	Greater than or equal
<	Less than
<=	Less than or equal
==	Equal
!=	Not equal

Logical Operators

Operator	Meaning
&&	AND
||	OR
!	NOT

Relational and Logical Operators

Relational and logical operators are used to produce TRUE/FALSE results and are often used together. In C, any nonzero number evaluates TRUE; however, a C relational or logical expression produces the number 1 for TRUE and 0 for FALSE. The relational and logical operators are shown in Table A-4.

The precedence of these operators is

Highest	!
	> >= < <=
	== !=
	&&
Lowest	||

For example, the following expression evaluates TRUE:

```
(100<200) && 10
```

Bitwise Operators

Unlike most other programming languages, C provides bitwise operators that manipulate the actual bits inside a variable. The bitwise operators can only be used on integers or characters. They are shown in Table A-5.

The truth tables for AND, OR, and XOR are as follows:

```
&|0|1
0|0|0
1|0|1
```

```
||0|1
0|0|1
1|1|1
```

```
^|0|1
0|0|1
1|1|0
```

Table A-5.   Bitwise Operators

Operator	Meaning
&	AND
|	OR
^	XOR
~	One's complement
>>	Right shift
<<	Left shift

These rules are applied to each bit in a byte when the bitwise AND, OR, and XOR operators are performed. For example,

```
  0 1 0 0    1 1 0 1
& 0 0 1 1    1 0 1 1
  ─────────────────
  0 0 0 0    1 0 0 1


  0 1 0 0    1 1 0 1
¦ 0 0 1 1    1 0 1 1
  ─────────────────
  0 1 1 1    1 1 1 1


  0 1 0 0    1 1 0 1
^ 0 0 1 1    1 0 1 1
  ─────────────────
  0 1 1 1    0 1 1 0
```

In a program you use the &, ¦ and $^\wedge$ like any other operator, as shown here:

```
main()
{
  char x,y,z;

  x = 1; y = 2; z = 4;

  x = x & y;   /* x now equals zero */

  y = x ¦ z;   /* y now equals 4 */

}
```

The one's complement operator (~) inverts all the bits in a byte. For example, if the character variable **ch** has the bit pattern

```
0  0  1  1   1  0  0  1
```

then

```
ch=~ch;
```

places the bit pattern

1 1 0 0   0 1 1 0

into **ch**.

The right shift and left shift operators move all bits in a byte or a word right or left by some specified number of bits. As bits are shifted, zeros are brought in. The number on the right side of the shift operator specifies the number of positions to shift. The general forms of the shift operators are

variable >> number of bit positions
variable << number of bit positions

For example, given the bit pattern

0 0 1 1   1 1 0 1

a shift right yields

0 0 0 1   1 1 1 0

while a single shift left produces

0 1 1 1   1 0 1 0

A shift right is effectively a division by 2 and a shift left is a multiplication by 2. The following code fragment will first multiply and then divide the value in **x** by 2:

```
int x;
x=10;
x=x<<1;
x=x>>1;
```

Because of the way negative numbers are represented inside the machine, you must be careful when you try to use a shift for multiplication or division. Moving a 1 into the most significant bit position causes the computer to think that the number is a negative number.

Remember: the bitwise operators are used to modify the value of a variable—they differ from the logical and relational operators, which produce a TRUE or FALSE result.

The precedence of the bitwise operators is as follows:

Highest   ~

                        >> <<

                        &

                        ^

Lowest |

Pointer Operators

Pointer operators are important in C: not only do they allow strings and arrays to be passed to functions, but they also allow C functions to modify their calling arguments. The two pointer operators are & and *. (Unfortunately, these operators use the same symbols as the multiply and bitwise AND, which are completely unrelated to them.)

The & operator returns the address of the variable it precedes. For example, if the integer **x** is located at memory address 1000, then

```
y = &x;
```

places the value 1000 into **y**. The & can be read as "the address of." For example, the previous statement could be read as "Place the address of **x** into **y**."

The * operator takes the value of the variable it precedes and uses that value as the address of the information in memory. For example,

```
y = &x;
*y = 100;
```

places the value 100 into **x**. The * can be read as "at address." In this example, it could be read as, "Place the value 100 at address **y**." The * operator can also be used on the right-hand side of an assignment. For example,

```
y = &x;
*y = 100;
z = *y/10;
```

places the value of 10 into **z**.

These operators are called pointer operators because they are designed to work on *pointer variables*. A pointer variable holds the address of another variable; in essence, it "points" to that variable as shown in Figure A-2.

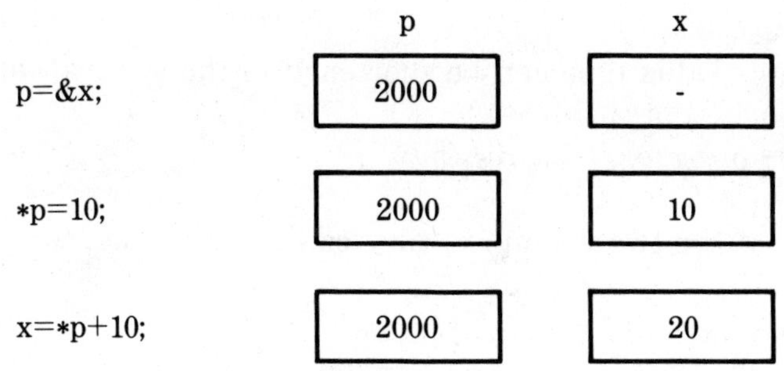

	p	x
p=&x;	2000	-
*p=10;	2000	10
x=*p+10;	2000	20

Figure A-2.   Pointer operations for character pointer **p** and integer **x**, with **x** at memory location 2000

Pointers of Type void

A pointer of type **void** is a generic pointer and can be used to point to any type of object. This implies that a pointer of any type can be assigned to pointers of type **void** (and vice versa) if you use the appropriate type casts. To declare a **void** pointer you use a declaration similar to the following:

```
void *p;
```

The **void** pointer is particularly useful when various types of pointers are manipulated by a single routine.

Assignment Operators

In C, the assignment operator is the single equal sign. However, C allows a convenient "shorthand" for assignments of the general type

variable1 = variable1 operator expression;

For example,

x = x+10;
y = y/z;

Assignments of this type can be shortened to the general form

variable1 operator = expression;

In the case of the two examples, they can be shortened to

x += 10;
y /= z;

The shorthand notation is used often in C programs written by experienced C programmers, so you should become used to it.

The ? Operator

The ? operator is a ternary operator (that is, it takes three operands). It is used to replace **if** statements of the general type

> **if** *expression1* **then** x=*expression2*
>   **else** x=*expression3*

The general form of the ? operator is

> *variable* = *expression1* ? *expression2* : *expression3*;

If *expression1* is TRUE, then the value of *expression2* is assigned to *variable*; otherwise, *variable* is assigned the value of *expression3*. For example,

```
x = (y<10) ? 20 : 40;
```

assigns to **x** either the value of 20 if **y** is less than 10 or the value of 40 if **y** is not.

The ? operator exists because a C compiler can produce very efficient code for this statement—much faster than the equivalent **if/else** statement.

Miscellaneous Operators

The . (dot) operator and the → (arrow) operator are used to reference individual elements of structures and unions. The dot operator is used on the structure or union itself. The arrow operator is used when only a pointer to a structure or a union is available. For example, consider the following global structure:

```
struct date_time {
  char date[16];
  int time;
} tm;
```

To assign the value "3/12/88" to element **date** of structure **tm**, you would write

```
strcpy(tm.date, "3/12/88");
```

The , (comma) operator is used mostly in the **for** statement. It causes a sequence of operations to be performed. When it is used on the right side of an assignment statement, the value of the entire expression is the value of the last expression of the comma-separated list. For example, consider the following:

```
y=10;

x = (y=y-5,25/y);
```

After execution, **x** has the value 5 because the original value of **y** (10) is reduced by 5, and then that value is divided into 25, yielding a result of 5.

Although **sizeof** is also considered a keyword, it is a compile-time operator used to determine the size of a data type in bytes, including user-defined structures and unions. For example,

```
int x;

printf("%d", sizeof(x));
```

prints the number 2.

Parentheses are considered operators that increase the precedence of the operations inside of them. Square brackets perform array indexing.

A *cast* is a special operator that forces the conversion of one data type into another. The general form is

(*type*) *variable*

For example, for the integer **count** to be used in a call to **sqrt( )**, which is the square root routine in C's standard library and requires a floating-point parameter, a cast forces **count** to be treated as type **float**:

```
float y;
int count;

count = 10;

y = sqrt((float)count);
```

Figure A-3 lists the precedence of all C operators. Note that all operators—except the unary operators and ?—associate from left to right. The unary operators (*, &, −, and ?) associate from right to left.

FUNCTIONS

A C program is a collection of one or more user-defined functions. One of the functions must be **main()** because execution begins at

---

Highest () □ → .

     ! ~ ++ −− − (type) * & size of

     * / %

     + −

     < <   > >

     < <= > >=

     == !=

     &

     ^

     |

     &&

     ||

     ?:

     = += −= *= /= %= >>= <<= &= ^= |=

Lowest ,

Figure A-3.   Precedence of C operators

this function. Historically, **main( )** is usually the first function in a program; however, it could go anywhere.

The general form of a C function is

type function__name(*parameter list*)
parameter declaration
{
   body of function
}

If the function has no parameters, no parameter declaration is needed. The type declaration is optional. If no explicit type declaration is present, the function defaults to integer. All functions terminate and return to the calling procedure automatically when the last brace is encountered. You may force return prior to that using the **return** statement.

Except those declared as **void**, all functions return a value. The type of the return value must match the type declaration of the function. If no explicit type declaration has been made, then the return value is defaulted to integer. If a **return** statement is part of the function, then the value of the function is the value in the **return** statement. If no **return** is present, then the function returns 0. For example,

```
f1()
{
  int x;

  x = 100;
  return(x/10);
}
```

returns the value 10, whereas

```
f2()
{
  int x;

  x = 100;
  x = x/10;
}
```

returns the value 0 because no explicit **return** statement is encountered.

If a function is going to return a value other than an integer, then its type must reflect this fact. Also, it will be necessary to declare the function prior to any reference to it by another piece of code. This can best be accomplished by making a function declaration in the global definition area of the program. The following example shows how the function **fn()** is declared to return a floating-point value:

```
float fn();

main()
{
   .
   .
   .
   printf("%f", fn());
   .
   .
   .
}

float fn()
{
   return 12.23;
}
```

Because all functions, except those declared as **void**, have values, they may be used in any arithmetic statement. For example, beginning C programmers tend to write code like this:

```
x = sqrt(y);

z = sin(x);
```

whereas a more experienced programmer would write:

```
z = sin(sqrt(y));
```

Remember that in order for the program to determine the value of a function, it must be executed. This means that the following code reads keystrokes from the keyboard until a "u" is typed:

```
while((ch=getche())!='u') ;
```

This code works because **getche()** must be executed to determine its value, which is the character typed at the keyboard.

The Scope and Lifetime of Variables

C has two general classes of variables: global and local. A global variable is available for use by all functions in the program, while a local variable is known and used only by the function in which it was declared. In some C literature, global variables are referred to as *external variables* and local variables are called *dynamic* or *automatic variables*. This appendix uses the terms *global* and *local* because they are more commonplace.

A global variable must be declared outside of all functions, including the **main()** function. Global variables are usually placed at the top of the file before **main()**, because this makes the program easier to read and because a variable must be declared before it is used. A local variable is declared inside a function after the function's opening brace. For example, the following program declares one global variable, **x**, and two local variables, **x** and **y**:

```
int x;
main()
{
  int y;

  y = get_value();
  x = 100;
  printf("%d %d", x, x*y);
}

f1()
{
  int x;

  scanf("%d", &x);
  return x;
}
```

This program multiplies the number entered from the keyboard by 100. Note that the local variable **x** in **f1( )** has no relationship to the global variable **x**, because local variables that have the same name as global variables always take precedence over the global ones.

Global variables exist during the entire program. Local variables are created when the function is entered and are destroyed when the function is exited. This means that local variables do not keep their values between function calls. You can use the **static** modifier, however, to preserve values between calls.

The formal parameters to a function are also local variables, and except for receiving the value of the calling arguments, they behave and can be used like any other local variable.

The main( ) Function

As previously mentioned, all C programs must have a **main( )** function. When execution begins, **main( )** is the first function called. You must not have more than one function called **main( )**. When **main( )** terminates, the program is over and control passes back to the operating system.

The only parameters that **main( )** is allowed to have are **argc** and **argv**. The variable **argc** holds the number of command-line arguments. The variable **argv** holds a character pointer to those arguments. *Command-line arguments* are the information that you type in after the program name when you execute a program. For example, when you compile a C program, you type something like

CC MYPROG.C

where **MYPROG.C** is the name of the program you wish to compile.

The value of **argc** is always at least 1, because C considers the program name to be the first argument. The variable **argv** must be declared as an array of character pointers. This is shown in the following short program, which prints your name on the screen.

```
main(argc, argv)
int argc;
char *argv[];
{
    if(argc<2)
      printf("enter your name on the command line.\n");
    else
      printf("hello %s\n",argv[1]);
}
```

Notice that **argv** is declared as a character pointer array of unknown size. The C compiler automatically determines the size of the array that is necessary to handle all of the command-line arguments.

Command-line arguments give your programs a professional look and feel, as well as allowing the programs to be placed into a batch file for automatic usage.

STATEMENT SUMMARY

This section is a brief synopsis of the keywords in C. The memory model keywords (**far, near, huge, _es, _ds, _ss,** and **_cs**) are discussed in Chapter 4.

auto

The **auto** keyword creates temporary variables that are created upon entry into a block and are destroyed upon exit. For example, in

```
main()
{
  for(;;) {
    if(getche()=='a') {
      auto int t;
      for(t=0; t<'a'; t++)
        printf("%d ", t);
    }
  }
}
```

the variable **t** is created only if you type an "a." Outside of the **if** block, **t** is completely unknown and any reference to it generates a compile-time syntax error.

break

The **break** keyword is used to exit from a **do**, **for**, or **while** loop, bypassing the normal loop condition. It is also used to exit from a **switch** statement.

The following is an example of **break** in a loop:

```
while(x<100) {
  x = get_new_x();
  if(keystroke()) break;  /* key hit on
                             keyboard */
  process(x);

}
```

In this example, if a key is pressed, the loop terminates no matter what the value of **x** is.

A **break** always terminates the innermost **for**, **do**, **while**, or **switch** statement, regardless of the way these might be nested. In a **switch** statement, **break** effectively keeps program execution from "falling through" to the next **case**. (Refer to the discussion on **switch** for details.)

case

Refer to the discussion on **switch**.

cdecl

The **cdecl** keyword is not part of the ANSI standard. It forces C to compile a function so that its parameter passing conforms with the standard C calling convention. You only use **cdecl** when compiling an entire file while using the Pascal option and when you want a specific function to be compatible with C.

const

The **const** modifier tells the compiler that the variable that follows may not be modified.

char

The **char** data type declares character variables. For example, to declare **ch** to be character type, you write

```
char ch;
```

continue

The **continue** keyword is used to bypass portions of code in a loop and force the conditional test to be performed. For example, the following **while** loop simply reads characters from the keyboard until an "s" is typed:

```
while(ch=getche()) {
  if(ch!='s') continue;   /* read another char */
  process(ch);
}
```

The call to **process( )** will not occur until **ch** contains the character "s".

default

The **default** keyword is used in the **switch** statement to signal a default block of code to be executed if no matches are found in the **switch**. (See the discussion of **switch**.)

do

The **do** loop is one of three loop constructs available in C. The general form of the **do** loop is

> **do** {
> *statement block*
> } **while**(*condition*);

If only one statement is in the statement block, the braces are not necessary, but they do add clarity to the statement.

The **do** loop is the only loop in C that always has at least one iteration, because the condition is tested at the bottom of the loop.

The **do** loop is commonly used to read disk files. The following code reads a file until an EOF is encountered:

```
do {
  ch=getc(fp);
  store(ch);
} while(!feof(fp));
```

double

The **double** data-type specifier declares double-precision floating-point variables. To declare **d** to be of type **double**, you write

```
double d;
```

else

See the discussion of **if**.

enum

The **enum** type specifier creates enumeration types. An enumeration is simply a list of objects, and an enumeration type specifies what that list of objects is. Further, an enumeration type variable may only be assigned values that are part of the enumeration list. For example, the following code declares an enumeration called **color**, declares a variable of that type called **c**, and performs an assignment and a condition test:

```
enum color {red, green, yellow};
enum color c;

main()
{
  c=red;
  if(c==red) printf("is red\n");
}
```

extern

The **extern** data-type modifier tells the compiler that a variable is declared elsewhere in the program. This modifier is often used in conjunction with separately compiled files that share the same global data and are linked together. In essence, **extern** notifies the compiler of a variable without redeclaring it.

As an example, if **first** were declared in another file as an integer, then in subsequent files the following declaration would be used:

```
extern int first;
```

float

The **float** data-type specifier declares floating-point variables. To declare **f** to be of type **float**, you write

```
float f;
```

for

The **for** loop allows automatic initialization and incrementing of a counter variable. The general form is

> **for**(*initialization*; *condition*; *increment*) {
> *statement block*
> }

If the *statement block* is only one statement, the braces are not necessary.

Although the **for** allows a number of variables, generally the *initialization* is used to set a counter variable to its starting value. The *condition* is generally a relational statement that checks the counter variable against a termination value, and *increment* increments (or decrements) the counter value.

The following code prints the message "hello" ten times:

```
for(t=0; t<10; t++) printf("hello\n");
```

The next example waits for a keystroke after printing "hello":

```
for(t=0; t<10; t++) {
  printf("hello\n");
  getche();
}
```

goto

The **goto** keyword causes program execution to jump to the label specified in the **goto** statement. The general form of **goto** is

> **goto** *label*;
> .
> .
> .
> *label*:

All labels must end in a colon and must not conflict with keywords or function names. Furthermore, a **goto** can only branch within the current function, and not from one function to another.

The following example prints the message "right," but not the message "wrong":

```
goto lab1;
  printf("wrong");
lab1:
  printf("right");
```

if

The general form of the **if** statement is

> **if**(*condition*) {
> *statement block 1*
> }
> **else** {
> *statement block 2*
> }

If single statements are used, then the braces are not needed. The **else** is optional.

The condition may be any expression. If that expression evaluates to any value other than 0, then *statement block 1* executes; otherwise, if it exists, *statement block 2* executes.

The following code fragment can be used for keyboard input and to look for a "q," which signifies "quit."

```
ch=getche();
if(ch=='q') {
  printf("program terminated");
  exit(0);
}
else  proceed();
```

int

The **int** type specifier declares integer variables. For example, to declare **count** as an integer, you write

```
int count;
```

interrupt

The **interrupt** type specifier is not part of the ANSI standard. It declares functions that are used as interrupt service routines.

long

The **long** data-type modifier declares double-length integer variables. For example, to declare **count** as a long integer, you write

```
long int count;
```

pascal

The **pascal** keyword is not defined by the ANSI standard. It forces C to compile a function so that its parameter passing convention is compatible with Pascal, rather than with C.

register

The **register** declaration modifier forces either an integer or a character to be stored in a register of the CPU, instead of being placed in memory. It can only be used on local variables. To declare **i** as a register integer, you write

```
register int i;
```

return

The **return** keyword forces a return from a function and can be used to transfer a value back to the calling routine.

For example, the following function returns the product of its two integer arguments:

```
mul(a, b)
int a, b;
{
   return(a*b);
}
```

Remember that as soon as a **return** is encountered, the function returns and skips any other code in the function.

sizeof

The **sizeof** keyword is a compile-time operator that returns the length of the variable it precedes. For example, the following prints a 2 for most computers:

```
printf("%d", sizeof(int));
```

The principal use of **sizeof** is aiding the generation of portable code when that code depends upon the size of the C built-in data types.

signed

The **signed** type modifier produces a **signed** data-type.

short

The **short** data-type modifier declares 1-byte integers. For example, to declare **sh** as a short integer you write

```
short int sh;
```

static

The **static** data-type modifier instructs the compiler to create permanent storage for the local variable that it precedes. This enables the specified variable to maintain its value between function calls. For example, to declare **last—time** as a **static** integer, you write

```
static int last_time;
```

struct

The **struct** keyword creates complex or conglomerate variables (called *structures*) that are made up of one or more elements of the five basic data types. The general form of a structure is

> **struct** *structname* {
> *type element 1*;
> *type element 2*;
> .
> .
> .
> *type element N*;
> } *structure—variable—name*;

The individual elements are referenced by using the dot or arrow operator.

switch

The **switch** statement is C's multiway branch statement. It is used to route execution one of several different ways. The general form of the statement is

```
switch(variable) {
  case (constant1): statement set 1;
    break;
  case (constant2): statement set 2;
    break

        .

        .

        .

  case (constant n): statement set N;
    break;
  default: default statements;
}
```

The length of each *statement set* may be from one to several statements. The **default** portion is optional.

The **switch** works by checking the **variable** against all the constants. As soon as a match is found, that set of statements is executed. If the **break** statement is omitted, then execution continues until the end of the **switch**. Think of **case** as a label. Execution will continue until a **break** statement is found, or the **switch** ends.

The following example can be used to process a menu selection:

```
ch = getche();

switch (ch) {
  case 'e': enter();
      break;
  case 'l': list();
      break;
  case 's': sort();
      break;
  case 'q': exit(0);
  default: printf("unknown command\n");
      printf("try again\n");

}
```

typedef

The **typedef** keyword creates a new name for an existing data type. The data type may be either one of the built-in types, or a structure or union name. The general form of **typedef** is

typedef *type_specifier new_name*;

For example, to use the word **balance** in place of **float**, you write

```
typedef float balance;
```

union

The **union** keyword assigns two or more variables to the same memory location. The form of the definition and the way an element is referenced are the same as for **struct**. The general form is

union *union_name* {
type *element 1*;
type *element 2*;

.

.

.

type *element N*;
} **union** *variable_name*;

unsigned

The **unsigned** data-type modifier tells the compiler to eliminate the sign bit of an integer and to use all bits for arithmetic. This has the effect of doubling the size of the largest integer, but restricts it to only positive numbers. For example, to declare **big** to be an unsigned integer, you write

```
unsigned int big;
```

void

The **void** type specifier is primarily used to explicitly declare functions that return no meaningful value. It is also used to create **void** pointers (pointers to **void**), which are generic pointers capable of pointing to any type of object.

volatile

The **volatile** modifier tells the compiler that a variable may have its contents altered in ways not explicitly defined by the program. These may include variables that are changed by hardware such as real-time clocks, interrupts, or other inputs.

while

The **while** loop has the general form

```
while(condition) {
   statement block
}
```

If a single statement is the object of the **while**, then the braces may be omitted.

The **while** tests its *condition* at the top of the loop. Therefore, if the *condition* is FALSE to begin with, the loop will not execute at all. The *condition* may be any expression.

The following example of a **while** reads 100 characters from a disk file and stores them into a character array:

```
t = 0;

while(t<100) {
  s[t]=getc(fp);
  t++;
}
```

THE C PREPROCESSOR

C includes several preprocessor commands that give instructions to the compiler. These are examined here.

#define

The #define preprocessor command performs macro-substitutions of one piece of text for another throughout the file in which it is used. The general form of the directive is

#define *name string*

Notice that no semicolon appears in this statement.

For example, if you wish to use the word TRUE for the value 1 and the word FALSE for the value 0, you would declare the following two macro #defines:

#define TRUE 1
#define FALSE 0

This causes the compiler to substitute a 1 or a 0 each time the name TRUE or FALSE is encountered.

#error

The #error preprocessor directive forces the compiler to stop compilation when it is encountered. It is used primarily for debugging. Its general form is as follows:

#error message

When **#error** is encountered, C displays the message and the line number.

#include

The **#include** preprocessor directive instructs the compiler to read and compile another source file. The source file to be read in must be enclosed between double quotation marks or angle brackets. For example, the following code instructs the C compiler to read and compile the header for the disk-file library routines:

```
#include "stdio.h"
```

#if, #ifdef, #ifndef, #else, #elif, #endif

These preprocessor directives selectively compile various portions of a program. These are of the greatest use to commerical software houses that provide and maintain many customized versions of one program. The general idea is that if the expression after an **#if**, **#ifdef**, or **#ifndef** is true, then the code that is between one of the preceding and an **#endif** will be compiled; otherwise it will be skipped over. The **#endif** directive marks the end of an **#if** block. The **#else** can be used with any of the above in a manner similar to the **else** in the C **if** statement.

The general form of #**if** is

#**if** *constant expression*

If the *constant expression* is TRUE, then the block of code will be compiled.

The general form of #**ifdef** is

#ifdef *name*

If the **name** has been defined in a #**define** statement, the block of code following the statement will be compiled.

The general form of **#ifndef** is

#ifndef *name*

If **name** is currently undefined by a #**define** statement, then the block of code is compiled.

For example, here is the way some of the preprocessor directives work together:

```
#define ted 10

main()
{
#ifdef ted
   printf("Hi Ted\n");
#endif
   printf("bye bye\n");
#if 10<9
   printf("Hi George\n");
#endif
}
```

This code prints "Hi Ted" and "bye bye" on the screen, but not "Hi George."

The #**elif** directive creates an **if/else/if** statement. Its general form is

#elif *constant-expression*

The #**elif** may be used with the #**if**, but not the #**ifdef** or #**ifndef** directives.

THE C STANDARD LIBRARY

Unlike most other languages, C does not have built-in functions to perform disk I/O, console I/O, and a number of other useful procedures. The way these things are accomplished in C is by using a set of predefined library functions supplied with the compiler. This library is usually called the "C Standard Library." Library functions can be used by your program at your discretion. The compiler automatically links the functions during the link process.

The C language contains a large number of library functions and these should be fully described in your C user manual. Also, *C: The Complete Reference*, by Herbert Schildt (Berkeley, Calif.: Osborne/McGraw-Hill, 1987) discusses the library functions in considerable detail.

B

DIFFERENCES BETWEEN UNIX C AND ANSI-STANDARD C

As has been mentioned numerous times in this guide, the proposed ANSI standard has defined a version of C that is slightly different and expanded in comparison to the de facto UNIX standard, defined by Brian Kernighan and Dennis Ritchie in their book, *The C Programming Language* (Englewood Cliffs: Prentice-Hall, Inc., 1978). Each of these differences is thoroughly covered in the chapters of this guide. The purpose of this appendix is to provide a convenient, quick reference to the most important differences.

KEYWORD DELETIONS

The proposed ANSI standard deletes the unused keyword **entry**, which had been reserved for future use.

KEYWORD EXTENSIONS

The proposed ANSI standard adds the following five keywords:

const
enum
signed
void
volatile

Each of these will be examined briefly in the following sections.

const

The type modifier **const** is used to inform the compiler that the values of the variable that follows it may not be changed except for an initialization. For example,

```
const int user_code = 2001;
```

informs the compiler that **version** may not occur on the left-hand side of an assignment statement. The code also sets the initial value to 2001.

Variables to type **const** have two main purposes. The first is to allow the compiler to place them in ROM (read-only memory). For example, the "combination" of a garage-door opener may be in ROM to prevent tampering. The second use is to ensure that arguments to functions are not modified by that function. Consider this example:

```
char *match_string(p)
const char* p;
{
   .
   .
   .
}
```

Because **p** is declared as a **const**, no code in the function may modify its value.

enum

The type specifier **enum** is used to create enumeration types. An enumeration is a list of named constants that a variable of that type may have. For example, the declaration that follows defines an enumeration type and two variables:

```
enum names = {Herb, Sherry, Jon, Rachel, Sasha, Josselyn};
enum names child, parent;
```

Now the following statements are legal:

```
parent = sherry;
child = Jon;
if(child == Jon &&  parent != Herb) ...;
switch(parent) {
  case Herb:
    .
    .
    .
  case Sherry:
    .
    .
    .
}
```

The values associated with the named constants are integer values. The first constant in the list is 0, the second 1, the third 2, and so on.

signed

The type modifier **signed** was added to the proposed ANSI standard to allow the type **signed char** to be specified. Previously, some compilers defaulted to signed characters and others defaulted to unsigned. The modifier **signed** helps standardize the use of type **char**.

void

The type **void** is used in two ways. First, functions that do not return values may be declared to be of type **void**, which tells the compiler that no values will be returned. This prevents any accidental use in an expression. For example, since this function does not return a value, it is declared as being of type **void**:

```
void shwo_stack_size()
{
  printf("Size of stack is %d", MAX_STACK_SIZE);
}
```

Second, generic pointers may be created as **void** * variables. In this case you would then use an explicit type cast to a pointer of the type you desired.

volatile

The type modifier **volatile** is used to tell the compiler that the variable that follows may be modified in ways that are not under the direct control of the program. For example, a variable may be updated by the system clock every tenth of a second. The purpose of declaring a variable as **volatile** is to prevent certain compiler optimizations from being made that might prevent the value of the variable from being accessed precisely as the expression indicates. Here is an example:

```
volatile int clck;
int time1;

time1=clck;
if(time1==clck) ...;
```

If **clck** were not declared as **volatile**, then some compilers could optimize the two expressions in such a way that the value of **clck** was only examined once.

PASSING STRUCTURES

Some early versions of C were not capable of passing structures to functions. Rather, they would only pass the address of the structure in much the same way that arrays are passed. However, in newer versions and in the proposed ANSI standard, structures are passed to a function in their entirety on the stack. If you wish to pass the address instead, you must precede the structure name with the operator **&**.

FUNCTION PROTOTYPES

The proposed ANSI standard allows the types of the arguments as well as the return type of a function to be declared in advance so that strong type checking can be enforced for arguments as well as return values. This is called function *prototyping*. For example, the function **func1()** is prototyped in this example:

```
float func1(int, float);   /* declare the function */

main()
{
  int x,
  float y;

  x = 10;
  y = 10.12;

  printf("%f", func1(x, y));
}

float func1(a, b)
int a;
float b;
{
  return (float) a + b;
}
```

STANDARD LIBRARIES

One of the most important aspects of the proposed ANSI standard is that it defines a standard set of library functions that will be supplied with a C compiler. This enhances the portability of the programs that you write. It is permissible for a compiler's developer to supply additional library functions other than those defined by the ANSI standard. However, there is no guarantee that they will be portable.

ADDITIONAL PREPROCESSOR DIRECTIVES

The following C preprocessor directives have been added by the proposed ANSI standard to those usually provided by the K & R standard:

#elif	**#line**
#error	**#pragma**

In addition, the standard defines these built-in macros:

Macro	Meaning
LINE	Number of current line
FILE	Name of source file
DATE	Current system date
TIME	Current system file
STDC	1 if a standard implementation

TRADEMARKS

INDEX

The manuscript for this book was prepared and
submitted to Osborne/McGraw-Hill in electronic form.
The acquisitions editor for this project was Jeffrey
Pepper, the technical reviewer was Scott Kissinger,
and the project editor was Dusty Bernard.

Text design by Judy Wohlfrom, using Century
Expanded for text body and display.

Cover art by Bay Graphics Design Associates. Color
supplier is Phoenix Color Corporation. Book printed
and bound by R.R. Donnelley & Sons Company,
Crawfordsville, Indiana.